E G L I

SOCIAL ORGANIZATION AND THE APPLICATIONS OF ANTHROPOLOGY

Essays in Honor of Lauriston Sharp

LAURISTON SHARP

SOCIAL ORGANIZATION AND THE APPLICATIONS OF ANTHROPOLOGY

Essays in Honor of Lauriston Sharp

Edited by ROBERT J. SMITH

CORNELL UNIVERSITY PRESS

ITHACA AND LONDON

First published 1974 by Cornell University Press.
Published in the United Kingdom by Cornell University Press Ltd., 2-4 Brook Street, London W1Y 1AA.

International Standard Book Number 0-8014-0891-1
Library of Congress Catalog Card Number 74-4721

Printed in the United States of America by York Composition Co.

Contents

6   Contents

Introduction

ROBERT J. SMITH

In the course of a long and fruitful career in teaching and research at Cornell University, Lauriston Sharp has influenced a diverse group of students and colleagues. A number of us, along with some of his friends and professional associates, have joined together on the occasion of his retirement from Cornell to present him with this book, the first of two in his honor.* Our aim is both to mark his contributions to anthropology and Asian studies and to indicate the degree of our indebtedness to him for his guidance and example over the years. It is our hope that these books will be found useful by many readers who share his interests in the several fields in which he has worked.

The diversity of the contributions to these two volumes is readily apparent; they tell us a great deal about the man and his intellectual concerns. Above all, he has taught us that man's behavior is comprehensible in human terms, and that our understanding of the constructions of the world made by men of other times and places must always be informed by an essential humanism. He has further urged the view that such understanding can be put to practical use.

The generation of scholars to which Sharp belongs has made important theoretical, methodological, and substantive contributions to anthropology, often on the basis of a wide spectrum of field experiences not likely to be matched by future generations. As an active researcher, Sharp has known the American Indians of the Plains and Southwest, the Berbers of North Africa, the

---

* The second volume is to be *Change and Persistence in Thai Society,* edited by G. William Skinner and A. Thomas Kirsch.

7

Australian aborigines, and for over twenty-five years he has had sustained contact with the peoples of Southeast Asia, particularly in Thailand. A number of his scientific papers, notably "Steel Axes for Stone Age Australians," "People without Politics," and "Cultural Continuities and Discontinuities in Southeast Asia," have been so frequently reprinted as to have attained the status of anthropological classics.

Sharp's teaching and research have been informed by two broad intellectual concerns. One has been to view the peoples of the non-Western world always in the larger cultural context of the region or area in which they are found. The second has been to explicate the interplay of the cultural forces of modernization as they have impinged on indigenous cultures. These two concerns are clearly evident in his years of service at Cornell, where he played the paramount role in establishing a department of anthropology which for much of its existence has been geared to the application of anthropological knowledge, and in setting up both the university's Southeast Asia Program and its Center for International Studies.

Lauriston Sharp was born on March 24, 1907, in Madison, Wisconsin. His father, Frank Chapman Sharp, was professor of philosophy at the University of Wisconsin. As a philosopher, the elder Sharp had reacted strongly against the extreme cultural relativism expressed by William Graham Sumner in his influential book *Folkways*. In challenging Sumner's contention that "the mores make all things right," he used, among other materials, the scattered reports on the Australian aborigines, who were later to be studied at first hand by his son.

Sharp attended primary and secondary schools in Madison and entered the University of Wisconsin in 1925. While still a senior in high school he had met Clyde Kluckhohn, already then a student at the university. With John King Fairbank and other friends, Sharp and Kluckhohn formed a "Sanskrit letter" society which met weekly for intellectual discussion; their aim was to provide a counterweight to the conventional "Greek letter" fraternities and their more social concerns. The friendships formed and the interests developed in these undergraduate years were to persist throughout his career.

In the summers of 1927 and 1928, Kluckhohn, J. J. Hanks, and Sharp undertook a reconnaissance of the Kaiparowitz Plateau in Arizona and Utah. On these two trips he first came into contact with the contemporary Indians of the region and saw the archeological remains left by earlier peoples. Although majoring in philosophy at the time, Sharp had grown increasingly disenchanted with the subject, which he felt had become divorced from concern with the concrete experiences of real people and with the impact of cultural factors in shaping their lives. Anthropology appealed to him as a discipline within which he could pursue these interests, bringing together data and abstractions.

In 1929–30, having taken his B.A. in philosophy, Sharp served as a Freshman Dean at the University of Wisconsin. This was the first year of Ralph Linton's tenure at Wisconsin, and Sharp attended his lectures. In 1930 he joined an expedition to North Africa sponsored by the Logan Museum of Beloit College, in which Sol Tax and John Gillin also participated. This sustained field experience with the Berbers crystallized his preference for ethnography and ethnology over archeology and physical anthropology. It had the further effect of convincing him of the absolute necessity for the cultural anthropologist to be thoroughly grounded in the history and language of the people with whom he works. He also acquired a perspective on culture which has led him always to emphasize the study of areas and regions rather than the more conventional concentration on a single group or society.

Two areas of the world were then still largely *terra incognita* to anthropologists—Latin America and Southeast Asia. The latter seemed to Sharp to hold the greater potential for future research, and he sought advice on how to achieve his goal of carrying on field investigations there. Robert H. Lowie suggested that he enroll in the University of Vienna, where Robert Heine-Geldern, one of the leading students of Southeast Asian culture of the time, was a *Privat Docent*. Ralph Linton advised him to enter the doctoral program at Harvard. Sharp followed both suggestions. He went directly from North Africa to the University of Vienna, where he was awarded the Certificate in Anthropology in 1931. He entered the Harvard doctoral program in anthropology in the fall of 1931, studying under Alfred E. Tozzer, Earnest A. Hooton, and Roland B. Dixon, and taking courses with the sociologist Talcott Parsons and the Sanskritist W. E. Clark. In the summer of 1932 he and Sol Tax were together again, this time on the Fox Indian project in Iowa. Sharp received the M.A. in anthropology at Harvard on the basis of this research.

The mid-1930's were not an easy time for securing financial support for overseas research in anthropology. Funds were so scarce that when W. Lloyd Warner's recommendation of Sharp to A. R. Radcliffe-Brown, who was then at the University of Chicago, produced an opportunity for research in Australia, Sharp set aside his plans for Southeast Asia and accepted it. Under the auspices of the Australian National Research Council, he was with the aborigines of Cape York Peninsula in North Queensland from 1933 to 1935. The bulk of his time was spent with the Yir Yoront. It is ironic that a career so heavily focused on the study of complex societies should have been initiated with research in a hunting and gathering society. Nevertheless, as is probably the case with most anthropologists, Sharp was profoundly impressed by his first lengthy field experience, and the Yir Yoront played a formative role in the development of his continuing interest in problems of social organization and role theory.

Before returning to Harvard to serve as a teaching assistant in the Department of Anthropology, he was able to make brief visits to New Guinea, China, and Southeast Asia. He received the Ph.D. in anthropology from Harvard in 1937; his dissertation was entitled "The Social Anthropology of a Totemic System in North Queensland, Australia."

In 1936 Sharp began his long association with Cornell University. There was no department of anthropology or of sociology at that time, and his initial appointment was as instructor of anthropology in the Department of Economics. The demographer Walter F. Willcox had long been interested in expanding the social science offerings at Cornell and had brought another demographer, Julian Woodward, to the university in 1928. President Edmund Ezra Day was instrumental in bringing Leonard S. Cottrell, the social psychologist, in 1935. Willcox, Cottrell, and Sharp set up the combined Department of Sociology and Anthropology in 1939, with strong informal links to the internationally renowned Department of Rural Sociology in the New York State College of Agriculture. Although President Day was eager to see expansion of the social sciences and to establish a full-fledged graduate program, the members of the new department were inclined to move more slowly. Sharp in particular felt that there were already enough well-established anthropology departments with the resources to produce an adequate number of professional anthropologists. He argued that for Cornell to establish a minimally acceptable program would require too great a drain on scarce resources and that the result would in any event be redundant. Although the impact of World War II would lead him to change his mind, at the time Sharp was urging that Cornell concentrate on undergraduate education in the social sciences. The only anthropologist to receive an advanced degree at Cornell before the war was David M. Schneider, whose 1941 master's thesis in social psychology was entitled "Aboriginal Dreams." It was not until 1951 that the first Cornell Ph.D. in anthropology was awarded to Charles S. Brant for his research on the Kiowa Apache.

With the entry of the United States into World War II, it became painfully clear that there was a severe shortage of people trained in both the social sciences and area studies. The federal government set up a number of crash programs at American universities designed to train language and area personnel quickly.

Academics, businessmen, and missionaries with firsthand knowledge of Asia and the Pacific were in great demand, and like most
with such special competence, Sharp was sought out. He had
been chairman of the Department of Sociology and Anthropology from 1942 to 1945, and in 1945–46, while on leave from the
university, he served as assistant chief of the Division of Southeast
Asian Affairs in the Department of State. There he worked
closely with Cora DuBois, Rupert Emerson, Raymond Kennedy,
Kenneth Landon, and Abbot Low Moffat. In 1947–48 he conducted his first field research in Thailand.

Upon his return to Cornell, Sharp set about organizing a program of instruction and research in applied anthropology center-
ing on the problems of change and modernization among tribal
and peasant societies. Leonard S. Cottrell, then dean of the College of Arts and Sciences, helped in the development of the joint
department, to which Sharp invited Morris Edward Opler, Allan
R. Holmberg, and John Adair. Under a grant from the Carnegie
Corporation, coordinated studies in North India, Thailand, Peru,
and the Navaho Reservation were initiated. Alexander H. Leighton's work in social psychiatry in the Canadian Maritimes was
closely associated with these studies, and Leighton himself was
involved in the Navaho project. Graduate training and field research proceeded under what become known as the Cornell University Studies in Culture and Applied Science. The program involved personnel from the other social sciences and from many
technical fields, particularly agricultural economics, plant science,
nutrition, rural sociology, and education.

In 1947, with the Carnegie support mentioned above, Sharp
had established the Cornell-Thailand Project, which has served
as the primary focus of his research ever since. Bang Chan, a
village in the Central Plains, was chosen for intensive long-term
study in 1948. A number of Cornell students and other colleagues
have participated with Sharp in the study of this community as
it has changed from an isolated "rice village" to an adjunct of
the ever-expanding Bangkok metropolis. In collaboration with

Lucien Hanks, Sharp is currently completing a social history of Bang Chan based on more than twenty-five years of periodic study. In recent years his research interests have shifted to northern Thailand and particularly to the problems of integrating upland minority peoples into contemporary Thai society.

The aim of the Cornell-Thailand Project has been not simply the study of a rice village. Still operating on his assumption that such research must be set in a larger historical, regional, and national context, Sharp encouraged the study of other villages in the Central Plains area and in the north and northeast regions. Nor has the project been limited to the village level; under Sharp's direction it sponsored studies of the Chinese community in Thailand, of Thai national politics and Thai linguistics, of Thai society in the eighteenth and early nineteenth centuries, and of nineteenth-century national educational reform. The bibliography of works engendered by the Cornell-Thailand Project now includes more than 250 items. In all of this activity Sharp encouraged Thai scholars to participate and young Thai to be trained who could provide their own perspective on their society. He recruited Thai students to come to Cornell for advanced training in many scholarly fields—in agricultural economics, comparative education, nutrition, economics, government, and rural sociology, as well as anthropology. Many of these Cornell-trained Thai scholars have assumed prominent positions in Thai educational institutions and are pursuing their own teaching and research. In recognition of his contributions to the study of Thai culture a group of Sharp's students have established a Lauriston Sharp Essay Prize, awarded annually since 1967, as well as a Lauriston Sharp Scholarship Fund aimed at promoting social science research in Thailand.

Although Thailand came to dominate his own research interests, Sharp encouraged his students at Cornell to carry out similar broadly conceived studies in other areas of the world. These studies include work on marriage and family patterns in Taiwan, the social organization of North American Indian tribes, eco-

nomics and social structure of Burmese communities, social stratification in North India, and community organization in Japan
and Peru.

While pursuing his own active field research, Sharp also
chaired the Department of Sociology and Anthropology from
1949 to 1956. Despite a full regimen of teaching and research,
not to mention his administrative responsibilities, he nonetheless
found the time to establish with Rockefeller support Cornell's
Southeast Asia Program, of which he was director from 1950 to
1960. In 1960–61 he chaired the faculty committee whose report
led to the establishment of the Center for International Studies.
Both the Center and the Program are flourishing, and Sharp
leaves an independent Department of Anthropology four times
as large as the original group which he had assembled in the
joint department.

Lauriston Sharp is the co-author of *Siamese Rice Village*
(1953), *Handbook of Thailand* (1956), *A Report on the Tribal
Peoples in Chiengrai* (1964), *Ethnographic Notes on Northern
Thailand* (1965), a series of comparative studies on cultural
change (1966–67), and *The Dream Life of a Primitive People*
(1969). He is the author of monographs, articles, and reviews
on the cultures and political problems of Southeast Asia and the
western Pacific for professional journals, government agencies,
and the American Institute of Pacific Relations. He has held
visiting appointments at Sydney University, Yale University,
Haverford College, the University of California (Berkeley), the
University of London, the Army War College, and, as Fulbright
Research Professor, at Kasetsart University in Bangkok. In
1967–68 he was awarded a Guggenheim Fellowship. He is a life
member of the Siam Society, one of the founders of the Society
for Applied Anthropology, and has served on the governing
boards of the American Anthropological Association, the Asia
Society, the Pacific Science Board of the National Research
Council, and as director and past president of the Association for
Asian Studies. He is a Fellow of the Royal Anthropological In-

stitute and corresponding member of the Australian Institute for Aboriginal Studies. He has been a consultant for the Department of State and has served on various committees of the Agency for International Development, American Council of Learned Societies, Institute of Pacific Relations, International Congress of Orientalists, International Union of Anthropological and Ethnological Sciences, National Research Council, National Science Foundation, Pacific Science Board, Social Science Research Council, and UNESCO. At present he holds the position of Goldwin Smith Professor of Anthropology and Asian Studies Emeritus.

Reflecting the anthropological concerns of Sharp's own work, the papers in this volume focus on the understanding of social organization and on the application of anthropological knowledge in the context of tribal groups as well as civilizations.

The first three, squarely in the classic anthropological tradition, are studies in kinship and social organization. As the reader will quickly discover, however, these are not presentations of such systems as comprehensive constructs of logical purity. Rather, the authors deal with a variety of situations which demonstrate the elusive and variable character of the phenomena of kinship terminologies and kinship groupings.

Firth, utilizing materials obtained over the course of almost thirty years, tells us that the Malays of the Kelantan coast use a kinship idiom to assist them in cooperating for general purposes and for social display. The "kin frame" is termed *waris,* and it is essentially a bilateral consanguineal one which may include some, but not necessarily all, affines. Religious constraints on marriage and inheritance are such that there are both "official" and "unofficial" definitions of *waris.* It soon becomes clear that while there may indeed be something called "the Malay kinship system," this system cannot be said to serve as evidence of the existence of uniform institutions and behavior patterns of "Malay society," for Firth convincingly demonstrates the presence of a considerable virtuosity in the selection of kin ties for activation on specific occasions by this particular group of Malays. The selections made are shown to be related to ecological, economic, and demographic conditions which must be analyzed in order to understand Malay kinship in this single regional context.

Goodenough, back on the familiar ground of Truk after a seventeen-year absence, takes us on an intellectual adventure which says a great deal about what has happened to anthropology since the end of World War II. In 1947 he had collected data which revealed that the Crow pattern of usage of kinship terms was the common one on the island of Romónum. But early in his second stay there, in 1964, he found that the Hawaiian pattern was in widespread use, and he was even assured by informants that it had always been an alternative. As his paper shows, the matter cannot be simply explained by his incomplete understanding of the situation in 1947, and we are left with a prime puzzle. Has there been a shift in kin terminology reflecting ecological and legal changes, or have the people of Romónum tried to become "more American" in this respect? Goodenough is obliged to leave the question open, but the reader will find his discussion of the materials an arresting example of the anthropologist at work.

Schneider's paper, based on reanalysis of field research on Yap some twenty-five years ago, is also concerned with change. Specifically, the focus is on the effects of demographic change, in this case depopulation which had occurred prior to the study, on the cultural definition of the kin group called *tabinau*. His conclusion is that in spite of depopulation and many associated changes, there has been no accompanying shift in the definition of the *tabinau,* the rules of inheritance of these estates, or their constitution as an element in the organization of the village community.

Hanks gives us an intriguing insight into the variety of functions served by the recitation of patrilineages among the Akha living in Thailand, and several contexts in which such recitations occur. The interplay between sociological and historical factors is only one of the themes taken up in the process of showing how among the Akha the recitation of the patrilineages serves to affirm the unique identity which has set them apart from the welter of groups among whom they have lived for centuries, thereby retarding their absorption into other more powerful societies.

With Wolf's paper, we move to the very large-scale society of China and are invited to consider the implications of the existence of a great variety of forms of marriage and adoption in northern Taiwan. The focus is on the customary law of the period 1900 to 1920; the field data are from the 1960's. From a detailed consideration of the character of the "major form of marriage," Wolf leads us first into the alternative "minor forms of marriage" and then into "second and secondary marriages." We are left with a new understanding and no choice but to ignore all previously published general statements about marriage in Chinese society which treat it as a unitary phenomenon.

Madge's paper continues our venture into complex, large-scale Asian societies with an overview of the process of modernization as it relates to demography and family patterns in Southeast Asia, using comparative materials from India, China, and Japan. The primary emphasis is on the absence of indigenous drives toward urbanization and industrialization in the countries of Southeast Asia and the link to demographic characteristics of those societies.

In the first of the papers on applied anthropology, Eggan offers a valuable account of its little-explored development in the Philippines in a period well before the term itself was coined. The reader versed in the history of American anthropology will find many familiar names here and will be introduced to a generation of Filipino scholars who now carry forward the application of anthropological knowledge to the solution of social problems in their own society.

With Judd's contribution, we move to another level of the analysis of change through a diachronic study spanning a decade. Essentially the paper examines a Thai community to see how well predictions made in 1958 held up in 1967. Many applied anthropologists make recommendations and predictions; few have the opportunity subsequently to see what the course of change has actually been. Judd shows us a community in which little of what has happened resulted either from planning within the village or from effective intervention by the government. His finding that change has proved to be piecemeal rather than structural will be of interest to anyone who has ever undertaken applied work.

In Kaufman's paper on a Vietnamese fishing cooperative we meet the limiting case where the applied anthropologist's plans were overwhelmed by political forces and historical developments completely beyond his control. The program of action is meticulously laid out; the character of fishing and its financing and organization are analyzed. The program for action outlined here is a model of its kind. The postscript's final dry sentence is its own tragic message.

Morris's paper on the mechanization of sago production among the Melanau of Sarawak gives us a poignant picture of a people who in the short space of three generations have seen most of their traditional values rendered irrelevant to the situation in which they now find themselves. And, as we have seen in other contributions to this volume, the recommendations of the applied anthropologist and others interested in making it possible for the people to retain something of their way of life have been ignored, as the irresistible sweep of change carries them inexorably into a world they have not made.

The paper by Freedman takes up an issue that has long been a central concern of Lauriston Sharp. The question is whether cultures and civilizations are the entities clearly demarcated "in the landscapes of time and space" that they are so commonly made out to be, or whether the anthropologist has done us all a disservice by overselling the "cookie-cutter" notion of culture. As Freedman convincingly suggests, perhaps few tests reveal the inadequacy of that notion more compellingly than the pursuit of its implications for our understanding of the relations between China and the countries of Southeast Asia. The Overseas Chinese play a crucial role in his argument, as does their "culture," which Freedman shows to be highly varied in time and space and not, as is so often argued, a mere approximation of the "culture of China."

There are, then, in the following pages recurrent themes and emphases. Dissatisfaction with traditional ways of handling the classical anthropological preoccupations with kinship and social organization is one such theme. The utilization of anthropological knowledge is another, with strong support for the position that planning and programs are futile where they are not built solidly into the administrative systems which everywhere are staffed by those who make the final decisions by default or by design as to what will and will not be done. Throughout there runs a litany of great importance to anthropology and its practice, whether action-oriented or not: time is everywhere in these papers—in instances of increased understanding gained by scholars who see their analytic problems in a time frame; in historical propositions concerning cultural interrelations and the course of the development of civilization which free us from overly rigid categorization of life and experience; in the study of change through time as productive of insights not available through synchronic approaches, which have stressed far too exclusively the structures and boundaries of human society.

SOCIAL ORGANIZATION AND THE APPLICATIONS OF ANTHROPOLOGY

Essays in Honor of Lauriston Sharp

1. Relations between Personal Kin (*Waris*) among Kelantan Malays[1]

RAYMOND FIRTH

This essay is concerned with some basic aspects of kinship in rural areas of the state of Kelantan. Historically, recognition of the significance of kinship in this state appears in a rather unexpected reference. Nearly fifty years ago it was noted by the British Adviser that the smuggling of rice out of the state ceased when the embargo on rice export was removed. The frontier between Pasir Puteh in Kelantan and Besut in Trengganu was an artificial one and the population on the border was heavily intermarried. When there was a shortage of rice in Besut and the embargo was in force, "the relations" in Kelantan were certain to carry supplies across the frontier.[2] This official reference to kinship draws attention to the pervasiveness of kinship ties in a Kelantan locality and to their strength as expressed in economic action.

A convenient way of tackling this enquiry into rural Kelantan kinship is to examine the significance of the term *waris* as used by the fishermen and other inhabitants of the Perupok area, where I have worked on various occasions.[3]

[1] This essay was completed essentially in 1970, from an earlier draft. For various suggestions I am indebted to members of a seminar in the Anthropology Department of the London School of Economics and Political Science, and also to Kahar Bador, Michael Swift, Clive Kessler, Amin Sweeney, and Douglas Raybeck.

[2] This note was copied by me in 1939 from the Kelantan Administration Report of 1921, by H. W. Thomson, then in files in Kota Bharu and now, I understand, in the archives in Kuala Lumpur.

[3] My observations are based upon data obtained in a coastal community

Designation of Persons by Kinship Terms

To understand the meaning of the Kelantan concept of *waris* it is necessary first to consider the local system of designating persons by kinship. For official purposes Kelantan Malays follow Muslim usage of recording the personal name followed by *bin* or *binte* according to sex and then the father's name. Hence, say, Awang bin Hamid is distinguished from his brother Mahmud bin Hamid. But while many Muslim personal names are available, Malays have generally chosen only a few. Village folk of Kelantan as elsewhere in Malaya have been fertile in expedients for distinguishing persons by ancillary means. Legally, a man is designated by reference to his father. Socially, he may be designated by reference to his sibling order or seniority. So if a man Awang is called Awang Long[4] this indicates that he is the eldest son in the family and distinguishes him from his younger brother, also called Awang; Awang Muda refers to junior status. A custom common on the northeast coast, as also in some other parts of Malaya, is to designate a man or wife by reference to his or her spouse (or sometimes eldest child). So Awang-Petimoh is Awang the husband of Fatimah, to be distinguished from Awang-Limoh, husband of Halimah. This is regarded as quite a proper mode of referring to a person; Awang Long said, "That style is very fine." (To indicate the wife the names are reversed; so Petimoh-Awang is distinguished from Limoh-Awang.) Nicknames and abbreviations also help to give other modes of designation. So

---

in Kelantan during a year's study in 1939–40, about ten days in 1947, and about six weeks in 1963. On the first and third of these occasions I worked together with my wife, Rosemary Firth, to whom I am indebted for much help (see her book on domestic management in peasant households, 1966). A brief visit to Malaysia in 1967, under the auspices of the London-Cornell Project for East and South-East Asian Studies enabled me to check a few points. Other acknowledgments for assistance on these expeditions have been made elsewhere (Raymond Firth 1946, 1948, 1966).

[4] Standard Malay spelling is Long; I have written Lung in some earlier work.

Awang Tokor refers to a man who stumped along, while Dolloh or 'Loh can be distinguished from someone else called by the same name (Abdullah) in full. (Note the Malay practice of abbreviating some names by dropping off an initial syllable, whereas Europeans tend to drop off final syllables.) A further mode of designation is by characteristic such as occupation, especially when this is of a very restricted kind, implying status. To this the term To' (Tok) indicating grandparental generation or social seniority or considerable age is often prefixed. So To' Penghulu, To' Bidan, To' Mindok are respectful ways of addressing a headman, a midwife, and a spirit-healer, respectively. The personal name may be combined with these for reference, as To' Mamat Mindok. In effect these are titles of office. (Not so respectful are conceptualizations of peculiar personal qualities, as in To' Mandul (Old Barren), the name given to one man unsuccessful in producing any offspring.)

A widespread mode of designation is by kinship term, or by term which has kinship as primary referent. Allowing for the local dialectal pronunciation, the Kelantan system of kin terms is similar to that in general use among Malays[5] (see Figure 1.1).

The Malay system of kin terminology is specificatory (I prefer this term to "descriptive") rather than classificatory. Basically, it distinguishes collateral from lineal kin. It also distinguishes kin by generation and makes some distinction for seniority (including birth order) as well as for sex. But it applies bilaterally, and distinction between mother's kin and father's kin requires subsidiary

[5] For an example see Judith Djamour (1959:26–27), and Downs (1967:136–39) for some brief remarks. There is as yet no recognized orthography for Kelantan dialectal forms. C. C. Brown has provided a pioneer study of Kelantan Malay but has based the orthography of his texts on standard Malay. In his impressive scholarly study of shadow-play texts Amin Sweeney (1972) has preserved some features of Kelantan speech by using some nonstandard forms. I have attempted in earlier work to give an approximation to a phonetic rendering, e.g., *ano'* for *anak*. But Kelantan rural Malays themselves, now that they have become literate, write in standard orthography, and I have generally followed this convention here.

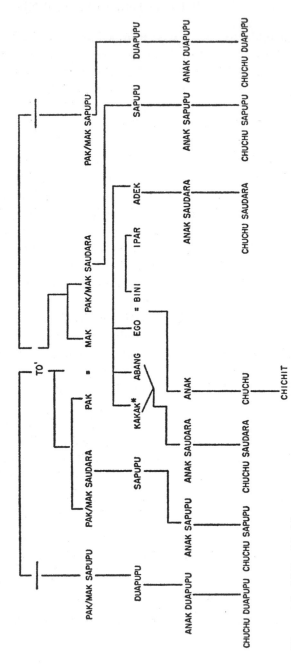

Figure 1.1 Malay kinship terms

* Sometimes used for elder male as well as elder female sibling.

description. The system of terminology is not a simple aggregate of different terms but follows an ordered development of its various levels, both conceptually and phonemically. So, conceptually in one descending series, *saudara* (relative; by inference, sibling) is followed by *anak saudara* (nephew/niece) and *chuchu saudara* (great-nephew/great-niece); in another series, *sapupu* (cousin) is followed by *duapupu* (second cousin) and *tigapupu* (third cousin) laterally, and *anak sapupu, anak duapupu, anak tigapupu; chuchu sapupu,* and so forth (first/second/third cousin's child; first cousin's grandchild, etc.) in descending order. Analogous expressions apply in an ascending order but dissolve into generalized "grandparent" forms. Phonemically, there is a relation between *chuchu,* grandchild, and *chichit,* great-grandchild; between *mentua,* parent-in-law, and *menantu,* son/daughter-in-law; and (in vernacular form) between *pak, mak* (in Kelantese form *po', mo'*) father, mother, and *to',* grandparent.

The specificatory character of the terminological system is not, however, complete. Although collaterals can be clearly distinguished from lineal kin, and commonly are so, in informal situations the specifying appellations may be dropped. So there is a tendency for *chuchu saudara,* grandchildren of siblings, to be termed simply *chuchu,* and the collective term *adek beradek,* siblings, tends to be applied to include first cousins. Indeed the term sometimes is used metaphorically of much wider kin; I once heard Awang Long say of two men who had had a row over fishing sales, "*Adek beradek* have parted, it is not good." Yet one was the wife's nephew of the other.

The effects of marriage and its concomitants, polygyny and especially divorce, call out some of the more ingenious applications of kin terms. The Malay system recognizes a particular relationship between affines who are the parents of a married pair; this is called *besan* and these people commonly address one another as To' Besan. A special link is also recognized between men married to sisters (*biras*). It would seem that Malays, recognizing the fragile nature of the marriage bond, try to emphasize the strength of the tie between affines. Thus, brothers-in-law may be spoken of as *adek beradek*, siblings, and as I shall show later, often may be found in cooperation. There is a strong tendency also for half-siblings and step-siblings, issue of other marriages of parents or parents' spouses, to be included in the sibling category. Yet while the frequency of divorce may impel toward strong recognition of the validity of relationships created by marriage as long as the marriage persists, Malay kinship terms are very effective in dealing with the separations which are the results of divorce. One might indeed put forward as a hypothesis that the specificatory nature of the system is particularly correlated with the frequency of divorce and remarriage and with the very specific inheritance rules from parents which obtain by Malay custom and by Muslim law.

An example of the application of kin terms in a situation of sequential marriages was given to me by Awang Long. I asked him about his relation to a goldsmith, Che 'Su' (Yusuf), who lived in the next hamlet. He explained that this man was not a kinsman (*waris*) of his; he was linked with him only because this man's *chuchu saudara* were his (Awang's) *adek* (younger siblings). The genealogy in Figure 1.2 illustrates this. Before Awang

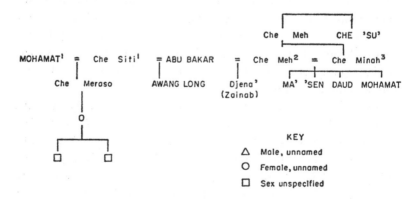

Figure 1.2. Awang Long and his half-brothers
Note: Capital letters indicate males. Numbers indicate marriage order.

Long's mother Che Siti married Abu Bakar she was married to Mohamat and had three children of whom only Meraso was alive in 1940; she was then an elderly woman, with grandchildren. Che Siti died after producing a family, and Abu Bakar then married Che Meh, whom he later divorced, and then Che Minah. Awang Long called his half brothers (then still in their teens) *adek*, younger siblings; on his father's death they inherited with him. Their mother, Che Minah, he called *mak muda* (junior mother) since she succeeded his own mother as his father's wife; conversely his half brothers would have called his mother *mak tua* (senior mother) if she had been living.[6] The grandchildren of his step-sister Meraso were called by Awang Long *chuchu saudara* (sibling's grandchildren). They in turn called him *to' ngah* (median grandparent) following their mother, for whom he was presumably an uncle junior to her parent's siblings, but of intermediate seniority vis-à-vis their other kin of that grade. Awang Long elaborated on this a little: "Their mother, my niece (*anak saudara*), she calls me Middle Father (*pak' ngah*); her children, they call me Middle Grandparent (*to' ngah*). If they get grandchildren in turn, they will call one differently, they will call Great-Grandparent (*to' nyang*)."[7]

A further point about these kinship terms, especially in the senior grades, is that they can be used to some extent as personal designations by any member of the community, irrespective of the precise kinship relation involved. In this way they come to serve as alternate personal *names*. In the village where my wife and I worked in 1963, the mother of our landlady was known to her daughter as *mo'* and to her grandchildren as *mo' wo'* (*mak wa'* or *mak 'ua*, grandma, lit. elder mother). Other people in the neighborhood, including my wife and I, referred to the old

---

[6] This is in line with terms for senior and junior wife in a polygynous marriage: *bini tua* and *bini muda*.

[7] Awang Long insisted pedantically that it was not *toh*, nor *to'*, but *tou'*; while this does accord with a recognized practice, it is my impression that *to'* is also used. (See also Wilkinson 1932:179, 595.)

woman by the same term. The special feature of such designations is that, unlike most of the other types of personal names, they tend to be *progressive*. In 1940 we knew Che Awang Long and Che Awang Muda; by 1963 they had become Pak Long and Pak Muda to local people of a younger generation. If they live many years longer they will become To' Long and To' Muda, this indicating grandparents' generation. What happens here is that a term of primary application in kinship relations comes to be used as a *generation indicator;* so the personal name now consists of an original or early individual component and a seniority category component. Various combinations of this kind occur. Thus Awang Long had an elderly kinswoman whom he, and as far as I know other people too, referred to as Mak Awang To'. He explained that she was his *to' sapupu,* the *mak sapupu* of his father. First cousin of a parent of his father, she was cousin by category and grandparent by generation to Awang Long, and this was precisely expressed in his definition. (Her reference name was, I think, teknonymous as well as expressing her seniority.) An interesting point was the difference between the structural and the organizational aspects of this relationship. Awang Long was her *chuchu sapupu*—but he added, "But she cares for me as if I were her own grandson!"

Two further points can be made about these kin terms. In accordance with the general specificatory character of the system a person may trace his relationship to another through more than one channel and so have a choice of terms and behaviors in regard to him. So in the instance shown in Figure 1.3, Bidah was great-grandchild (*chichit*) of Pak Che Mat and niece (*anak saudara*) of Meriam his wife. Bidah lived with them, since her mother had died in childbirth with another baby and her father's sister had acted as foster-mother to her. Pak Che Mat and Bidah behaved to each other as grandparent and grandchild. He called her by name and she (I think) called him *to' chu,* since there was a very considerable age difference.

The second point is that there is some flexibility in kin ter-

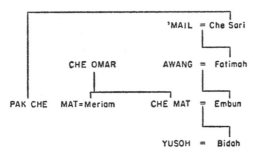

Figure 1.3.   Pak Che Mat and his wife's niece
Note: Capital letters indicate males.

minology even in a unitary relationship. Ordinarily a father-in-law is called *pak*, the same term as for a father, by his son-in-law. But Awang Long called his father-in-law *che*, equivalent to "sir," presumably an abbreviated form of *inche* (*enche*), the usual term prefixed to a male personal name in formal circumstances and applicable to people of the same generation. The reason given to us by him was that he used the same term as did his wife. "*Pak* would not be so good, because Che Mah (his wife) calls him *che*." Awang Long discussed such alternate terms of respect for parents-in-law further. "If one is not married to their children one calls men *pak ngah, pak do, po' chik, po' nik, pak chu, po' teh*, one can call them any one of these.[8] When one has married one of their children, if the child calls him *che*, one calls him *che* too; if the child calls him *pak*, the son-in-law calls him *pak* too. In the same way with uncles and cousins (*pak saudara, pak sapupu*), they are called similarly. Like my nephews and nieces, half call me *pak ngah*, half call me *'uo*, the elder ones call me *'uo*." He added that corresponding alternate terms for females were *mak ngah, 'uo meh*, and so on.

How general is the use of kin terms in specifying persons, and in distinguishing categories of persons, in Kelantan rural life?

---

[8] They are all abbreviations of terms for various kinds of junior uncles; *tengah*, middle; *muda*, junior; *kechil*, little, etc.; they are in effect diminutives. (The speaker used *Pak* and *Po'* forms indiscriminately, as given here.)

Downs (1960:56), who worked mainly in Pasir Puteh, states that kinship in Kelantan is of importance for relationships outside the village, but because so many of the people are related in some degree to one another, kinship is of minor importance as a discriminating factor within the village itself. I am inclined to put the matter rather differently. In my experience kin terms are often used in the village in providing a social description of persons, to set them in the general framework of personalities for identification. Expressions equivalent to "he is a sibling/first cousin's child/younger brother . . . of So-and-so" were very common wherever I went in Kelantan and served as most useful means of discrimination. Moreover, it was just because so many of the people *were* related that discrimination in kin terms had such meaning; if only very few had local kin, there would be little point in using kin terms in general social relations. The specificatory nature of the system, too, lent itself to the making of fine distinctions, as I have shown. What the use of kin terms as identifiers does, in particular, is to point up significant social alignments, symbolizing the recognition and implementation of social relationships.

What about the character of kin groups? Burridge (1956) has identified, from his examination of Malay villagers in Johore, what he describes as agnatic or patrilineal descent groups, albeit of shallow depth. How clearly these units are structured in Johore is perhaps a matter of interpretation, and perhaps a local phenomenon due to the ancestral Bugis incursions. But an obvious question is the degree to which they can be paralleled in rural Kelantan society. Here the evidence seems decidedly negative. Downs argues that kinship in Kelantan provides no basis for the formal organization of the community, and that while one has certain obligations to close relatives, friendship and proximity are equally important, if not more so, than kinship in the determination of subgroupings within the village. While not prepared to endorse these statements fully, I too have found very little to suggest that there is any corporate association of patrilineal kin beyond the sibling level, in any enduring form. Kin sharing of a house plot (*bekas rumah*) is perhaps the most usual form of permanent cooperation. But as sibling joint owners die, the heirs tend to divide the land on which their houses stand. An illustration of the process at work was given by residents of a plot near where we lived. The plot of land had been common property of a woman and her brothers; she and one brother were dead, and several houses were occupied by one surviving brother and the children and grandchildren of all the siblings. But already relations were bad between the children of the dead woman and those of the surviving brother, and there was prospect that the property would be split before long. In summary, among Kelantan peasants, the limit of corporate kin-group formation, holding property in common, was about three generations, and the kin ties were bilateral, not exclusively patrilineal. It does not seem appropriate, then, to speak of patrilineages in such circumstances. (Conditions among the Kelantan aristocracy are likely to be different.)

But the absence of unilineal (or bilateral) descent groups of a corporate character does not mean that the kin principle is unimportant for grouping of people on periodic occasions of ceremony. At a circumcision feast, celebration of a boy's completion of reading the Koran, marriage (particularly first marriage), or a funeral, people assemble very largely on a kin basis. Neighbors and friends attend, but kin are the core of the proceedings. And apart from personal crisis rites or achievement rites, more public occasions of celebration, such as the Birthday of the Prophet, often specifically involve the participation or entertainment of kin. All such occasions tend to involve persons in their capacity as *waris*.

Meaning and Delimitation of Waris

The Malay term *waris*, derived from the Arabic *warith*, means most simply "heir; inheritor." More generally, it is applied to anyone eligible to inherit under Muslim law—that is, normally, to specified kin. The prime principle of inheritance among Malays, as among Arabs, is consanguineal kin relationship based on common descent. The rules of inheritance in the Koran stress the position of males in the agnatic relationship, giving sons twice the inheritance portion of daughters unless the heirs should agree otherwise. Muslim law places great store on the importance of agreement, and in Malay society generally it seems to be common for daughters to be given portions substantially larger than the minimum shares specified by the Koran, even of the same approximate value as those given to their brothers.[9]

In Negri Sembilan, in the area following the *adat perpateh* customary rules, the stress on female rights emerges in matrilineal transmission of major property. Daughters tend to inherit from their mothers and not from their fathers, particularly with what is known as "customary land," the traditional property in which matrilineal descent groups have overrights. Succession to traditional offices and titles, held by men, is also matrilineal. Whereas then the term *waris* in Malay society generally applies bilaterally, with transmission of rights through men and women and a predisposition in favor of males, in Negri Sebilan it is unilateral, with the more specific meaning of a matrilineal descent group having defined social and economic functions, including rights of succession to traditional political office. These facts, which are very well known,[10] point up the contrast of the Kelantan situation.

[9] See, for example, E. N. Taylor (1937:8–10), Judith Djamour (1959:-40), Raymond Firth (1966:140).

[10] According to R. J. Wilkinson (1903), in Minangkabau states *waris* is used for "tribal officials who control the law of succession." Cf. *idem*, 1932. P. Favre (1875, Vol. 1:218) gives the meaning of *waris* in terms of inheritance alone—*héritier, legataire*, etc. M. G. Swift (1965:14–16, 176) translates *waris* as "heirs, in Negri Sembilan applied to the clan." J. M. Gullick (1958:38–42, 75–78) illustrates how the term is applied as a title to those matrilineal clans with special status. Downs (1967:136, 138) gives the Arabic form *warith* as if it were used by the Malays he studied, and equates it with "all relatives." In Perak the *Waris Negeri* is a large category of persons of specified royal descent in patrilineal form, theoretically eligible to succeed to the throne (Wilkinson 1932; Kahar Bador 1967).

In Kelantan, *waris* are not corporate descent groups of exclusive unilineal membership, nor is the accent in their relationship
primarily on inheritance. They are essentially *sets* of personal kin,
apparently equivalent to the *saudara* of other Malay areas (Burridge 1956:61; Djamour 1959:23). To explain their nature I
examine the following points: the genealogical significance of
the *waris* tie and the degree to which genealogical connection
can be assumed without demonstration; the relative significance
of links through males and through females; the erosion of *waris*
ties through genealogical distance; the degree of localization of
waris; differentiation between kinds of *waris;* who are not *waris;*
the social and economic significance of *waris* ties; the extent to
which people who are *waris* operate in individual or collective
terms.

The first question to consider is the definition of *waris* in
genealogical terms. To be counted as *waris* must a person have
a demonstrable genealogical link? And conversely, are all persons
with whom a genealogical link is traceable counted as *waris?*

Indubitably, the basis of the *waris* tie is genealogical connection. The use of what is ordinarily considered as a kinship term—
to', pak, mak—does not in itself entitle a person to be categorized
as one's *waris;* such terms may be simply part of the system of
status recognition of senior-generation persons. For inclusion in
the category of *waris* there must be a demonstrable or a presumptive genealogical relationship. Usually, someone who is *waris* can
be identified in alternative kin terms, as the son of a first cousin,
for example. In the use of the rather vague affirmative expression
waris-waris-lah, applied collectively to a set of people who are
"kinds of relatives," it is assumed that the links are known, or
could be traced if all the evidence were available. So in Fig. 1.4
old Belo was described by Awang Long as among his *waris,* as
his *to' sapupu,* though he said the precise link between them was
not known to him; he could not remember whether it was on his
father's or his mother's side. So even though a genealogical tie
may be known traditionally but not traceable in detail, if the
persons so involved wish it they may count each other as *waris.*

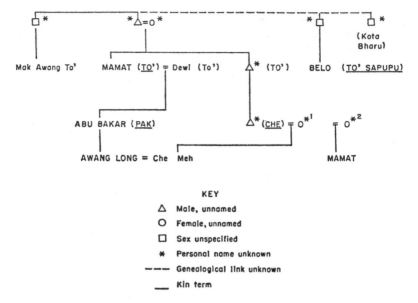

Figure 1.4. Some *waris* of Awang Long
Note: Capital letters indicate males.

Important here is the factor of local residence; if the people concerned see each other frequently and can have occasion for common participation in everyday and ceremonial affairs, there is a greater tendency for them to define their relationships in *waris* terms.

Recognition of such *waris* ties is bilateral. Contacts are maintained between men and women who are so related—as cousins, for example—and their children are reckoned as *waris*. For instance, two second cousins, fishermen, recognized the son of another second cousin as their *anak duapupu* and cooperated with him as such; all the links except the grandfather of one fisherman were women, and were valid for *waris* reckoning. (Other examples appear later.)

What is very clear is the shallowness of genealogical knowledge held by most peasants. The lack of a literary tradition in earlier

Kelantan education and rural life generally may have acted to some extent as an impeding factor. The absence of surnames among Malays[11] has also militated against simple identification of lineal kin over more than two generations. Again, Kelantan rural society is perhaps less interested in genealogical depth than are some other Malay societies, but the crucial point would seem to be the relation between memory, face-to-face encounter, and common interests. To have *seen* elderly relatives seems to be an important element in remembering them, and to have heard them talk of kin is a great aid in recognition of ties.

Where genealogical connection is traceable, it seems usually not to go further back in time than two direct kinship grades (Raymond Firth 1964:117–121) from any adult of middle age —that is, covering no more than five generations in all. So, Awang Long, when aged about forty, could give the name of his father and FF, and of his MFB, of his FM and MM, but not of his FFB or his FFF, nor did he know the name of his WFF (Figure 1.4). Our neighbor Awang-Yah and his sister Minah (Figure 1.5) could go no further back than their FF. Pak Che Mat, when in his sixties, could not even remember the name of his FF or any of his father's brothers. He said that he was the youngest child in the family, and that knowledge of this kind was obtainable only by word of mouth from people of an older generation.

Corresponding to the shallow genealogy, the tracing of *waris* often does not go beyond second cousins (grandparents' siblings' grandchildren), plus their children and grandchildren. *Sapupu* and *duapupu* were relatively commonly identified among *waris*, as were *anak sapupu* and *anak duapupu. Chuchu sapupu* and *chuchu duapupu* (grandchildren of first and second cousins) were occasionally cited. *Tigapupu* were also recognized in theory

[11] The demands of modern administrative record, often requiring evidence of ancestry, and the felt need for a system of personal identification of a character more easy to fit in with other systems elsewhere, has led to some change in practice among educated Malays.

and actually on the ground as *waris,* though not very often. Minah, our landlady, described Awang Long as among her *waris* in such terms, through the cousinship of their parents. Fourth cousins (*empatpupu*) can be recognized theoretically but are rarely identified. Asked if she could recollect any, Minah at first said she had none. But then she remembered that the old people talked of a fourth cousin of her mother's (with whom she had no social relations), and a few days later she herself referred to a son of Awang Long as *empatpupu* (strictly speaking he was *anak tigapupu*). Asked about the possibility of *limapupu* and *enampupu* (fifth or sixth cousins), Minah replied rather scornfully that she had never heard tell of such.

There are four points to be made here regarding the relation of *waris* membership to genealogical linkage. The first is that in general it is only consanguine links which entitle people to be included among one's *waris.* (The special position of immediate affines is discussed later.) The second point is that since consanguineal ties often become fairly rapidly eroded as the connecting links in the senior generations become lost to memory, people who could be recognized as *waris* remain unknown; normally they are people who live in other communities. The third point is that where face-to-face relations are frequent, even if knowledge of exact genealogical linkage is lacking, inclusion of persons—especially senior persons—among one's *waris* is still possible, although perhaps not common. The fourth point is the operational distinction between theoretical or inferential *waris* membership and empirical recognition. Genealogical admission of a fifth or sixth cousin is possible, but in practice this just does not happen; although the persons may be known, they are treated as too distant to count, and hence as non-kin.

Some of these processes in the delimitation of *waris* membership and the erosion of kin ties are illustrated by some of the relationships of Awang Long. He said in 1947 that he had *waris* only in Kelantan and Thailand; he had none in other states. (Consequently he professed entire ignorance of the term *adat perpateh* and its customs; he said he had never heard of them, because he had no *waris* in Negri Sembilan.) As regards Kelantan, he said at first that in the capital, Kota Bharu, he had no *waris*, then on reflection that he had a few. The old people had told him that they had first cousins there. "But they don't come here; I don't know them, they don't know me." (He knew no names of people in his great-grandparents' generation.) With this lapse of kin knowledge of people living twenty-five miles away was contrasted his kin position at Gutung, near Pasir Tumboh, about twenty miles from his home. There, he said, he had many *waris*, *adek beradek* of his mother's father, who lived there. These people were of grandparent category—*jadi to' to'*. So, grandparents' first cousins at a distance were *waris*, though not personally known, but were at first forgotten and were obviously passing out of range through lack of communication. Their descendants would soon cease to count as *waris*. But grandparents' siblings, at a lesser distance, were personally known and immediately recollected; their descendants would continue as *waris* for some time. Awang Long's FF, FM, and MM were local. Living locally, a grandparent's first cousin counted as *waris*, even though the precise genealogical link was not known.

A person's *waris* tends to be identified with particular localities, with particular reference to the home of his or her parents and grandparents. A marked distinction exists in the Perupok area as elsewhere in Kelantan between people who are locally born (*orang sini*, people from here) and those born elsewhere but now resident in the area (*orang lain*, different people, "foreigners"). It was said of an immigrant often that he had no local kin—*orang lain, ta'ada waris sini*. The definition of his immigrant status was given, in effect, in terms of lack of local kin. A locally born person tends to have a strong concentration of *waris* nearby. But a person's *waris* may be distributed in several communities, according to the origin of his parents and grandparents, as with Awang Long cited above. Again, Yah, the wife of one of our neighbors, came from Kubang Golok, a mile up the coast. Her husband said, "Perhaps her cousins together with her cousin's children—first cousins only—are two hundred people. In Kubang Golok there's not a nonrelative of hers; all are *waris* of hers." When I expressed surprise at the numbers, he explained that she had ten uncles and her siblings were very prolific; one had twelve children, all of one wife!

The significance of the locality factor in the distribution of *waris* is twofold. A local concentration of *waris* makes for strong support in all the ceremonial events which a man as husband and father is obliged to undertake in the course of his life in a community. They may help him with cash gifts, but in particular they give him services for which he otherwise would have to pay cash. So a man without *waris* locally is at a great disadvantage. But the existence of *waris,* especially in some numbers, in another community gives a person an occasion for social visits abroad, a point of entry for trading enterprises, a source of labor to assist him if his local supplies fail. The kin of a person's mother, if she has come from another community, tend to fill this latter position most effectively. As an example of the kind of relationship which *waris* tend to maintain in such circumstances, neighbors of ours had first cousins owning rice and rubber land in a community inland at some distance. The cousins had a private car, in which they occasionally came to our coastal village, bringing a load of durian, rambutan, and other fruit for sale. Combining pleasure and business, they used to visit their kin, usually bringing a gift of rice or fruit and getting some fish in return. Such ties with *waris* in other communities may be very highly regarded and given as a reason for actions not otherwise explicable. When the wife of Ja'par, a fishing expert, died she was buried in the cemetery at Bachok about a mile from her home, a long hot walk in the sun for the large procession. When I enquired of a casual bystander why she was not buried in the cemetery much nearer at hand the reply was, "Don't know—perhaps her *waris* are of Bachok." The point here is not whether this was the true reason, but that it was regarded as adequate.

In the light of the social support likely to be given by kin, it is of significance to have some idea of the number of *waris* whom a person may ordinarily have in recognized relationship, and their degree of localization in relation to the size of the local community. Any systematic calculation of such magnitudes would be a very laborious operation, but I did collect information from a few people. What seemed to be a case of ordinary kind was that of our landlady, sister of Awang-Yah (outlined in Figure 1.5).

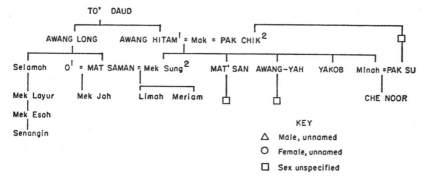

Figure 1.5.   Some close kin of Minah
Note: Capital letters indicate males. Numbers indicate marriage order.

She listed her *waris* in the vicinity as follows:

- a. Her mother, who lived with her (*mak*).
- b. Her son, aged twelve, who lived with her (*anak*).
- c. One sister and two brothers, living in the same village (sister and one brother being almost next door) (*adek beradek*).
- d. One brother living a mile away, inland (*adek beradek*).
- e. Two sisters' daughters (married); two brothers' daughters and three brothers' sons (unmarried) all living near; and one brother's son, married, working away but often returning home. All these were *anak saudara*.
- f. About a dozen children of nieces and nephew (*chuchu saudara*).

g. One mother's brother (*pak saudara*), a mile inland.
h. Six first cousins (*sapupu*)—one male, one female, father's brother's children, nearby; three male, one female, mother's brother's children—a mile away.
i. Six children of first cousins (*anak sapupu*), four male and two female, nearby.
j. One grandchild of a first cousin (*chuchu sapupu*) and one great-grandchild (*chichit sapupu*) both female, nearby.
k. Two second cousins (*duapupu*), one male, one female, nearby.
l. One third cousin (*tigapupu*), nearby.

It is sometimes said that all members of a Malay kampong are closely interrelated by kinship and marriage. But while valid for many members, this is not by any means true for all, in a large coastal community such as Perupok. Thus, within about a mile from her home this woman had about forty-five admitted *waris,* of whom the adult members comprised twenty-one males and twelve females. In addition, she had an unnumbered group of half a dozen or so in an inland village some twenty miles away; this included at least one male first cousin and they occasionally came to visit her in their motorcar. In addition, her nearby third cousin had sons, but she said these did not really count as *waris.*

The specification of these people as her *waris* was made very clearly by this woman, as is usual in such cases, and it was apparent that she was related by consanguinity to really only a very small fraction of the surrounding kampong population, which amounted at least to one thousand within much less than a mile. From other enquiries and some general observation, I would estimate that in this Kelantan rural area a set of *waris* whom a person would ordinarily recognize would comprise not more than fifty to sixty persons. In addition, specific social relationship is recognized with close affines; and special problems are presented in this recognition by the frequency of adoption and of divorce. But even if some affines be included in a set of *waris*, the total number of persons comprised under such a head for any individual cannot normally be put much above the figure mentioned. This applies to folk of long residence in the area, the "local people." For someone of recent arrival or even someone whose father or mother was an immigrant, the number of local *waris* may be very small indeed. The deceased husband of our landlady, who was not of local origin, had had very few *waris* living locally— two nephews, a niece, a grandniece, and a first cousin (FBD), making only five in all.

The *waris* category is by no means an undifferentiated one. Not only are persons categorized by the grades of their genealogical relationship, they are also divided according to whether their relationship is "near" or "far." This is a description in genealogical rather than in geographical terms. A member of one's *waris* may be described as being nearby or far away according to where he lives, but if he is described as *waris dekat* or *waris jauh* (near *waris* or far *waris*), this is primarily a matter of genealogy. *Waris dekat* includes siblings, first cousins, siblings of parents, nephews, and nieces. Second cousins and children of nephews and nieces may be included, but this seems optional. *Waris jauh* may include second cousins, and certainly does include their children and third cousins. There may be also, however, to some extent an affective quality in the application of these terms. Minah in 1963 described Awang Long, who was her third cousin (*tiga-pupu*), as *waris jauhjauh,* a rather far kinsman, and justified this by indicating that relations between them were tenuous. She said, "Minah is not up to coming to his house. He is a bit proud. He is a man of learning." She added that if he had a feast he did not invite her. I asked if other people of distant kinship were the same. "No," she said, some invited her, and cited a second cousin who had and to whom she went. (This man's sister, also a *waris jauhjauh,* was "a bit closer than Awang Long.") But she pointed out that the economic factor might enter also. "It is because I am a poor person he does not invite me. If he did invite me I would not go. I have not got the money." Minah noted rather acidly that before we came to live in her house Awang Long, who was an old friend of ours, never came to visit her. Once we were installed he came. She remarked on this to us and also twitted him about it.

Thus, of the set of persons characterized as *waris* there is a grading in operational terms. This grading corresponds in general, but not at all exactly, with genealogical distance. More distant *waris* may be mobilized for special occasions, but for ordinary social and economic purposes a person's operational set of *waris* comprises probably a score or so of closely related people with whom recognition is fairly regularly exchanged.

Waris *and Not*-Waris

To understand fully what *waris* means one must indicate who are not counted as *waris* though they may appear on a person's genealogy as related to him. For these people the expression *orang lain* (different persons) is used. The categories involved here are step-kin, half-kin, and affines.

Step-kin among Malays comprise (1) a person who is not one's parent but who is married to one's widowed or divorced parent; (2) a woman who is married polygynously to one's father; (3) a child of such a person by another spouse than one's parent; (4) a child of a person to whom one is married, but by a former spouse. For all of these persons the ordinary kin terms are used, with the adjunct *tiri* (step) added. But none of these persons is classed as *waris* to oneself because there is no consanguineal tie at all.

With half-siblings the situation is rather different. Patrilineal half-siblings are not only referred to by kin terms but are regarded as *waris* because they have a father in common. For instance, Awang-Yah said that a woman Mek Joh, though no relation to him, was a half-sister to his nieces (sister's daughters Limah and Meriam in Figure 1.5), being their father's daughter by an earlier wife. I asked, "Are they step-siblings (*adek beradek tiri*)?" He replied, "No! A different mother but real siblings; though a different mother, true siblings." Then he added significantly. "If Mek Jon were rich and she died, Limah together with Meriam would inherit." So, with a common father but different mothers, children are true siblings (*adek beradek betul*). But with a common mother and different fathers, children are classified apart. According to my informants, such cannot be *waris*. They are called *adek beradek saudara anjing*.[12] Minah said, "*Saudara anjing* are not able to become *waris;* they cannot become *waris* because they have a different father. If they have one father but different mothers they are true siblings because the same blood has entered each of them."

What this statement was expressing was not so much a patrilineal bias in the kinship system as the sense of male privilege which underlies much of Malay custom in this field and is consonant with the Muslim customs of polygyny and inheritance from the father. The asymmetry of the sex code is indicated particularly by the total absence of polyandry, plural husbands being inconceivable for a Malay woman, while plural wives are feasible and still enjoyed by some Malay men, to the indignation of many modern Malay women. Yet notwithstanding the asymmetry, not only is the kinship system in general bilateral, but also children of the same mother by different fathers *are adek beradek* and may well be closer in their social ties than patrilineal half-siblings. In fact, if their father came from another district and has been long divorced from their mother, it may be only on his death, when matters of inheritance arise, that the different position of some children of the same mother becomes obvious. Moreover, if one recognizes a mother's brother as *waris* it seems illogical to say that one's mother's other children are not *waris*. But the Malay position is in accord with the legal and conceptual

---

[12] Literally the term means "siblings of dog relationship" (see also Djamour 1959:26), but the expression can be offensive and is not commonly heard in Kelantan.

recognition of polygyny and not of polyandry. In the Malay view, a man can create one family by two wives; a woman cannot have one family by two husbands.

A cautionary note with respect to interpretation of such kinship data is worth a slight digression here. Awang Long had married his second cousin (Figure 1.4). He told me that she had a half-brother, Mamat, son of the same father but a different mother, and that this man was *waris* to him; had he been of a different father but the same mother as Awang's wife, then he would not have been *waris* to Awang. This may look like a patrilineal bias to the *waris* system. But it is a direct implication from the fact that the connecting link between Awang Long and his wife prior to their marriage was her father, who was Awang's FFBS; hence if the wife and her half-brother had been children of the same mother, not the same father, the half-brother and Awang Long would not have been consanguineal relations at all.

The third category of persons who appear on one's genealogy but who are normally not counted as *waris* is affines. For instance, Pak Che Mat (Figure 1.3) was married to Meriam, whose brother Che Mat was married to a *chuchu saudara* of Pak Che Mat. But Pak Che Mat said quite specifically that he and Meriam were not *waris;* they were *orang lain*. Again, Minah recognized one of her neighbors as *anak sapupu,* her cousin's son, and *waris,* but she classed his wife, a local person, as *orang lain* and not *waris*.

While this principle was definite for affines in general there was some ambiguity about the classification of immediate affines, such as brother/sister-in-law and son/daughter-in-law. Here I got some quite firm opinions. When Awang-Yah gave me a list of the men who attended a religious feast in his house he included brother, brother's son, and brother's son-in-law among his *waris* present. When I asked about the relationship of this last man to himself he said he was a nephew (*anak saudara*), adding, "If he marries an *anak saudara* of mine, then he becomes an *anak saudara* too." Later, Awang discussed another such case with me.

Again, he said, "If he marries with a *waris* of ours, he becomes *waris* of ours."

The situation from Awang's viewpoint was clear. An immediate affine, a person actually married to a *waris*, becomes *waris* himself. But it must be stressed that this is only for the period during which he remains married to the *waris* person; the *waris* tie terminates if there is a divorce, although of course any child of the marriage continues to be one's *waris*. This nominal admission to *waris* membership of immediate affines in full status may be idiosyncratic; I have no indication that it conveys any legal right whatsoever, and without carrying out any wide enquiry I suspect that many rural people would not endorse this classification. (Minah, sister to Awang-Yah, for instance, refused to admit her niece's husband as her *waris;* she insisted he was *orang lain.*) It is a theoretical, even somewhat artificial, inclusion. If a person becomes *waris* on marriage but ceases to be such when the marriage ends, he is not on the same footing as permanent consanguineal kin and in this sense is not true *waris*. (The term *sabit* may be used for immediate affines.) It is important to note that his affinal *waris* membership is only for certain limited purposes such as granting hospitality or requiring small services. He is not a legal heir and he is not classed as a *waris* of his spouse when the husband/wife groups happen to be opposed. But it is of distinct sociological interest that here is a principle of what may be called *contingent kinship*—membership of a kinship category as a matter of individual terminable recruitment for certain specified statuses. I will refer later to the more general relevance of this.

It is important to stress that the *waris* of such an affine are not themselves regarded as *waris* of Ego. Minah was categorical on this. She categorized her next-door-neighbor and his wife as not *waris* although the wife was the elder sister of her own brother's wife. Another neighbor was a nephew of her late husband and so a first cousin of her son, but she did not regard him as *waris* of hers. He was "nothing of significance (*tidak apāapa*)," meaning that he was not part of her sphere of kinship action. Parent and child have overlapping but not identical *waris*. Because Awang-Yah, Minah's brother, was more liberal in his *waris* definition, I tried very hard to see if Awang would admit the logic of his position: that if the husband of a woman who is *waris* to Awang also becomes *waris* to Awang so long as he is married to this woman (as Awang himself affirmed), then the husband's *waris* too should become part of Awang's *waris*. But Awang would not have this. It was clear that only the immediate affine himself was taken into the *waris* category. There is *contingent* but not *inferential waris* membership. Put more generally, *waris* may include an immediate affine of a consanguine, but not the consanguine of an affine and, even less, an affine of an affine. In particular, one has to distinguish the *consanguineal kin set* from the genealogical network.

Waris *as Operational Category*

How far can the *waris* of a person be considered as a kin *group?* Conceptually, I think, they are often so regarded by Kelantan Malays, especially when they are not dispersed but are in strong local concentration, able to assemble in a body for some collective action. They may be spoken of collectively, and as if acting corporately on some ceremonial occasions. But in practice there seems to be great latitude for individual interpretation of *waris* responsibilities and obligations, and very little action as a united body. Usually it seems to be only a small set of siblings and their children, with possibly parents or grandparents, who operate with any great consistency and regularity in group terms. Even then there is considerable selectivity in behavior. *Adek beradek* who are true siblings may be in bad relations and refuse to cooperate. *Waris* then is a *category* and *set of personal kin,* rather than a kin group.

In the field of marriage there is no notion of *waris* as an exogamous group or as a category of persons who should not marry. The ordinary peasant conventions follow Islamic rules,

laying down a set of near kin with whom marriage is forbidden—
including, for a man, aunt, niece, sibling, step-mother, grandchild, great-grandchild (*mak saudara, anak saudara, adek beradek, mak tiri, chuchu, chichit*). But first cousin, first cousin's
child, second cousin, and so on, are marriageable, although they
are *waris*, and many examples of such unions appear in my
genealogies. As an example, Mek Sung, sister of Minah and
Awang-Yah, was married to Mat Saman; her father and her husband's father were brothers. Hence Mat Saman was both consanguine and affine to Awang-Yah. As Awang said, "He's my
cousin once, and he's become my elder brother-in-law once—
waris twice over." The notion of kinship creating a good foundation for marriage was illustrated by the marriage of Minah.
When Minah was quite small her mother was divorced from her
father. When her mother remarried, Minah lived in her stepfather's house. Although she married and divorced several times,
she bore no children. In due course her stepfather said it would
be a good thing if she married his nephew; both were willing,
they married, had a son, and lived together for more than twenty
years until her husband died.

There are three spheres in Kelantan rural life in which the role
of *waris* is most clearly seen: informal social relations, small-scale
economic cooperation, and ceremonial occasions. Residentially,
little neighborhood groups often form, consisting of parents and a
married son or daughter; siblings and their children; an aunt or
uncle and a nephew or niece, with children. Members of such
households are apt to drop in on one another at any time of the
day, and a great deal of interchange of information and advice
takes place. Other *waris* living within a radius of a mile or so
commonly call from time to time. The spirit healer To' Mamat
Mindok, living in Kubang Golok, had no *waris* in Pantai Damat
except his *anak duapupu*, the junior wife of a local fisherman.
There was no economic bond to draw them together, but he
made a specific point of dropping by to see her when affairs
brought him that way. Similar interchanges may take place with
neighbors and friends, but what is significant is the selectivity in

the behavior of *waris* and the air of comparative freedom with which they enter the house of their kin.

In more general social relations the role of *waris* is diffuse but can be very important. Although there are no very highly formalized obligations for *waris*, there is often a distinct sense of moral responsibility. If, for instance, as occasionally though rarely happens, an unmarried girl becomes pregnant, not only her father but also her other *waris* are ashamed, as are the *waris* of the man concerned. When a woman is widowed her *waris* take counsel together about her remarriage. If a man gets a bad reputation his *waris* try to induce him to change his ways. In an argument or a fight a person expects his *waris* to stand by him and they usually do so. This characteristic of identification by *waris* was illustrated for me by a remark about a man who had not been able to build up any skilled position for himself in fishing. It was said that he was a person of little value; that his *waris* had use for him but nobody else had!

This identification by *waris* was exemplified in a rather odd symbolic way by Pak Che Mat. Toward the end of our stay in Perupok, To' Mamat Mindok died, and several accounts were given of his appearance after death. A cobra which was seen in the house was said to be his *penggawa*, his guardian spirit, looking for him. Pak Che Mat said he himself had seen To' Mamat, just before the seventh-day celebration after the burial, out at sea in a fishing boat toward morning. The dead man had appeared in the bow of the boat, with his usual black scarf around his neck. "He didn't say anything particular; he said only, 'I'd like one fish.' " Pak Che Mat replied, "That's all right, there are plenty," and the spirit disappeared. When the boat got to shore Pak Che Mat took a whole large fish and half of another and carried them up to the house of the dead man for the funeral feast. He said that the dead often appear like this. They come to the door of a house and look in, they want to see their relatives. They do not speak, but go away; they are angels. But sometimes they appear clad in their usual clothes and say, "I want you to take me and foster me." These are evil spirits (*iblis*), and can be told by their conduct. The kinsman appealed to replies, "I won't take you and foster you; it is not proper; go to another place," and they go. But if the dead do not say anything particular they are angels (*maláikat*). The point of this is the symbolization of *waris* ties by the behavior of spirits. Interest in living relatives, and attempt to pose as relatives and be cared for, conceived as spirit attitudes, are symbolic portrayals of sentiments felt to be proper between kin.

The role of *waris* in social relations is expressed and emphasized by their normally being among the first to be invited to participate in any celebration involving people outside the immediate household. In 1963, Awang-Yah gave a feast in celebration of the Prophet's Birthday. About thirty men were present, including a local shopkeeper, a schoolteacher, and a neighbor noted for his skill in Koranic chant. Awang said that there were many *waris* of his there, including some from inland; indeed in a grand sweep he said, "All my *waris* were there last night." This was an exaggeration, but I listed in that category his elder brother, two first cousins, two brothers' sons, four patrilineal second cousins, one nephew-in-law, and the husband of the adopted daughter of his former wife. In each case Awang described to me very carefully the precise genealogical relationship to himself. Of the second cousins he said, for example, that they were *"waris* a little way afar off, second cousins of mine; their father and my father were first cousins."

Economic relations between *waris* are very varied. It would need a much more elaborate record than I could make to differentiate in magnitude the interchange of goods and services between *waris* as a whole as against that between friends and neighbors. But types of such relations, which I believe to be significant, can be indicated by examples of this order: a net fisherman with a good catch giving some fish to another, his *sapupu,* who had none at the time; a lad going to sea with his brother and *pak saudara;* a man taking two sections of mackerel net belonging to his *pak saudara* and dividing the catch with him. These are simple transactions, paralleling those with non-kin. More complex, and more dependent on specific *waris* acknowledgment, was the case of a man with no net, boat, or other substantial property going to sea with his *sapupu,* who gave over to him the land on which his house stood and a stand of a score or so coconut palms to help provide food for his family; or of a man with buffalo or bullocks who ploughed for his elderly female relatives (*mak sapupu* or *mak saudara*) and who did not eat at their house but reserved for himself the grass in their compound as fodder for his animals.

It is notable that in such transactions affines, especially immediate affines, were included, and that the affinal tie was often given as the specific reason for the economic relationship. So, a man hands over his boat to his *adek ipar* (younger sister's husband or wife's younger brother) to run; a man goes out in the boat of his *menantu* (son-in-law); a man and his *kakak ipar* (elder sister's husband or wife's elder brother) go out fishing together—they are termed *adek beradek;* a fishing expert has as his selling agent his *biras,* a term indicating that they married two sisters. Consanguines and affines are often intermingled in a working party. So in the repair of a small boat the owner was helped by his *sapupu* and his *to' saudara* (his MZS and his MMB) and by the *adek ipar* of his *sapupu;* both the great-uncle and the cousin's brother-in-law were described as "nothing in particular" in relationship—just as kinds of relatives (*waris-waris-lah*). For this help no cash payment was made; the workers got a midday meal and a little rice afterward, but if they had been *orang lain* they would have been paid.

Not all economic transactions between *waris* are amiable. It was admitted by people in general that *waris* by no means always responded to their economic responsibilities in case of need; some cousins helped and others did not, and even siblings might behave in the same way. Tensions could grow, high words and even blows be exchanged—*ada baloh* in the local phrase. Awang-Yah told me how he sold his boat and bought a parcel of land for $500, from his *mak sapupu*. Since she was a relative he trusted her and did not change the name in the Land Register, a not uncommon means of evading fees. "I remembered that she was my mother, and that she would not get angry with me." But later bad relations developed between them, and, Awang alleged, she took the land back (since it was still in her name) without returning his money. He resented this betrayal keenly. Two second cousins had a dispute over a fishing lure at sea, and a lawsuit resulted. People in the village commented adversely on this as "not good, because they are *waris.*" Two fishing partners separated in anger, with mutual accusations of bad faith. One was the *anak saudara* of the wife of the other. "They are *waris,*" commented Awang Long, "*adek beradek* have parted. It is not good." Between *waris* such bad relations were regarded as especially shocking, much more so than between any ordinary non-kin, who were not expected by their fellow villagers to show the same moral solidarity.

The role of *waris* is of outstanding significance when life crises occur, either those of illness and death which cannot be planned in advance, or those like circumcision and marriage, which can be timed to some extent according to circumstances.

When a person is ill his *waris,* if they are able, are expected to visit him. Minah said of her dead husband, "Pak Su had only a few *waris.* When he was sick his *waris* didn't come. His nephew, living near, came only intermittently. He had only one uncle, but he was dead already. All my *waris* used to come, but his *waris* didn't." She obviously felt rather bitter about the lack of local kin support for her husband and the resulting burden laid upon her own kin.

An instance of such kin support occurred in a spirit healing performance we saw. We heard that To' Mamat Mindok was going to perform one evening at Kubang Golok. We arrived to find that the performance was to take place in the house next door to his own, the house of his wife's *sapupu,* and that the invalid over whom the rites were to take place was the *adek ipar* of the *sapupu*. This was an almost automatic kin service by a noted healer.

When a person dies his *waris* assemble and take a primary part in the various tasks, both technical and ritual, of holding the corpse while it is being cleansed and shrouded, carrying the bier to the cemetery, reciting the appropriate prayers, and preparing the funeral feast. They normally contribute such services without payment, and on the other hand make a larger contribution in cash than do non-kin to the necessary minimal funeral costs. At the funeral of a woman *sapupu* of his, Awang Long gave a dollar, as against the twenty or thirty cents given by men who were not kin. At another funeral, where the wife of the dead man was his *waris*, Awang Long stayed on shore instead of going fishing and helped to find the money to buy cloth and planks for shroud and coffin for the corpse; he was going to ask his wife for cash, and although she was not *waris* of the wife of the dead man he hoped she would give it. Neighbors and friends take part in the work— they may construct the coffin and bier, for instance—but *waris* are expected to be prominent. Put rather colloquially, men with plenty of *waris* should get a good funeral.

Waris are not invited to a funeral; they simply attend. But for ceremonial occasions of social achievement such as circumcision and marriage it is Kelantan custom to issue formal invitations to all guests except the closest kin. Here the *waris* tie gives a strong presumptive title to invitation. A generation or so ago, before literacy was common among the Kelantan peasantry, it was the custom to issue a verbal invitation to a feast accompanied by the present of a stick of Malay toffee (*dodol*) as a material token. Nowadays an invitation written or printed on a card is usual, and the toffee stick has been abandoned. In 1963 I saw an invitation to our landlady from her *waris* at Lundang, some twenty miles away, to attend a "small occasion" of a circumcision. The invitation was issued by her first cousin, a nephew of her mother (*waris sapupu, anak saudara mak*) and she was addressed as

"Mak Su Minah." (A similar invitation to a marriage specified "from 10 A.M. to 10 P.M.") For a circumcision ceremony relatives will come from considerable distances; I recorded that about a dozen traveled more than fifty miles upriver into the jungle to attend one such occasion.

Participation of *waris* on the larger ceremonial occasions can be of distinct economic importance, for they help with labor. For instance, at one such wedding celebration I recorded a host's elder brother, a second cousin, two father's sister's sons, a junior brother-in-law, and a son-in-law's brother all helping, as well as the bride's father. They were cutting up goat meat and grating coconuts, while their womenfolk were pounding up spices and preparing fish. But *waris* may also contribute substantially in cash. Among Kelantan peasants major social occasions are signalized by a feast, the cost of which is borne only partially by the host, who may in fact hope to recoup most if not all his expenditure from the contributions of his guests.[13] This is where a man who has few local *waris* is at a great disadvantage, and I have heard this given as a reason why a feast was a financial loss. On the other hand, the system of reciprocity in feast invitations, with long-term countercontributions, is such that local *waris* in particular can afford to be generous with their gifts of cash since the odds are that in the long run they themselves will be able to command equivalent contributions from their erstwhile hosts.

At weddings my wife and I attended in 1940, male kin and friends came mostly in the evening and partook of a meal, comprising rice, *lauk,* and *tepong* (flesh food and sweets). Afterward each man contributed a gift of money. Small contributions were handed to the host, between palms, and he received them likewise; both men made the gesture of greeting. Large contributions were handed to an official recipient, in front of whom was a metal stand on which he placed the money. Taking up some coins from a pile in front of him, he began to throw them down

[13] See Raymond Firth (1966:177–182), for details of the finance of such feasts and their economic implications.

on the stand, calling as he did so the name of the donor and the number of dollars contributed, "One, two, three," and so on. The ringing of coins was heard by the spectators, who also counted aloud if they wished. If "ten" was reached a shout went up, in special acknowledgment. A clerk at the side usually wrote down the name and occupation of the donor (to help in identification) and the amount contributed, against any future need for reciprocity. It was noticeable that while gifts of cash ranged from $1 to $15, those in the higher figures were usually from *waris*. In 1963 we attended similar celebrations during which money gifts were made without the publicity of the ringing of coins by the official recipient.[14]

[14] To make such contributions is known in Kelantan as *mengelan* (*pengelan*). (I have written the final, nasalized, syllable also *en*—Firth 1966:177.) I have not been able to identify this term in standard Malay. Some Malays have suggested that it may be derived from *panggilan* (invitation), but phonetically this is implausible; others have declared it to be a local word. Amin Sweeney, to whom I am indebted for comment on the Kelantan expressions in this article, informs me that the Kelantan word is indeed *ngélan,* meaning to go along with a contribution.

Usage of the term is illustrated by the following vernacular statement: "Kalau waris, dia pengelan kuat, dia ingat tidak hilang; kalau orang luar dia pengelan kuat, barangkali hilang saja" (If as a kinsman he contributes heavily, he calls to mind that he cannot lose; if he is a man from outside and he contributes heavily, perhaps he will simply lose). The reference here is to the possibility of reciprocity at a future feast; this is less certain with a stranger who has not the regular contacts of a kinsman.

In 1940 a person planning a formal feast bought *dodol* in large kerosene tins. One tin, holding toffee sticks for about one hundred people, cost $3.50. The toffee, made by Malays, was purchased in Kota Bharu. Awang Long used six tins for his feast; another man used four tins. Going round the invitees took quite a long time, the host usually starting about a fortnight before a feast. Summoning by written invitation (*surat*) had begun by 1940, but was rare. By no means everyone summoned came to the feast: poverty or lack of prestige of the host were among the reasons which kept people away.

In 1940 I recorded that an original invitee to a feast, if he were called by verbal invitation (mouth) only, could enlist others on his own initiative. He could say to friends, "I want ten gallons of rice or fifty coconuts," and they then brought the accumulation along with them to the feast. When they arrived the host would ask, "You have brought invited contributing

The presence of *waris* at a feast, particularly at a circumcision or a wedding, is intended to demonstrate their support of the occasion. They are not usually expected to give economic support unless they attend, but they are normally expected to attend if invited. If they do not attend, particularly if they are close kin, this is regarded as an expression of disapproval of what is taking place, even if as poor people it may be hard for them to afford a contribution. If a celebration such as a wedding is attended by relatively few people, the host will lose heavily in financial terms. But even if many people attend, and financially he is successful, the affair will still be lacking in some social sense if his close kin are absent.

General Observations

From this material certain general conclusions can be drawn. The Kelantan *waris* is a collectivity of kin, defined with reference to specific individuals, and to some degree by those individuals. The demarcation of *waris* shows considerable flexibility. *Waris* are kin, but genealogical demonstration of their kinship is not always insisted upon. Conversely, all kin are not necessarily included in a person's *waris*. The principle of *waris* inclusion is not automatic, but selective. Potential *waris* are eroded at the edges of the system by memory lapse or by refusal to admit the validity of distant kinship ties. Potential relatives are so many in the intermarrying sphere of peasant activity that for sheer economy of social responsibilities and energies an individual must limit his more definite relationships. Within the more immediate range of kin the emphasis given to male superiority and expressed in polygynous marriage and differential inheritance patterns finds its correlate in a formal denial of *waris* relationships to children of the same mother by different fathers, even though these are admitted as kin in other respects. Yet the personal associations

persons. How many are they?" The quantities contributed were entered on a list which served as witness to later reciprocal contributions. The term used for the secondary contributions is *perbawakan*, from *bawa*, to convey.

created by marriage have their pragmatic appeal, and some people are willing to admit as *waris* near affines who would be excluded by the more formal definition of other people. For any individual, then, his or her *waris* is a bilateral set of personal kin, with an optional element in the demarcation of the boundary of the set.

The flexibility of the concept emerges also in the relation of *waris* to *adek beradek*. In one sense a distinction is made between relatives in general and siblings, members of one's own natal family. But the concept of *adek beradek* is generally enlarged to include *sapupu* (first cousins) and when the emphasis is put on the kinship tie between parties, the term may be applied even more widely. Although *waris* and *adek beradek* may seem to merge on occasions, there is a broad distinction in intensity between the *waris* concept of general cooperation and the *adek beradek* concept of kin intimacy.

The notion of *waris* is associated with the notion of moral responsibility, in a two-way process. If a person commits an offense against morality, his *waris* are ashamed; on the other hand, their responsibility toward him is more specific or more socially definable than that of his neighbors and friends. This notion of responsibility emerges in contribution of service; it is the role of *waris* to support their kinsman in practical affairs, and appeal will be made on this basis to a *waris* who lives some distance away rather than to a near neighbor. In particular, when their kinsman is emphasizing his position in society, it is expected of them that they will rally to his cause and give him physical support, services on a noncash basis for which others would be paid, or cash to help meet his commitments. But while *waris* may act collectively on occasion—as in subscribing for a shroud and coffin for a dead kinsman, with one of them acting as holder of the subscriptions—they rarely act in any representative manner but behave with individual freedom in interpretation of their obligations. Hence lack of contribution by *waris*, especially more distant *waris*, is common; this is a source of ill feeling and facilitates the lapse of recognition of that particular *waris* tie. To understand the meaning of the *waris* concept it is necessary to look at it in operational as well as structural terms.

I have described the *waris* situation as I have found it on one section of the Kelantan coast. My hypothesis broadly has been that Malays of this area have an interest in cooperation for general purposes and for social display and have found it convenient to use a kin frame to assist them in this. The kin frame they use, termed *waris,* is primarily a bilateral consanguineal one, but they are accustomed to include near affines in it. Whether these affines are called *waris* or not is a matter of choice. At the same time, they take account of the formal framework of Islam, with its rules of marriage and inheritance, so that in effect there are both official and unofficial definitions of *waris.*

In comparative anthropological discussion it is not unusual to talk of "the Malay kinship system." While this expression is probably valid for the system of basic kinship terms, it can be misleading if it implies a uniformity of institutions and behavior patterns throughout Malay society. Aristocrats and peasants, urban and rural dwellers, fisherman, agriculturalists, and forest exploiters all probably have variant patterns of kinship. The Kelantan situation I have described is that of a particular type of rural area. It is marked by relatively large-scale concentrated settlement with no very clearly marked boundaries or well-developed communication facilities. This permits a high degree of selectivity in kin ties. The preponderance of fishing as an activity, with its ancillaries of craft work and marketing, give many opportunities for cooperation in labor and skill, and hence for use of kin facilities in contrast to those of non-kin. The opposed yet close relation of the coastal fishing strip to the inland agricultural plain leads to considerable exchange of fish for rice and vegetables, even if through a cash medium, and promotes kin interchange at an informal level. I think that factors such as these may well be significant for the form, operation, and intensity of the kinship relations of these Malays. Further comparative studies elsewhere, of the kind which Burridge, Downs, Inge Rudie, Swift, Kessler, Raybeck, Wilder, and others have made, should show more clearly the common factors and the variations in Malay kinship in different areas and conditions, and the relevance of demographic, ecological, and economic factors to these.

References Cited

Bador, Kahar
  1967 Traditional and Modern Leadership in Malay Society. Unpublished doctoral dissertation, University of London.
Brown, C. C.
  1927 Kelantan Malay. Papers on Malay Subjects (Second Series). Singapore: W. T. Cherry, Government Printer.
Burridge, Kenneth
  1956 The Malay Composition of a Village in Johore. Journal of the Malayan Branch of the Royal Asiatic Society 29 (3) : 60–77.
Djamour, Judith
  1959 Malay Kinship and Marriage in Singapore. London: Athlone.
Downs, R. E.
  1960 A Rural Community in Kelantan, Malaya. *In* Studies on Asia. Lincoln: University of Nebraska Press. Pp. 51–62.
  1967 A Kelantanese Village of Malaya. *In* Contemporary Change in Traditional Societies, Vol. 1: Asian Rural Societies. Julian H. Steward, ed. Urbana: University of Illinois Press. Pp. 105–186.
Favre, P.
  1875 Dictionnaire Malais-Français. Vienna: Imprimerie Impériale et Royale. 2 vols.
Firth, Raymond
  1946 Malay Fisherman: Their Peasant Economy. London: Kegan Paul, Trench, Trubner.
  1948 Report on Social Science Research in Malaya. Singapore: V. C. G. Gatrell, Government Printer.
  1964 Essays on Social Organization and Values. London: Athlone.

1966 Malay Fisherman: Their Peasant Economy. London: Routledge & Kegan Paul. 2d ed., rev.
Firth, Rosemary
1966 Housekeeping among Malay Peasants. 2d ed., rev. London: Athlone.
Gullick, J. M.
1958 Indigenous Political Systems of Western Malaya. London: Athlone.
Sweeny, P. L. Amin
1972 The Ramayana and the Malay Shadow-Play. Kuala Lumpur: National University of Malaysia.
Swift, Michael G.
1965 Malay Peasant Society in Jelebu. London: Athlone.
Taylor, E. N.
1937 Malay Family Law. Journal of the Malayan Branch of the Royal Asiatic Society 15 (1) :1–78.
Wilkinson, R. J.
1903 A Malay-English Dictionary. Singapore: Kelly and Walsh.
1932 A Malay-English Dictionary (Romanized). Mytilene: Salavopoulos and Kinderlis. 2 vols.

2. Changing Social Organization on Romónum, Truk, 1947–1965

WARD H. GOODENOUGH

Ideally, ethnographic accounts of cultural change should be based on a record of continuous observation over an extended period. Anthropologists are rarely in a position to obtain such records, however, and commonly resort to the next best strategy, which is to make ethnographic studies of the same community at two or more different times. A comparison of the separate ethnographic records will presumably indicate how the local culture has changed in the interim. To control for the possibility that recorded differences reflect differences in the ethnographic observers rather than changes in the culture, it is preferable to have later studies done by the ethnographers who did the earlier ones. Repeat studies of this kind are regarded with favor by anthropologists as an appropriate strategy for examining change.[1] In 1964 I had an opportunity to return to the small island of Romónum in Truk, Micronesia, where I had been a member of an ethnographic team seventeen years earlier.[2] I did not have a study of change as my principal concern when I went back, but I tried to check my understanding of Romónum's social organiza-

[1] Examples are Margaret Mead's return to the Manus in the Admiralty Islands, Raymond Firth's return to Tikopia, and Lauriston Sharp's return to the Yir Yoront in Australia.

[2] In 1947 I spent seven months on Romónum as a member of a research group from Yale University, led by Professor G. P. Murdock, sponsored by the Pacific Science Board of the National Research Council, and financed by the Office of Naval Research. My return in 1964 was made possible by a research grant from the National Science Foundation (NSF–GS–340).

tion as I had published it in 1951 by such further inquiry as my other research responsibilities allowed me.

This report recounts such changes in family and kinship as I was able to observe and calls attention to some problems that can arise in the course of doing return studies.

Material Evidence of Change

In 1947, Romónum's large interior plateau was covered largely by vegetation that was only two years old. This area had been completely cleared by the Japanese during the war and the population settled entirely along the island's coastal flats (Map 2.1). All but one of the dwelling houses were constructed of sawn lumber, largely salvaged from the Japanese barracks, with floors raised off the ground on piles and corrugated iron roofs from which rain water was caught in fifty-gallon gasoline drums, and in many cases with sliding glass windows.

In 1964 the interior plateau was fully planted in breadfruit and coconut groves. The sweet-potato and manioc gardens that had dotted the bush here in 1947 were entirely gone. About half of the population had moved its dwellings up onto the plateau (Map 2.2), where all dwellings had been located in precolonial times. Most houses were now of traditional frame and thatch construction, corrugated iron being used only for siding, especially on sides exposed to the wind. Houses, moreover, were more widely scattered. The main path along the south shore had fallen into disrepair and in two places had been entirely destroyed by the sea. In other ways, the people seemed to be a little more prosperous than in 1947. The food supply was somewhat better, and there was more cash, mainly from the sale of copra. Several people had boats powered by outboard motors. In effect, the things that had resulted from or been made possible by the Japanese presence, such as roadways and houses with raised floors, had disappeared or were in a state of advanced decay; but the resources of the island were now being much more fully exploited, and the

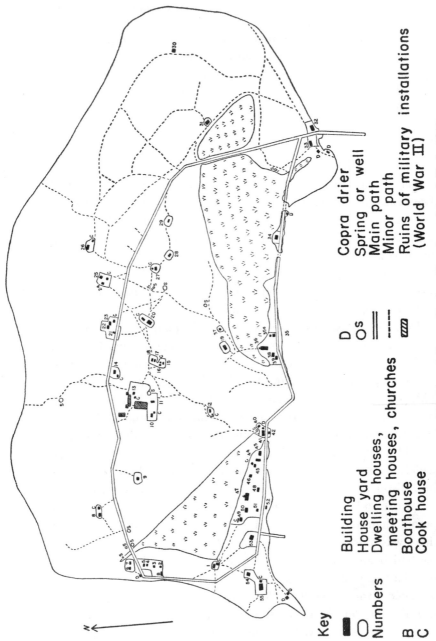

Key

■   Building
◯   House yard
Numbers   Dwelling houses,
           meeting houses, churches
B   Boathouse
C   Cook house

D   Copra drier
Os   Spring or well
═══   Main path
-----   Minor path
▨▨▨   Ruins of military installations
           (World War II)

Map 2.1.   Housing clusters of lineages in Winisi and Corog districts, Romónum Island, Truk, 1948

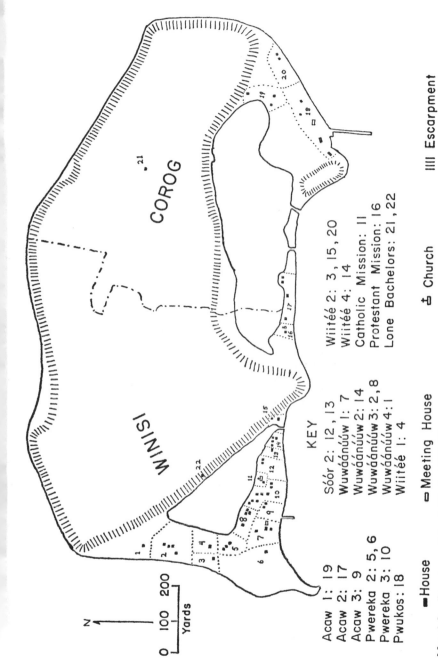

KEY

Acaw 1: 19	Sóór 2: 12, 13
Acaw 2: 17	Wuwáánúúw 1: 7
Acaw 3: 9	Wuwáánúúw 2: 14
Pwereka 2: 5, 6	Wuwáánúúw 3: 2, 8
Pwereka 3: 10	Wuwáánúúw 4: 1
Pwukos: 18	Wiitéé 1: 4

Wiitéé 2: 3, 15, 20	
Wiitéé 4: 14	
Catholic Mission: 11	
Protestant Mission: 16	
Lone Bachelors: 21, 22	

■=House ▭=Meeting House ⚲ Church ‖‖ Escarpment

Map 2.2. Romónum Island, Truk, 1964–65

overall standard of living showed a corresponding modest improvement.

In 1947, Romónum's resident population was 242 persons, including some who were not members of lineages based on Romónum.[3] Residing elsewhere were eighteen persons who were members of lineages or sublineages based on Romónum. In 1964, Romónum's resident population had grown to 296 persons, and the number of Romónum-based individuals residing elsewhere had increased to forty-seven. The increase of 22 per cent in the resident population is small in comparison with the increase of approximately 60 per cent in Truk's total population during the seventeen-year period (from c. 10,000 to c. 16,000). Although there were many more births (148) than deaths (89) on Romónum,[4] the island lost more residents through emigration (24) than it gained through immigration (19). I cannot say that the rate of population movement to and from Romónum has changed since before World War II, for I lack information for earlier periods. Table 2.1 gives a detailed picture of population changes since 1947.

These physical and demographic changes do not in themselves imply any significant change in Romónum's social organization. To show what seems to be happening here it will be necessary first to give a sketch of the traditional social system.[5]

Traditional Social System

In precolonial times, property in land was held both individually and corporately by lineages and sublineages (*eterekes*). In

[3] A lineage (or sublineage) is said to be based on Romónum if its members have permanent rights in land there.

[4] Given an average population of 266 and average number of births per year of 8.7 and deaths per year of 5.5, the average crude birth rate for the period 1947–1964 is 33 per thousand per year, and the average crude death rate is 21 per thousand per year.

[5] The picture of Romónum's social organization outlined in my earlier report (Goodenough 1951) seems to have been reasonably accurate as far as it went. I was able to add considerably in 1964 to my understanding of its workings. The account given here takes advantage of this additional information.

the case of individually owned property, full title (Goodenough 1951) passed to a man's or a woman's children and became their corporate property. If a woman had children by different husbands, the children pooled whatever holdings they acquired from their respective fathers into a single estate, which they held collectively. Illegitimate children had equal rights with legitimate ones in this corporate estate.[6] The resulting corporation of siblings became the beginning of a sublineage, the children of the sisters among them being added to its membership. If title passed to an only child, the property remained, in effect, under individual rather than corporate ownership.

Under corporate ownership the rights of individuals derived from their membership in the owning group. The corporation held title and there was no inheritance until the group was without childbearing female members. Heirs to the corporation's property were the children of its male members, its *éfékúr*, who were regarded as the corporation's children. Authority over the corporation's property lay with its senior male member. He was the eldest brother among a group of uterine siblings, and the eldest son of the eldest woman in the senior female line in the case of groups several generations deep. In such groups, however, if he was not the lineage's eldest male, he shared the authority with that individual, the latter serving as the group's executive head and the former as its symbolic head until he reached middle age and thereby became old enough to assume executive as well as symbolic leadership.

Whoever exercised authority over the corporation's landholdings was called the *sowuppwún* (lord of the soil). No one else could harvest anything from it without his permission. At the same time he was responsible for the needs of his junior kinsmen within the corporation. This responsibility is dramatized in a story about the demigod Wonofáát, who selfishly refused to allow

---

[6] The minimal familial unit in Romónum reckoning is the *owunnun*, consisting of an adult woman, all of her children, and her current husband. The closest possible sibling bond is between the children of one mother.

Table 2.1. Changes in Romónum's population between December 1947 and December 1964

Lineage or sublineage*	1947		1964		Between 1947 and 1964						
	On Rom.	Off Rom.	On Rom.	Off Rom.	Died On	Off	Born On	Off	Born & Died†	Emigrated	Immigrated
Acaw 1	19	0	16	3	6	0	5	0	3	3	1
(Maasané)	4	–	9	–	0	–	6	–	0	1	0
Acaw 2	21	0	36	1	3	0	19	0	1	1	0
(Fesinimw)‡	0	–	5	–	0	–	3	–	0	0	2
(Sóór)§	0	–	4	1	0	–	3	–	0	0	1
Acaw 3	2	2	8	1	1	0	6	0	0	0	1
Pwereka 1	1	0	0	0	1	0	0	0	0	0	0
Wuwáánúúw 5	3	1	2	1	1	0	0	0	0	0	0
(Fesinimw)‡	2	–	0	–	0	–	0	–	0	2	0
(Maasané)	4	–	0	–	0	–	0	–	0	4	0
Pwereka 2a	6	0	9	1	1	0	5	0	0	1	0
Pwereka 2b	3	0	2	0	1	0	0	0	0	0	0
Sóór 1	2	0	2	0	0	0	0	0	0	0	0
Pwereka 3a	32	0	37	0	14	0	19	0	3	0	0
Pwereka 3b	2	0	2	0	0	0	0	0	2	0	0
(Wuwáánúúw)	1	–	0	–	0	–	0	–	0	1	0
Pwéénll	3	0	2	0	2	0	1	0	0	0	0
Pwukos	16	8	23	23	4	1	13	14	1	2	0
Sóór 2a	9	0	5	1	4	0	1	0	0	1	0
Sóór 2b	5	0	4	0	1	0	0	0	0	0	0
Sóór 2c	10	0	4	2	5	0	1	0	0	2	0

Wiitéé 1	10	0	16	0	1	0	7	0	0	0	0
Wiitéé 2a#	13	1	22	1	4	0	13	0	0	0	0
Wiitéé 2b	6	0	3	0	3	0	0	0	0	0	0
Wiitéé 2c	2	0	2	0	0	0	0	0	0	0	0
Wiitéé 2d	8	5	8	10	2	2	3	7	0	2	1
(Pwéén)	0	–	1	–	0	–	0	–	0	0	1
Wuwáánúúw 1	8	0	3	0	5	0	0	0	0	0	0
Wuwáánúúw 4	10	0	15	3	1	0	9	0	0	3	0
Wuwáánúúw 2	3	1	2	0	2	0	0	0	0	0	1
(Wiitéé 4)	12	–	22	–	1	0	10	–	7	1	2
Wuwáánúúw 3a	14	0	9	0	6	0	1	0	0	0	0
Wuwáánúúw 3b	11	0	13	0	3	0	5	0	0	0	0
(Nuuken Fénú)§	0	–	2	–	0	–	0	–	0	0	2
(Maasané)§	0	–	7	–	0	–	1	–	0	0	6
Affil. unknown	0	–	1	–	0	–	0	–	0	0	1
Totals	242	18	296	47	72	3	131	21	17	24	19

* Lineages and sublineages are grouped according to their association together in a *fanag* (hearth). Each *fanag* is a political unit within a *sóópw* (district); its members working together to prepare first fruits for presentation to the district chief. Lineages are listed here as in my earlier report (Goodenough 1951) by their sib names. A number is added when a sib is represented by more than one lineage, and letters designate important sublineages. Sib names in parentheses represent groups or individuals who belong to lineages that are not based on Romónum. For reckoning purposes, all adopted persons are counted with their lineages or sublineages of birth except when the adopted person came from another island. In the latter event the adopted person is counted with his lineage of adoption and reckoned as a birth on Romónum, if he was born after 1947, rather than as an immigrant.

† On Romónum only.

‡ These two groups of Fesinimw outsiders are from the same lineage on Uman Island.

§ Members of these sibs make a related group of immigrants from Losap.

‖ Associated with Wiitéé 1 in 1947 and with Sóór 2a in 1964.

This had become a separate lineage, Wiitéé 5, by 1964.

his sisters and their children access to food on their corporate property. One of his sisters lured him into incestuous relations with her, declaring that if he did not treat his sisters as kin then they need not treat him as kin either, so shaming him into more responsible behavior. Thus, failure to provide for one's junior *eterekes* mates was portrayed as a violation of kinship responsibility on a par with incest.

The *sowuppwún* might allocate certain properties to junior members of the owning group for their personal use. He might also make such properties available to a junior male member's own children, who were not members of the corporation. In the latter case, the children continued to enjoy the use of the land after their father's death, holding it collectively as a matrilineal corporation subject to the residual authority of the *sowuppwún* of their father's corporation. They had to use the land and not leave it idle; they had to look after it; and, most important of all, they had to render gifts of first fruits (*mmwen ppwún*) to the head of their father's corporation, who continued to hold the title of *sowuppwún* for these lands. Any improvements they made on the property were theirs under full title. If they failed to render first fruits and the *sowuppwún* decided to exercise his right to demand return of the property, he was required to render compensation for the labor represented by the improvements.

In theory, such grants or gifts of land to a corporation's children required the consent of all its members; but in practice strong corporation heads often acted on their own and sometimes favored their own children with such grants at the expense of their junior corporation mates. Indeed, when a man died, the legal status of the properties subject to his authority was likely to be disputed by his surviving children and corporation mates. To prevent such disputes, a dying man customarily issued a "death instruction" (*emwirimá*) to his assembled kinsmen so that his intentions and desires regarding the land under his authority would be clear to all.

Grants of land to a corporation's children, as the foregoing indicates, resulted in two corporations having interests in the same land. One, the grantee, had the rights and privileges that went with physical possession. The other, the grantor, had right to the first fruits, to the title of *sowuppwún*, to confiscate if the grantee misused the property, and to the ultimate return of physical possession upon extinction (in the female line) of the recipient corporation. As children and heirs of the granting corporation, the recipient corporation had the right to acquire full title in the event that the granting corporation died out. Either party might prevent such dying out by resort to adoption.[7]

This grantor-grantee relationship between corporations, in which the grantee acquires a provisional title (which may eventually become a full title) and the grantor retains a residual title (which may eventually revert to a full title), is the key to understanding much of Romónum's traditional social organization and, consequently, to understanding how it has been changing in recent years.

Traditionally, Truk's islands were divided into small districts (*sóópw* or *sópwun fénú*). A district was a territory with a matrilineal corporation holding residual title to its space, as distinct from tracts of soil, *ppwún*, within it. The head of this corporation was chief of the district, the *sómwoonun fénú*.[8] In theory a group of siblings had established a full title to the space when the island was first inhabited and held this title thereafter as their corporate property. Rights to portions of the space were then

[7] Adoption on Romónum is described at length by Ruth Goodenough (1970).

[8] This expression is now used for the elected office of mayor of Romónum Municipality under the Trust Territory government, and *sómwoonun sóópw* now refers to the traditional district chief. If the symbolic chief and executive chief were not the same person, they were distinguished as the *sómwoonun mwégé* (chief of food) and the *sómwoonun kkapas* (chief of talk), respectively. The word *sómwoon* (chief) seems originally to have meant "top father" or "big father," being derivable from a Proto-Micronesian *tama-ulu*. For the shift of *t* to *s*, *l* to *n*, *au* to *oo*, and *a* to *ó*, see Dyen (1949). Cf. Trukese *sómwo-mw* (your father), *wunu-ug* (summit).

granted to the children of men in this corporation. By developing their grants, they acquired full title to tracts of soil. The resulting junior corporations, sired by the chiefly one, owed first fruits to the chief for their use of the space. They, in turn, sired other corporations to which they gave grants of soil (*ppwún*) and from which their respective *sowuppwún* were entitled to first fruits as well. Intermarriages among these corporations and successive grants of soil back and forth resulted in a number of larger and smaller corporate groups, some contained within others. Two corporations might be independent with respect to some recently acquired properties but be part of a larger one with respect to holdings acquired many generations earlier. A maximal corporation of the latter kind, one that is not part of a larger one, I have called a lineage (Goodenough 1951).

The active-use rights people had in land were as likely to come from holdings whose soil they held under provisional title as from holdings whose soil they held under full title, even when they were members of long-established lineages. What distinguished the older corporations from the younger ones was the extent of holdings to which they had a residual (or full) title—holdings, that is, of which their head could claim to be *sowuppwún*. The chiefly corporation was entitled to first fruits from all holdings within the district. The older corporations were entitled to first fruits from extensive tracts of soil. The most junior corporations were entitled to no first fruits at all, holding only provisional title to tracts of soil. The size of these provisional holdings was important for their economic well-being but irrelevant for reckoning their political rights within the district.

Only corporations with full or residual rights to soil whose heads could claim to be *sowuppwún* of some land within the district's territory could claim full membership in the district. They were the corporations that owed first fruits to the chief directly. The others owed first fruits to these and were called upon by them to assist in preparing presentations of first fruits to the district chief. Junior lines in older corporations remained joined in common lineages with the senior lines down which the title of *sowuppwún* descended, even though these junior lines might be corporations in their own right with extensive provisional holdings. A junior line might declare itself independent of the senior line when it acquired full title to soil in its own name, thus becoming a new lineage. A new minor corporation resulting from an interdistrict or interisland marriage associated itself with the corporation of its local founding father, the grantor group taking in the grantee group as its political client. Without full or residual title to soil, the client group could not render first fruits directly to the chief in its own name, thereby presenting itself as a full-fledged constituent of the district.

A lineage with full political rights maintained a *fanag* (hearth, lit. ashes), where it prepared food for presentation of first fruits to the district chief. Dependent corporations and in-married residents from other districts attached themselves to the *fanag* of their father's, spouse's, sibmate's, or other available kinsman's lineage. Lineages with a right to their own *fanag* temporarily joined with other lineages with which their members had kinship ties if their numbers were too depleted to enable them to mobilize an effective work force. The *fanag,* then, were the immediate constituents of a district, each consisting of an established lineage with full or residual title to soil in the district's territory, together with attached individuals and lineages lacking such title.

With its right to first fruits, its reversionary rights, and its right to district membership, residual title to soil obviously played a key role in the workings of the precolonial social order. It provided incentive for lesser corporations to stay together as larger lineages, even when all use rights to common holdings had been given to other groups under provisional title.

The members of a corporation often acquired holdings in more than one district. It was not uncommon for a group to function as a major corporation, a lineage, in one district while at the same time enjoying membership rights with sibmates in another district in a corporation with more ancient land holdings there.

Such extended lineages, or subsibs as I have called them (Goodenough 1951), resulted both from interdistrict marriages and
military conquest.

When one district defeated another in war, the chiefly lineage
of the conquering district might expropriate all of the holdings
of the chiefly lineage in the defeated district, the members of the
defeated group taking refuge with kinsmen in other districts and
islands. Other lineages in the defeated district might be allowed
to remain on their lands as before, in return for which favor they
now owed first fruits to the chief of the conquering district.
Members of the conquering lineage might take up residence in
the defeated district and function locally as the new chiefly line,
but they remained a junior line within the larger, extended lineage that wielded the chiefship in both districts. The new local
chief was expected to render first fruits on behalf of his entire district to the head of the senior line in the conquering district. In
this way, the chiefly lineage of Núkúnúféw District on Udot
Island once claimed overlordship of neighboring Peniya District
and of the whole of Romónum Island, which comprised another
district.

Extended family households were the standard domestic form
in precolonial Romónum (Goodenough 1951, 1956a). Ideally,
all the women of a lineage or sublineage lived together in one
house with their husbands and children. The number of adult
women per household seems not to have been large, ranging from
a minimum of two to as many as five or six. It was important
that there be at least one middle-aged woman, for it was felt that
two or three young women in their late teens and early twenties,
relatively inexperienced in the care of children, ought not to form
a separate household by themselves. When there were only one or
two younger women left in a household, they went to reside with
the women of their father's lineage, or they resided in a separate
house near the women of their respective husbands' lineages,
with whom they cooperated in a single domestic economy. In the

latter case, the separate dwelling was required by a tabu against lineage brother and sister sleeping together in the same house except when the brother was ill and under his sister's nursing care. A house was identified with the lineage or sublineage whose women resided in it. The lineage's men kept their valuables there in the care of their mothers and sisters.

A lineage entitled to maintain its own *fanag* might also maintain an *wuut* (meeting house, or men's house), where its unmarried young men slept and where the lineage head might himself reside with his wife and children in a small apartment at one end. If for any reason a lineage lacked a meeting house, its young men slept in the meeting houses or dwellings of their respective fathers' lineages. A chiefly lineage regularly maintained a meeting house. Map 2.3 shows the distribution of houses and meeting houses on Romónum circa 1900 as remembered in 1947 by a man who was about fifteen years old when Germany established its administration in 1903.

The classification of kinsmen reflected the corporate organization of property relationships. The relationship between grantor and grantee was commonly between a corporation and the children (or descendants) of its men. It was understood to result from a father's obligation to provide for his children. The corporation as provider was therefore in a collective parental relationship to the children of its men. These same children were the corporation's children in another sense: they were heirs to whatever it held under full title, and would actually inherit if the corporation died out in its female line. From this perspective, a person regarded all members of his or her father's lineage as belonging to the parental generation of kinsmen. Complementarily, all children of men of one's own lineage were regarded as belonging to a junior generation, and all children of men of one's father's lineage were equated with one's own generation.

The resulting system of kinship classification (Goodenough 1951, 1956a), as reflected by the use of kinship terms for reference purposes, was one of "Crow" type (Murdock 1949; Louns-

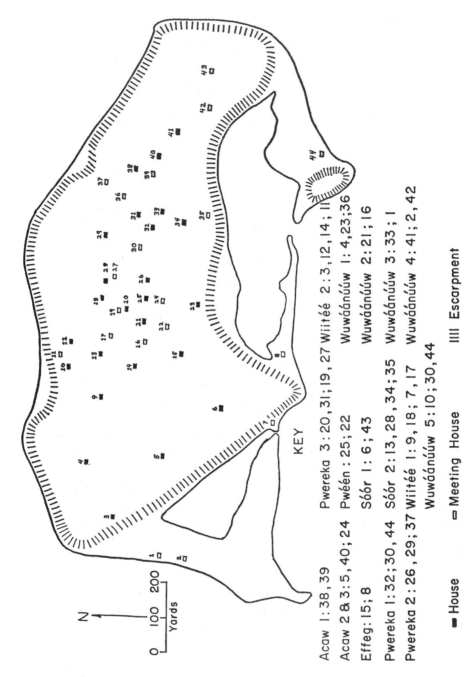

KEY

Acaw 1: 38, 39 Pwereka 3: 20, 31; 19, 27 Wiitéé 2: 3, 12, 14; 11

Acaw 2 & 3: 5, 40; 24 Pwéén: 25, 22 Wuwáánúúw 1: 4, 23, 36

Effeg: 15; 8   Sóór 1: 6; 43   Wuwáánúúw 2: 21; 16

Pwereka 1: 32; 30, 44 Sóór 2: 13, 28, 34; 35 Wuwáánúúw 3: 33; 1

Pwereka 2: 26, 29; 37 Wiitéé 1: 9, 18; 7, 17 Wuwáánúúw 4: 41; 2, 42

             Wuwáánúúw 5: 10; 30, 44

■ = House □ = Meeting House ||||| Escarpment

Map 2.3. Houses of lineages on Romónum Island, Truk, c. 1900. Numbers indicating meeting houses follow semicolons.

bury 1964). The conceptual model of the system, however, remained one of "generation" and "Hawaiian" type (Murdock
1949), for informants gave as a general principle that all relatives in a senior generation were "father" or "mother," all those
in a junior generation were "child," and all those in one's own
generation were "sibling of the same sex," "sibling of the opposite
sex," "spouse," or "sibling-in-law of the same sex." What ac-
counted for the Crow pattern was not a skewing rule based on an
equivalence of kin types, as discussed by Lounsbury (1964), but
a rule regarding the reckoning of generation membership in the
context of lineage membership (Goodenough 1956b).[9]

Social Change since 1947

The beginnings of change away from the traditional social
system go back to the imposition of the German administration
in 1903, which put an end to warfare. This made it more difficult for chiefs to enforce their hegemony over districts on other
islands.[10] It was the German administration, apparently, that
settled the long-standing quarrel among the several Pwereka
lineages on Romónum as to which was senior and hence entitled
to Romónum's chiefship and the first fruits and other perquisites

[9] Lounsbury's skewing rules can, of course, be used, together with merg-
ing and other appropriate rules, to account for the distribution of Romónum
kinship terms. The Romónum system can, therefore, be placed in Lounsbury's typology of Crow and Omaha systems when there is reason to do so
for comparative purposes. Within the framework of Romónum culture,
however, the Crow skewing is an artifact of the following rule: In any
collateral relationship involving a common ancestress and the presence of
one or more male links in either or both lines of descent, all female links
between the ancestress and the first descendant male link in each line are
ignored for purposes of reckoning generation distance. Thus people
recognize generation distance throughout the genealogical structure but
operate with a rule as to when generations will and will not be counted
for purposes of classifying kin.

[10] This had been difficult before. At about the time when Germany took
over Truk, for example, the local chief of Romónum murdered emissaries
from Núkúnúféw on Udot—his own extended lineage mates—who came to
inquire about his failure to keep up with Romónum's first-fruits obligations
to Nukúnúféw.

that went with it. Their division of Romónum into two districts, each with its own chief, was still in effect in 1964. The island continues to be a single community, however, with land holdings and residences scattered all over it to such an extent that the chiefly line of one district has its own major land holdings and its household in what is physically regarded as the other district.

The effect of the division was to award to each of two political factions control of half the traditional spoils. When Romónum was made a single municipality by the American administration after World War II, with elected island officials, a new set of spoils came into existence. The two districts now function in some ways as political parties or organized voting blocks, competing for control of the islandwide municipal offices.

The German administration also made a registry of land holdings. The registry was incomplete, and corporation titles were registered in the names of the corporation heads, the *sowuppwún*. Often thereafter they were treated as if they were individual rather than corporate holdings, the written deed being used as evidence of individual ownership in court. These deeds are still important legal documents in Truk's courts today, serving as crucial evidence in many disputes, although the courts, now well aware of the fraudulent use to which these deeds were sometimes put in the past, seek to investigate each case as best they can. The Japanese encouraged transmission of property from parent to child and apparently sought to weaken the matrilineal lineages, looking with little favor upon matrilineality as a principle of organization.

In 1947, only two years after the Japanese surrender of Truk to the United States, the American government was still an unknown quantity to Romónum's people. Administrative policy held that local custom was to be respected unless it seriously conflicted with American conceptions of justice and fair play or created especially difficult problems for effective administration. Romónum, a small island on the other side of the Truk lagoon from administrative headquarters, was left almost entirely to itself. The policies, prejudices, and ignorance of the administration could not be exploited as a means of bypassing the requirements and obligations of the traditional social and property system, except by a very few people who did not live on Romónum. The Japanese had gone, and the changes they had instituted were presumably no longer in force. The traditional system was functioning with minimal interference.

As soon as courts were re-established, they were deluged with property disputes. The Japanese had treated grants of corporation land to the children of one of its men as if they were an inheritance by a man's children of his individually owned land. The result was that many disputes coming before the American high court were between the members of a corporation and the children of its men. The latter were disputing the residual title of the former and claiming full title for themselves, and the former were asserting their confiscatory and reversionary rights under traditional residual title. The court undertook seriously to follow local custom, but some witnesses presented the rulings of the Japanese courts as representing local custom whereas others presented the traditional system as local custom, depending on which representation was to their immediate advantage.[11] The high court, I am told, chose to follow the precedent set by the Japanese and ruled that if it could be established that a corporation grant to the children of one of its men had been made with the consent of the corporation's members, then the children had

---

[11] Trukese terminology makes it difficult to distinguish between individually owned land that has passed to the owner's children by right of inheritance and corporately owned land that has been given as a grant to the children of one of the corporation's male members. The Trukese refer to either as *fénúwen naaw* (land of the child) or *fénúwen saam* (land of the father)—depending on whether they are looking at it from the father's or child's viewpoint—adding *seni eterekes* (from the matrilineal corporation) when they wish to make it clear that the holding is a grant from a corporation. The Trukese manner of speaking emphasizes not the difference in the nature of the children's title but the fact that in each case control of use rights lies with the children rather than with their father's lineage or with other members of their own lineage.

the same rights as if it had been their father's personal property.

The effect of this ruling was to deprive the granting corporation of its residual title; once the grant was made, the grantee had full title. The grantee need not now render first fruits or obtain the grantor's approval for transactions he wished to arrange. The head of the granting corporation could no longer claim to be *sowuppwún;* this title now belonged to the head of the recipient corporation if he wished to claim it. Some people on Romónum continue to follow traditional practice and continue to render gifts of first fruits to the traditional *sowuppwún* as a matter of courtesy, and there are some who still try to assert their right to first fruits under the traditional system. No one is compelled to follow traditional practice and a number of people no longer do so. It is my impression that scarcely anyone would do so if he felt that he would be seriously inconvenienced by it.

The value of residual title to tracts of "soil" had helped to hold lesser corporations of immediate siblings together in lineages in the traditional social system. Except as other interests countervail, Romónum's traditional lineage organization has been weakened. Indeed, before I learned about rulings of the courts, I had gained an impression that Romónum's lineages were less frequently a unit of reference in community affairs than they had been in 1947. Talk of dissension within the lineages led me to the intuitive judgment that the lineage organization was weaker and looser than it had been. I cannot pretend to have examined all the different possible causes of this, but if my impression was correct, the court's ruling regarding the jural relations of grantor and grantee in land transactions seems likely to have been an important contributing factor.

Old lineages, whose corporate assets consisted largely of holdings under residual title, derived their cohesion in good part from the value of a residual title. The ruling of the court has not only deprived the traditional residual title of much of its former value, but it has also made it possible for junior and dependent corporations to acquire full title to what they had formerly held only under provisional title.[12] They are now freer than they formerly were to establish themselves as independent lineages with their own *fanag* and with full political rights within the district. What was a sublineage within a larger one on Romónum in 1947 had taken this step by 1964, establishing itself as a constituent lineage of the district other than the one to which its parent lineage belonged.[13] In this, it was acting in a thoroughly traditional manner. Some of Romónum's older lineages were established in the same way. The point remains that sublineages now have more options and seem to be functioning with somewhat greater autonomy than before. The effect of the court's ruling has not been and will not be to do away with corporate ownership of land. What it has done is diminish the importance of the larger corporations with considerable generation depth, the lineages, and enhance the relative importance and autonomy of siblings sets and sublineages with shallower generation depth.

In 1964 the lineages were still looked upon as the constituent units of Romónum's two districts. The lineages sent representatives to meetings called by the chiefs, for example, but the heads of sublineages within them might all attend and argue with one another in public over matters at issue, something regarded as distinctly bad form by traditional values.

The traditional chiefs still wielded authority in 1964 over the conservation of food resources in their districts, tabooing for a

---

[12] Thus Boutau, chief of Corog District, comments on the residual title to several plots that the two major sublineages within the Neepiikóów lineage (Pwerka 2) hold in common. "Today it does not really mean anything, because the *éfékúr* [children of Neepiikóów men] have taken all these plots and under present law control them outright. Under traditional law, the Neepiikóów lineage would still control *ppwún* [soil], and Maateewus [senior in age of the two sublineage heads] would be *sowuppwún* of these lands."

[13] The main holdings that made this move possible had come to them from lineages in Corog District including its chiefly lineage, whereas the other sublineages of the parent lineage were intimately tied through marriage and grants of property with lineages of Winisi District.

time the harvesting of coconuts for copra in one district, for example, and controlling the times when harvesting and eating fresh breadfruit, preserved breadfruit, and taro might begin. There were, however, no ceremonial presentations of first fruits to either district chief in 1964–65, as there had been in 1947. The chiefs of the two districts consulted with one another to coordinate the timing of the opening of the different harvest seasons, but they were free to act independently and did so when they felt the occasion required it.

There has been little modification in the selection of traditional chiefs on Romónum. The executive, as distinct from the symbolic, office is now filled by election in Corog District. Those elected have been of chiefly rank, however, and Corog's executive chief in 1964 was also its proper symbolic chief according to traditional principles of primogeniture. According to him, the people of Corog have agreed to regard only persons of chiefly rank (men in the chiefly lineage or their sons) as eligible for the executive chiefship. In Winisi District, the succession has followed the same principles. In 1964, the chiefly office was divided between the symbolic chief and a somewhat older cousin in his lineage who functioned as executive chief. For a time the executive chiefship has been held by the son of a former chief, but he later stepped down in favor of maturing members of the chiefly lineage.

Romónum's municipal government, created in 1952, was responsible for the upkeep of paths, keeping the peace, and providing a school (but not for teachers' salaries). The municipal chief or mayor was elected by those who had registered their names on Romónum's electoral roll, rather than on some other municipal roll. These were people who regarded Romónum as their continuing place of residence. A municipal judge was nominated by the electorate and his appointment confirmed by the District Administrator of the Truk District.[14] In 1964 responsibility for

[14] Under American administration, the Trust Territory of the Pacific Islands is divided into six administrative districts. The Truk District is the largest in population (but not in land area), with about 26,000 inhabitants

the maintenance of paths had been delegated by the municipal chief to the two traditional district chiefs. What was used as the school building was in fact the traditional meeting house of the chiefly lineage of which the principal and other teacher were both members. The municipal chief confined his activity to making occasional reports to the District Administrator's office and to collecting personally the municipal taxes, the spoils of office. The traditional political organization and the Protestant and Catholic churches were the effective institutions for community action and social control on Romónum.[15]

Household composition seemed to me to have changed considerably in the interval between 1947 and 1964. Already in 1947 the extended families associated with lineages and sublineages were not housed under one roof to the extent that they seemed to have been earlier. A house usually contained a woman and her daughters or several uterine sisters, together with their husbands. If the older women of a lineage or sublineage tended to have separate houses of their own, their several adjacent houses formed clusters. In 1964 the individual houses tended to have the same composition, but they were much more scattered and did not so frequently cluster by lineage and sublineage. I interpreted this as further evidence of the weakening of lineage cohesion on Romónum. Consideration of other evidence, however, has forced me to abandon this interpretation. When I counted up the number of distinct households as recalled in 1947 by Simiron of Romónum for around the time the Germans first came to Truk in 1903 (Map 2.3), it turned out that there were very nearly as many as in 1964 (Table 2.2). It is difficult to imagine that Romónum's population was any larger in 1900 than it was in 1964. Consequently, I conclude that the average num-

---

in 1964, and includes Truk, the Mortlock Islands to the southeast, the Hall Islands to the north, and Namonuito, Pulap, Tamatam, Puluwat, and Pulusuk Islands in the west.

[15] Another man has since been elected municipal chief. By 1967 there was a new municipal school building, obtained under a building program of the Trust Territory, and a school lunch program.

Table 2.2. Lineages, house clusters, and meeting houses on Romónum, 1900, 1947, and 1964

Lineage	Distinct houses or house clusters			Meeting houses		
	c. 1900	1947	1964	c. 1900	1947	1964
Acaw 1	1	1	3	1	0	0
⎰ Acaw 2*	1	1	4	⎰ 1	0	0
⎱ Acaw 3	1	0	0	⎱	0	0
Effeg	1	–	–	1	–	–
⎰ Pwereka 1	1	0	–	⎰ 2	⎰ 0	⎰ 0
⎱ (Wuwáánúúw 5)	1	0	0	⎱	⎱	⎱
Pwereka 2	2	2	3	1	0	1
Pwereka 3a	1	1	3	1	1	1
Pwereka 3b	1	0	0	1	0	0
Pwukos	–	1	1	–	0	1
Sóór 1	1	0	0	1	0	0
Sóór 2	3	2	2	1	0	0
Pwéén	1	0	0	1	0	0
Wiitéé 1	2	1	1	2	0	0
⎰ Wiitéé 2	2	3	3	⎰ 1	⎰ 1	1
⎱ Wiitéé 5†	1	1	2	⎱	⎱	0
Wiitéé 3	–	–	–	–	–	–
Wuwáánúúw 1	2	1	0	1	0	0
⎰ Wuwáánúúw 2	1	⎰ 1	⎰ 1	1	⎰ 0	⎰ 1
⎱ (Wiitéé 4)	1	⎱	⎱	–	⎱	⎱
Wuwáánúúw 3	1	2	2	1	0	0
Wuwáánúúw 4	1	1	1	2	0	0
Maasané	–	–	1	–	–	0
	25	18	27	19	2	5

* Brackets indicate shared meeting houses.
† A sublineage of Wiitéé 2 in 1947.

ber of persons to a household in 1900 was as small as in 1964. The situation in 1947, when the house clusters seemed larger, represented the adjustments Romónum's people had made to the Japanese military having taken over much of their island. The people had been crowded into the beach areas. They built near their lineage mates, because it was through them that they could get access to land on which to build. When the interior of the island was rehabilitated after the war, there was then a return to former conditions rather than a change toward new ones. What had changed between 1900 and 1964 was the distribution of population among the lineages. There had earlier been more smaller ones with houses of their own, and in 1964 some lineages had grown considerably in numbers while others had become too reduced to maintain distinct households at all. It is evident from this analysis that it is methodologically unsound to draw conclusions regarding social trends from only two observations in time. Interpretation of the apparent change between 1947 and 1964 was entirely altered when data from 1900 were taken into account.

One change in residential practice was clear, however. In 1947 I knew of no instance in which an adult brother and sister (uterine or classificatory) were domiciled together under the same roof. Informants agreed that such an arrangement was taboo. In 1964 there were several cases in which uterine and lineage brothers and sisters were so housed. Informants recognized them as definite departures from older custom and as reflections of a changing attitude toward the traditional code governing relationships among kinsmen.

A truly difficult problem of interpretation, which confronted me at the outset of my return in 1964, was what appeared to be a change in the use of kinship terminology. In 1947 I had systematically worked through the genealogies with an elderly informant, Simiron, obtaining from him the "Crow" pattern of usage that I subsequently published (Goodenough 1951, 1956b). With another informant, Eiue, who was then in his early thirties, I had called the name of every resident of Romónum, asking him to tell me for each name what category of kinsman, if any, the indicated person was for him. On the basis of the genealogies I had already collected I predicted what his response would be for every name. My predictions were realized without exception, and in every instance his usage conformed with the Crow pattern. I used kinship terms and had them used to me constantly by many people without my encountering, or at least registering, a single instance in which cross-cousins were classed as siblings. The behavior I observed between young men and women who were cross-cousins was entirely different from that I observed between those who were parallel cousins and siblings. I should add, moreover, that the contexts in which the Crow patttern of usage was obtained were unstructured and devoid of any reference to property, and the contexts in which I experienced the use of kinship terms in everyday affairs were varied. Moreover, when lineages as corporate bodies were the objects of reference, kinship terms were used with first-person-plural possessive pronouns rather than with first-person-singular pronouns.

I stress this because a few years later, Swartz (1960, 1962) observed instances in which cross-cousins on Romónum were referred to as "siblings" rather than as "parents" or "children." He concluded that the Crow pattern of usage obtains only in contexts in which the inheritance of property or corporate relations are involved, but that "in all other contexts" (1962:359) cross-cousins are referred to in the Hawaiian pattern as "siblings." This conclusion, derived from two observations (Swartz 1960), simply did not accord with what I had observed. That there were certain situations in which a Hawaiian pattern of usage might occur seemed reasonable, but that it was the prevailing pattern in all contexts except those where property was a consideration was controverted by my own data and experience.

In 1964, within the first week of my return to Romónum, I heard my landlord's wife refer to a classificatory father's sister's son as her "brother" rather than as her "father." Startled, I questioned her usage. An older man present agreed that the man in question might also be classed as her "father," but she, a young woman of twenty-five, expressed herself as having no knowledge of any such possibility. The kinsman in question was her "brother" and nothing else. Satisfied with confirmation of my understanding by the older man, I dismissed the incident as indicative of youthful ignorance by a young woman who had spent some years in mission boarding school. Two weeks later her husband, Boutau, a man in his middle forties, the adopted son of my former elderly informant Simiron, and the symbolic as well as executive chief of Corog District, also casually referred to a cross-cousin as his "brother." I expressed my surprise and he replied that one normally referred to cross-cousins as siblings. As *éfékúr* (heirs) of one's lineage, mother's brother's children might be referred to as one's "*éfékúr*-children," but otherwise they were to be classed as "siblings." He went on to say that this was the way it had always been done on Romónum and that his father, Simiron, must have been deliberately misleading me if he had told me otherwise.

What was I to believe now? In consternation I asked Eiue about it, for it was from him that I had earlier obtained the complete roll call of Romónum that had accorded perfectly with my predictions. He replied that, of course, the Hawaiian pattern was an alternative usage and always had been. "Look at me and Teriwo," he said. "Teriwo is a member of my father's lineage, but I prefer to deal with him as my 'brother.' " Teriwo was in fact Eiue's father's sister's daughter's son and specifically listed by Eiue as his "father" in the 1947 roll call. By the Hawaiian pattern he would have been Eiue's "child" rather than his "brother." But Teriwo was now also Eiue's wife's younger sister's husband and, as such, his "brother" by marriage (*winipwúnú*). The significance of this latter fact did not strike me until after Eiue's death a few months later, and for the moment I could only conclude that somehow I had managed to miss a common alternative pattern of usage in my earlier study.

But I was still troubled, for I could not see how I could have missed it if it had been at all common. I had been confronted with it quickly enough on my return and had had ample opportunity to be similarly confronted with it before. I decided to repeat the roll-call approach I had used earlier with Eiue. This time I did it with Boutau, asking him to tell me his relationship, if any, to every person on Romónum as I called off his or her name. The result was a perfect Hawaiian pattern. Since the matter had already become an issue between Boutau and me, this was not too surprising. Even so, I had hoped that I might catch him out in some inconsistencies, but he was ready for me. Whatever the truth regarding past usages might have been, there was no doubt that Boutau was able to conceive of the entire terminological system according to Hawaiian principles and do so accurately and consistently. I then decided to try the same procedure with Suuta, one of Romónum's oldest living men. What I got from him was even more baffling. The bulk of his answers conformed to the Crow pattern of usage, except that he switched to the Hawaiian pattern for his father's most immediate matrilineal kin. His father's more distant matrilineal kinsmen, in whose property he had *no* interest as an heir, he classed as "fathers" and "mothers" without regard to generation. He could not explain why he classed his father's more immediate sister's children (nearly all of whom were dead) as "siblings" and the more distant ones as "parents." That was just the way they had been and were to one another. At least I was reassured that the Crow pattern was a reality, but it was also apparent that various considerations affecting individuals could produce Hawaiian patterns of usage as well. What these considerations were, however, remained obscure.

In the meantime, I was becoming increasingly aware of a problem in my relations with Boutau, who was working closely with me as one of my principal informants. The problem arose from the fact that the brief history of Romónum Island that I had published (1951) was based almost entirely on information supplied me by Simiron, Boutau's father by adoption. Included in this account were names and alleged facts with which Boutau was unfamiliar. I had been privileged to receive information from his father that he had not received himself. This, it became apparent, was disturbing to Boutau. He had personal reasons for wanting to question the truth of what his father had told me.

By bringing his father's name into my original query about his use of kinship terms, I had injected into the situation this more basic issue of our rivalry in relation to his father.

When I became aware of this problem between us, I asked Boutau to review with me my version of Romónum's history with the object of correcting its mistakes and getting the record straight. He decided whom we should consult as the presumed most knowledgeable living person. The upshot of our deliberations was Boutau's finally saying that he could see that none of the versions of Romónum's history that contradicted the one Simiron had given me was acceptable when projected against my genealogical records. These other versions were obviously much more fragmentary. Boutau finally said that he could see now that my version of Romónum's history would have to stand, for whatever the mistakes in it, there was now no one alive who knew enough to be able to correct them. He also told me that he now knew from other things we had discussed that Simiron had not lied to me, even in connection with some land holdings where it might have been in his personal interest to have done so.

Shortly after this I began with Boutau to make an inventory of behaviors that were obligatory or tabu in at least some social relationships. I also prepared a list of the social relationships in which some behavior was obligatory or tabu with the object of examining how obligations and tabus were distributed in these relationships. Boutau agreed that it would be proper to look at cross-cousins as being both in a sibling relationship and in a parent-child relationship when we charted the distributions of obligatory acts. When cross-cousins were classed as siblings, he invariably indicated that the obligations between them were those of classificatory siblings (parallel cousins), and when cross-cousins were classed as parents and children, he invariably indicated that the obligations between them were those of classificatory parents and children (that is, parents' siblings and siblings' children). After we had listed these alternatives, I regularly asked Boutau which pattern of obligation was the more binding one. He invariably answered that the pattern for the parent-child relationship took precedence over the sibling pattern. In other words, when behavioral considerations came into the picture, the Crow pattern of kinship took priority over the Hawaiian pattern. Boutau remarked in relation to this one day that Simiron had often reminded him when he was young that it was important to remember that cross-cousins were also like siblings and that it was appropriate to treat them as such. In other words, cross-cousins were basically in another category, but were also like siblings.

My wife, meanwhile, was gathering detailed information about every case of child adoption that she could find. It turned out that adoption had been very common. There were a great many cases of which I had been quite unaware. There was a tendency, moreover, for younger people to be unaware that older people had been adopted. In one instance a woman did not know that her own older sister had been adopted by the same woman who had adopted her. The reason is that the adopting parent is almost always a close relative of the child. Furthermore, adoption transfers primary parental rights from the original to the adopting parents, but it in no way alters the child's right to membership in his natal lineage or his place in his natal sibling set, nor does it remove all parental rights from the original parents. Only primary parental rights (as against secondary rights such as are held by parents' siblings) are transferred and only for the lifetime of the adopting parents. Older persons who were adopted in childhood are usually functioning as members of their natal lineages just as if they had not been adopted at all. Adopted persons, however, grow up looking upon the members of their adopted mother's lineage as lineage mates and regarding their siblings by adoption as siblings. In many cases the adopting mother is already a member of the child's lineage, for example, the child's mother's sister, but often she is the child's father's sister. In the latter case, the child's paternal cross-cousins become lineage mates by adoption and "siblings" instead of "parents." Thus Boutau's two maternal cross-cousins (mother's brother's sons) had been adopted by Boutau's mother and mother's sister. Since they were the last surviving members of their natal lineage, they continued to operate as members of Boutau's lineage as adults and to regard him as an older sibling. The significance of all of this for the problems of kinship usage that I had encountered did not strike me until I had returned home from Truk. The young woman who had insisted that her paternal cross-cousin was her "brother" and nothing else, it turned out, was quite right, because she had been adopted by her father's sister.[16] Adoption by a father's sister would explain the peculiar pattern of usage I had obtained from Suuta, who referred to his immediate paternal cross-cousins as "siblings" but to the remote ones as "parents." But he was one of Romónum's oldest inhabitants and beyond the age limit for which we had information for adoption in childhood.

There remained, of course, Boutau's own stated preference for dealing with his paternal cross-cousins as "siblings" rather than as "parents," except when the roles were in conflict. It also remains that Swartz encountered the use of sibling terms as an alternative usage, although I cannot corroborate his statements regarding the contexts for it.[17] I should add that in 1966, Trukese instructors at a Peace Corps training program with which I was associated in Key West, Florida, used sibling terms as the translation for English *cousin* as well as for *brother* and *sister*. When I called attention to the Crow pattern of usage, they acted surprised that an American should understand this peculiar Trukese way of classifying kinsmen.

What are we to make of all of this? Is kinship usage changing from a Crow to a Hawaiian pattern? Have there been alternative

---

[16] I did not know that she had been adopted, even in 1947, when she was yet a child. She had been assigned to her natal lineage in our census.

[17] Swartz tells me in personal correspondence that according to his recollection one of his two examples involved Isitaro, himself adopted. Isitaro is one of two last surviving members of a lineage that has incorporated in it as client members the descendants of one of its men. They were first reported to me as belonging to Isitaro's sib in 1947, although Isitaro's was Wúwáánúúw and theirs was Wiitéé.

patterns of usage right along? If so, is the Hawaiian pattern being used in a wider range of contexts than before? And if so, does this reflect a shift toward what Romónum's people regard as an American pattern? Or does it reflect the changing relations people have with the members of their fathers' lineages now that property relations have been changed by action of the courts? I cannot answer these questions.[18] My main concern in 1964 was simply to reassure myself that what I had understood in 1947 was, indeed, true: the Crow pattern was the common pattern at the time on Romónum at least, whatever alternative patterns may also have existed. It was a familiar pattern on other islands in Truk too, but Hawaiian usage could have been common there without my knowing it. On this last point, however, Tolerton and Rauch (n.d.: 39–40) report a Crow pattern of usage of the same terms for Lukunor in the Mortlock (Nomoi) Islands to the southeast of Truk; and in 1947 two different sets of informants from Puluwat, to the west of Truk, gave me the Crow pattern as the standard one there, also.

I must leave the matter there. I cannot say what change in usage of kinship terms has actually taken place on Romónum, but I can report a considerable change in how certain I am about my knowledge of usage. I can also illustrate how personal relationships on return studies can be affected by relationships in earlier studies in ways that make the assessment of change very difficult indeed.

[18] Information on kinship usage is, unfortunately, too ambiguous in the earlier ethnographic sources (Krämer 1932:266–267, Bollig 1927:103–104) to clarify matters.

References Cited

Bollig, Laurentius
1927 Die Bewohner der Truk-Inselin. Anthropos Ethnologische Bibliothek, Vol. 3, No. 1. Münster: Aschendorffsche Verlagsbuchhandlung.

Dyen, Isidore
1949 On the History of the Trukese Vowels. Language 25:420–436.

Goodenough, Ruth G.
1970 Adoption on Romónum, Truk. *In* Adoption in Eastern Oceania. Vern Carroll, ed. Honolulu: University of Hawaii Press. Pp. 314–340.

Goodenough, Ward H.
1951 Property, Kin and Community on Truk. New Haven: Yale University Publications in Anthropology, No. 47.
1956a Residence Rules. Southwestern Journal of Anthropology 12:22–37.
1956b Componential Analysis and the Study of Meaning. Language 38:195–216.

Krämer, Augustin
1932 Truk. *In* Ergebnisse der Südsee-Expedition, 1908–1910, Series II, Subseries B, Vol. 5. Hamburg: L. Friedrichson.

Lounsbury, Floyd G.
1964 The Formal Analysis of Crow- and Omaha-Type Kinship Terminologies. *In* Explorations in Cultural Anthropology. Ward H. Goodenough, ed. New York: McGraw-Hill.

Murdock, George Peter
1949 Social Structure. New York: Macmillan.

Swartz, Marc
1960 Situational Determinants of Kinship Terminology. Southwestern Journal of Anthropology 16:393–397.
1962 Recruiting Labor for Fissionary Descent Lines on Romónum, Truk. Southwestern Journal of Anthropology 18:351–364.

Tolerton, Burt, and Jerome Rauch
n.d. Social Organization, Land Tenure and Subsistence Economy of Lukunor, Nomoi Islands. Coordinated Investigation of Micronesian Anthropology, 1947–1949, Report No. 26. Mimeographed.

3. Depopulation and the Yap *Tabinau*

DAVID M. SCHNEIDER

The relationship between cultural definitions and changing population size is an especially interesting one on Yap, which was beginning to recover from a period of severe depopulation when I worked there in 1947–48. In this paper I will focus only on those relationships between population size and culture which concern the Yap *tabinau* (Schneider, 1953, 1955, 1957, 1962). The aim of the paper is to enquire into the possible significant effects of depopulation on the *tabinau* as it is culturally defined.[1]

Table 3.1 describes the situation in detail, village by village, for the districts of Rumung, Map, and Rul in 1947–48. Table 3.2 summarizes the data for these three districts. For purposes of these computations I have defined the married couple as a nuclear family. When the *tabinau* included no more than one married couple, with or without unmarried offspring or other unmarried kin, it was rated as "one nuclear family or less." Such a *tabinau* might be made up of a single woman, a single man, two unmarried men, a father and his married or unmarried son,

[1] The ethnographic present of this paper is 1947–48, when I worked on Yap sponsored by the Peabody Museum of Harvard University and the Coordinated Investigation of Micronesian Anthropology. Since that time David Labby, Sherwood Lingenfelter, John Kirkpatrick, and Charles Broder have worked extensively on Yap and have all courteously made their findings available to me. Their reports will soon be appearing in the form of monographs and journal papers as well as in papers in symposia organized by the Association of Social Anthropology of Oceania.

a mother and her married or unmarried son, a parent and daughter, or a man and his wife with or without unmarried offspring, and so on. If two married couples were present, with or without other unmarried kin, the *tabinau* was rated as "two nuclear families." Thus a married couple and their married son were rated as "two nuclear families," as was a *tabinau* composed of two brothers and their wives. Where three married couples were present, with or without additional unmarried kin, the *tabinau* was rated as "three nuclear families." I have included, in the last columns of Tables 3.1 and 3.2, the number of *tabinau* on the point of extinction. Reference is made to these data below.

As Table 3.2 indicates, 83 per cent of all the *tabinau* of Rumung, Map, and Rul districts consist in one nuclear family or less, while only 13 per cent contain two nuclear families. The percentage drops to 3 per cent for *tabinau* of three nuclear families. Only one *tabinau* of the 231 extant in 1948 in Rumung, Map, and Rul contained five nuclear families.

The crucial point to be made about these figures is that there is no reason to believe that the *tabinau* of Yap were, in the discernible past, ever very large or wide in scope. The evidence for this statement can be indicated only briefly here as follows. Maps of the villages of Fal, Ri, and Eng on Rumung were drawn to show plot boundaries, the name of each plot, its use, the name of the *tabinau* or estate of which each plot was a part, its owner, the location and name of each stone and rubble house platform, the *tabinau* or estate of which it was a part, its owner, and various other features.

The map of Fal showed fifty-seven differently named *tabinau* or estates. Although many of these contained plots now owned by different owners, and were therefore at this time parts of different estates, my informants said that "at one time long long ago" each of these had been the estate of a single *tabinau*. They explained the dispersion of plots into different *tabinau* at the present time as a consequence of inheritance and land transfers since that earlier time. Thus, what was at one time a single estate called *fonigeler* is now divided between two *tabinau*.

Of the fifty-seven differently named estates in the village of Fal in Rumung, twenty-six had only one house platform each, fifteen had two house platforms each, and the remaining eighteen had three to seven house platforms each.[2] If it is assumed that for each house platform there were four people, of whom two were adult males, each the center of his own nuclear family, then just under half of the *tabinau* were made up of either father and son (both married) or two married brothers. Even if we assume three adult males to each house platform, it would be difficult to describe the *tabinau* of which they formed the core as anything but small and shallow at best. In any case, there are not now nor, according to my oldest informants, were there ever formal bonds between any two of these fifty-seven estates. There is thus some reason to believe that *tabinau* containing only one nuclear family or less are not a new phenomenon. They were probably present in sufficient numbers in the past to constitute a significant proportion of the *tabinau* at any given time.

By "the past" I mean the period of peak population prior to the period of depopulation. Census data from the late nineteenth century to 1947–48 collected by Spanish, German, Japanese, and then Americans, provide a rate of population decline. From this rate, an estimate of when the decline first started can be made by extrapolating back until the population size reaches that estimated by the census of house sites, as indicated above. A variety of different estimates has been prepared using a variety of different assumptions of population decline rate and average housesite occupancy, thus providing outer boundaries between which actual population size and time of beginning of depopulation can be judged most probable. The period of depopulation prob-

[2] It is possible that the very few estates with four or more house platforms each are the result of consolidations just beyond my informants' memories. Although I enquired into this possibility, the evidence was not conclusive.

ably began no later than the turn of the nineteenth century, perhaps a little earlier. Thus the period of peak population occurred prior to the turn of the nineteenth century. How long that peak population—a period of overpopulation and of land and food shortage—prevailed is not possible to say at this time and with the data available.

The proportion of *tabinau* containing only one nuclear family has increased, while the proportion of *tabinau* of two or more nuclear families has declined. Two important consequences follow from the increased proportion of *tabinau* composed of a single nuclear family or less. The first is that the proportion of *tabinau* at the point of extinction is probably higher now than during the period of maximum population. The second bears on the relations among *tabinau* members, a point discussed further below.

Table 3.1 summarizes the data for each village in Rumung, Map, and Rul with respect to the number of *tabinau* on the point of extinction. As Table 3.2 indicates, 89 (38 per cent) of the 231 *tabinau* in these three places are on the point of extinction. By "point of extinction" I mean that the *tabinau* either has no offspring at all, and because of the age of the members there is neither practical prospect of offspring nor likelihood of adoption, or that all the offspring are female and there is no prospect of further offspring or adoption. In short, these are *tabinau* in which there are no male offspring or any prospect of them.

Here, again, there is reason to believe that this is in itself not an unprecedented phenomenon. It can be assumed that a time of maximum population preceded the period of depopulation. Given small and shallow *tabinau* and a low birth rate, the probability is that a small but significant number of *tabinau* became extinct in each generation. Although adoption probably reduced this number somewhat, it must have failed to forestall extinction in some cases, since adoption was always arranged prior to the birth of the child. When the child thus adopted proved to be a girl, extinction was not averted.

Table 3.1. Composition of *tabinau* in Rumung, Map, and Rul, 1947-48*

District and village	Number of nuclear families per *tabinau*					Number of *tabinau*	Number of *tabinau* at point of extinction‡
	1†	2	3	4	5		
Rumung							
Biluol	2					2	1
Fal	4	3				7	1
Ganuun	4					4	1
Mecuol	1	1	2			4	1
Ri	9	2				11	4
Wenfra	5	1				6	5
Map							
Bechel	2					2	1
Cool	9					9	4
Malon	4					4	3
Macieu	4					4	3
Nulul	3					3	1
Numudul	1					1	1
Omin	10	3				13	8
Palau	8	3	1			12	2
Talangith	7					7	3
Toru	7					7	4
Woned	6	2				8	3
Weloi	3	2			1	6	1
Wocolob	6					6	3
Wurile	2	1				3	0
Rul							
Balabat	16	5	2			23	5
Benik	3					3	0
Ducungir	3					3	1
Dulukan	7					7	2
Gitam	2	2				4	1
Inuf	11		1			12	8
Lamer	9	2				11	3
Ley	2					2	0
Luec	5	3	1			9	3
Ngari	7	1				8	4
Ngof	2					2	2
Ngolok	11					11	3
Tabnify	5					5	2
Talagu	4					4	2
Worowa	8					8	3

* From *tabinau* lists collected with 1948 census.
† One nuclear family or less (see text)
‡ No male child or reasonable expectation of one.

Table 3.2. Summary of composition of *tabinau* in Rumung, Map, and Rul, 1947–48

| District | Nuclear families per *tabinau* | | | | | | | | | | Total of nuclear families | | *Tabinau* at point of extinction | |
| | 1 | | 2 | | 3 | | 4 | | 5 | | | | | |
	#	%	#	%	#	%	#	%	#	%	#	%	#	%
Rumung	25	73	7	21	2	6	–	–	–	–	34	100	13	38
Map	72	85	11	13	1	1	–	–	1	1	85	100	37	43
Rul	95	85	13	12	4	3	–	–	–	–	112	100	39	35
Total	192	83	31	13	7	3	–	–	1	.4	231	100	89	38

I assume a stationary population at this time of peak population, which means that on the average each couple would have only two children who lived to reproduce. In *tabinau* of one nuclear family, the pattern of offspring could be two sons, a son and a daughter, or two daughters. A *tabinau* made up of two nuclear families, each centered on a brother, could have four sons, three sons and one daughter, two sons and two daughters, one son and three daughters, or four daughters. Where adoption failed to provide a son, the *tabinau* with four daughters would have reached the point of extinction. The *tabinau* of two nuclear families stood a better chance of survival than the *tabinau* composed of only one nuclear family. Because *tabinau* were rarely large enough to be certain of producing one viable son, some of them must have become extinct in the normal course of events. At present, the large proportion of *tabinau* of only one nuclear family is consistent with the large proportion of *tabinau* on the point of extinction.

Since neither *tabinau* extinction nor *tabinau* consisting of only one nuclear family is a new phenomenon, we might expect that *tabinau* organization and inheritance rules are adapted at least in part to cope with these eventualities. *Tabinau* organization is in fact sufficiently elastic so that a small but steady rate of extinction and a small proportion of *tabinau* of only one nuclear family would be of no great consequence for the major cultural values of *tabinau* organization.

The elements of elasticity in the pattern for *tabinau* organization with respect to single-nuclear-family *tabinau* and *tabinau* extinction are as follows: First, the *tabinau* is structured as a nuclear family. The roles and statuses not only do not require more than a single nuclear family, but are phrased as if the *tabinau* contained but one nuclear family (Schneider 1953). Thus any shrinkage in the number of nuclear families within the *tabinau* has no immediate bearing on its functioning. Second, there is no set definition of the size of an estate, what its geographical boundaries must be, or where within a village it should be located. Thus the place it occupies geographically has no immediate bearing on its size. Third, inheritance rules provide for the consolidation of estates, so that after one generation this enlarged estate can be viewed as if it had always been one. For example, a woman who inherits an estate when the *tabinau* is on the point of extinction must leave it to her children, who in turn will inherit their father's estate. When this happens, the two estates are consolidated, passing down through the male line as if they had always been a single unit.

The second point which can be made in describing the present situation is that a large proportion of the *tabinau* which contain living fathers and their sons or which are centered on brothers have overlapping land holdings such that the son holds land in his own right as well as an interest in the estate of his *tabinau*, and each brother has distinct holdings in his own right as well as sharing an interest in the estate of his *tabinau*.

In Fal, Rumung, three of the seven *tabinau* contain adult sons. In one *tabinau* one son owns an estate inherited from his mother. In another, two of the three sons each hold separate estates inherited from their respective mothers. In the third, neither of the two adult married sons holds land in his own right, although their mother does and will leave it to them when she dies. In Ri none of the eleven *tabinau* contains adult sons.

No *tabinau* in Fal has an elder brother as its head. In Ri two of the eleven *tabinau* have elder brothers as heads. In both cases the younger brother holds land in his own right, inherited from his mother who is not the mother of the elder brother.

The third point is that a significantly high proportion of women now own estates, in addition to such individual plots as they may have received on marriage. In the village of Fal three *tabinau* heads are living with their wives, and in each case the wife owns one or more estates within the village. In Ri eight *tabinau* heads are living with their wives, and in four cases the wife owns one or more estates in her own right either in Ri or another village. Of the thirty-one persons who own estates in the village of Fal, eight are women and the remaining twenty-three are men. Of the twenty-seven persons owning estates in Ri, seven are women. The land of Fal and Ri, however, is owned by only forty-three people, including fourteen women. Fourteen individuals, one a woman, own estates in both Fal and Ri.

The elasticity of *tabinau* organization with respect to *tabinau* extinction and one-family *tabinau* is effective if events such as those discussed above occur relatively infrequently. Does the picture change if they occur very frequently? When a *tabinau* becomes extinct either one woman inherits the estate or it is divided among two or more women, depending on the number of surviving women. When the inheriting woman dies the estate goes to her oldest son. The woman's husband administers the land while his wife is alive and may continue to exercise control over it while his son is young. Nevertheless, it belongs to the son and he can have recourse to it with or without his father's consent if he is no longer a child.

Such a situation need not necessarily be inconsistent with or threaten the major values of *tabinau* organization. If such a situation arises only occasionally among all the *tabinau* of the village, it means that the major value, the exclusive interest of father and son in but one estate, is still the dominant feature of the situation. It would be possible for the son to break away from his father and live on the land inherited from his mother, but should he do so he would contravene the values of obedience to his father and solidarity with his brothers.

When, on the other hand, women increasingly inherit land as a result of the extinction of *tabinau,* many sons find themselves in a position of potential independence from their fathers. Equally important, when women inherit land the children of different brothers by different mothers find themselves similarly differentiated by virtue of inheriting separate land holdings from their respective mothers. The sons of brothers, it will be recalled, are brothers, and their order of inheritance in the *tabinau* is determined by their relative age. A woman, on the other hand, transmits land only to her own son, not to the son of her husband's brother.

Both of these patterns are illustrated in Figure 3.1. The estate of the *tabinau* (A) is first held by the eldest brother, but all the males have rights in it and the order of inheritance is by relative age within generation. However, son 2 has inherited a portion of estate X and son 4 has inherited estate Y. Each therefore has some land holdings different in part from those of the other.

Figure 3.1. *Tabinau* holding patterns with respect to *tabinau* of mothers and fathers

There are two other ways in which this pattern is further complicated and accelerated, but to the same end, where women own land with some frequency. The first is when a woman who has borne a son dies, her husband remarries, and another son is born to the second marriage. The second is when a woman divorces after bearing a son and remarries, bearing a son to another husband. The effect of the first situation is for the sons by different mothers to have a common interest in the father's estate, but different land holdings as well, each derived from his own mother. The effect of the second situation is precisely the same from the point of view of the sons but has the added effect of dividing one estate between two *tabinau*.[3] Figure 3.2, a portion of a genealogy from the village of Fal, illustrates these points.

A (which may stand for both the person and the estate) first married Y, who died after bearing a son, AY. A then married X who bore a son, AX. A's two sons, by X and Y, now have common interest in estate A, but each has land through his mother as well. AX has the whole of estate X from his mother.

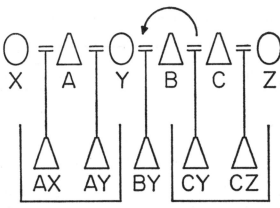

Figure 3.2.   Diffusion of *tabinau* holding patterns

AY has only a portion of estate Y, since his mother had been married earlier to B, by whom she bore a son, BY. Before marrying B, Y had been married to C. Thus estate Y was divided among her sons by her three husbands. Although B had no children by subsequent marriages, C remarried after being divorced from Y and his next wife Z bore a son, CZ. Thus no two sons of the same father have identical land holdings or land rights, nor has any of them rights or holdings identical to those of his father.

Finally, adoption itself may contribute to the individuation of

[3] The remarriage of widowers and the divorce and remarriage of women who have borne children appear not to be new patterns in themselves. It is possible, however, that the rate of both has increased since the time of maximum population, although I cannot present conclusive evidence to support the statement.

land holdings under certain rare conditions. Although an adopted child loses formal rights in his natal *tabinau,* he may regain them by fulfilling the obligations of a child to his true parents. If the adopting parents die and the child's true parents are still living, he may, if he is not old enough to be self-sufficient, return to them. In one such case in the village of Ri, two brothers were adopted by different *tabinau.* Both sets of adopting parents died and the brothers returned to their mother's house. Both inherited from their adopting parents and will inherit from their mother when she dies. Each brother in this reconstituted *tabinau* thus has separate land holdings, and both will share in the estate of their mother.

The fourth point to be made in describing the present situation is that land within a given village is now often owned by persons who live elsewhere. Of the thirty-one persons owning estates in Fal, fifteen are not residents of the village. Of the twenty-seven persons owning land in Ri, seven live elsewhere. It is noteworthy, however, that all nonresident landowners live in other villages on Rumung, with the exception of only two married women.

Ideally, land in a village should be held only by residents of that village, and should it be inherited by someone resident elsewhere every reasonable effort should be made to recover it. According to informants, this was in fact the situation in the past. When village endogamy was possible and could be practiced systematically, the likelihood of a woman's marrying outside the village was low and the likelihood of her inheriting land lower still. When land is held by persons residing outside the village, and when two persons owning land in each others' village can be found, it is felt that an exchange should be arranged so that each will hold land only in his village of residence. Because such exchanges obviously depend on just the right combination of land holdings and individuals, they are not always possible.

At the present time, 40 per cent of living Yap females of all ages live in a village other than that in which they were born. Some live in the village of their adoptive parents, and others have moved to villages in which they hold land. However, most live in a village other than their natal one because a very large number of women now marry exogamously, although village endogamy is still preferred. This puts them in the position where, if they do inherit land in the village of their birth, there is a strong possibility that ownership of that land will remain outside the village in which it is located. Thus the high rate of village exogamy, along with the high rate at which women now inherit, has greatly increased the chances that village land will be held by outsiders.

One of the consequences of the inheritance of land outside the village of one's birth is that one may now choose which village one wishes to live in. A man born in Biluol came to Fal because he found it "an easier place to live" and he held land there. Another man's father had moved from Ri to Fal, "because," he said, "I had more land in Fal." This trend accounts for the depopulation of some villages.

The fifth point is that there is a considerable difference between the size of land holdings of different persons, some people having much larger holdings than others. There is plenty of land now and no one feels a shortage or complains that he has too little, but this does not mean that all estates are of equal size, or that every individual has access to as much land as his neighbor.

The differential size of land holdings brings out two distinct but related points. First, taking the land within the village as the reference point, it is clear that much of it is held by a few people. Second, taking the individual owner as the reference point, it is equally clear that some own far more land than others. If a man owns a great deal of land, his holdings tend to be concentrated within his own village.[4] When land is held outside one's own

---

[4] As has been suggested above, there is a slight tendency for a man to become a resident of the village in which his major land holdings are located. The mere volume of holdings is not crucial to the decision to move, however. The rank of the land, whether it contains inhering status or not, the class of the village as compared with that of his natal village, as well as the attitude of the people in the village to which he might move, are all more important in affecting such a decision than the mere volume of his holdings. In 1948 15 per cent of all males lived in villages

village, holdings tend to be comparatively small. Hence whether a man is a large or a small landowner within his village, he tends to own little land outside his village if, indeed, he owns any at all.

The extent of land holdings outside one's natal village, although still not high today, may represent a change from the period prior to the early nineteenth century. As I have indicated, land is said to have been held very rarely by persons living outside the village in the past. On the other hand, the variable size of total land holdings is a phenomenon which I cannot demonstrate to be new; there are good reasons to believe that even at the time of maximum population, some *tabinau* had much more land than others.

The effect of depopulation has been to reduce the number of nuclear families per *tabinau* and thus increase the proportion of *tabinau* composed of one nuclear family or less. This, in conjunction with the lowered birth rate and increased death rate, has increased the proportion of *tabinau* which become extinct in any one generation. The effect of the increased frequency of *tabinau* extinction has been to increase the rate at which women inherit and so own estates in their own right. Because of the rule that a woman's land is inherited by her own children, and not the children of other wives of her husband, the high proportion of women who own estates results in a high proportion of sons who own estates apart from their fathers, and brothers who own estates apart from each other. Further, as the rate of marriages between persons of different villages has necessarily risen owing to the increasing difficulty of finding a spouse in one's village, the rate at which individuals own land in villages other than their own has also necessarily increased.

Depopulation has reduced the number of people without, of

---

other than those into which they were born. Some of this movement was enforced during Japanese times when a few villages were bulldozed into landing strips. Some follows from the fact that adopting parents may reside in another village. But a small proportion of the movement—I am unable to measure it precisely—is the result of a man's holding land in a village other than the one he was born in and simply choosing to change his residence.

course, affecting the volume of land, and so increased the amount of land available per person. But depopulation alone need not necessarily have had the effects described above. A different set of inheritance rules might still have permitted concentration of land in the hands of the father or the elder brother. Specifically, if a woman's land were inherited by her husband or the children or her husband regardless of who their mothers were, and held nominally by the eldest male child, the estates might still have been held intact without the division of interest between father and son and between brothers which characterizes the present situation. Instead, depopulation, in conjunction with the rules of inheritance on Yap, has led to the situation described above.

What has been the effect of these changes on the structure of the *tabinau* as it is culturally defined? Are any of the rules unworkable? Has the definition of the *tabinau* as a unit of Yap culture shifted perceptibly? Has the pattern for the relationship of its members shifted? It is not unreasonable to expect a change in the structure of the *tabinau* with respect to some of the patterns of relationship of its members. A son should be obedient to his father, and a younger brother should obey his older brother. These relationships are pivotal to the structure of the *tabinau*. Informants say that a son's obedience is in some degree enforced by the fact that he has only his father's land to live on or take food from, and the punishment for disobedience is disinheritance. In the same way, brothers are forced to be solidary when they have no land other than the estate in which they share interests to live on or take food from. This was true, at least, in the past at the time of maximum population prior to the turn of the nineteenth century when land was scarce and food short. Under such conditions the splitting of a *tabinau* and its lands could hardly have worked to anyone's advantage.

But today it is only the exceptional adult son who does not have land of his own to which he can repair if he cares to break with his father. Today it is the exceptional younger brother who does not have an estate of his own to which he could go and become the head of his own, independent *tabinau*. Sons and fathers, and brothers, no longer systematically share interests in the same estate but are instead differentiated by virtue of the estates they own. More important than the mere differentiation of their interests by land holdings is the high frequency with which sons and younger brothers are in fact in a position where authority over them cannot be enforced because they are able to repair to their own holdings and so greatly reduce the efficacy of the threat of disinheritance.

Further, the increased size of each estate, a function of the increased amount of land available per person under conditions of depopulation, has changed the situation with respect to *tabinau* splitting. Whereas in the past splitting of a *tabinau* worked to no one's real advantage, today there is so much land that such a split would still leave ample land for each party.

As a consequence of these factors, one might reasonably expect a high rate of splitting between father and son and between brothers. In point of fact, however, I was unable to uncover a single instance on Rumung where a son had separated from his father to live on his own estate as head of his own *tabinau*. Nor was I able to discover a single instance on Rumung of brothers who had thus separated since the Spanish arrived on Yap. In short, *tabinau* splitting, although stipulated in the pattern as a possibility, occurred very rarely in the past and occurs equally rarely today.

When I first enquired into concrete cases of *tabinau* splits, I was disturbed to find none. It somehow seemed unreasonable, for by that point in the field investigation, I was well aware of the strains involved in the relations between father and son and between brothers. In view of the magnitude of those strains and the frequency with which I heard accounts of friction and dispute between father and son and between brothers, I simply could not believe that *tabinau* never split on Rumung. When I went on to discover the frequency with which sons held estates in their own right and brothers held different estates while sharing interest in another, it seemed even less credible that splits had not occurred. I suspected that splits were kept quiet because they were disvalued and so increased the diligence of my search, but to no avail. I approached the matter obliquely through genealogies, inheritance histories, ownership histories of selected plots, and by such subterfuges as seeking information from women and children, and men in their cups. Men in their cups proved to be excellent informants on other subjects, but they provided no concrete case of *tabinau* splitting more recent than "long, long ago; long before Spanish times." These cases I had already collected.

I had, however, in the person of one of my closest informants, a very good case history of friction between a father and his adult son. I therefore turned my question about and asked why, in this particular case, the *tabinau* had not split. The *tabinau* in question consisted of my informant, a man in his late sixties, his deceased older brother's son and daughter, and his brother's son's wife. My informant and his brother's son were thus father and son to each other. It would have been very difficult to infer from their behavior that these people were all of one *tabinau,* since my informant and his son never spoke. Indeed, the sister and brother were not on speaking terms either, nor was she on speaking terms with her father. This situation was of such long standing that I was unable to date its beginning accurately.

My informant lived at the north end of the village; the brother's son and his wife lived toward the center of the settlement. I never once observed any direct communication between them, and other informants said that they never spoke to one another. The land on which each lived belonged to the estate of the *tabinau.* Nonetheless, the son had holdings in his own right inherited from his mother, to which he could have moved had he cared to do so.

On one formal occasion, when the ritual catch of fish was delivered to the village meeting place and divided by *tabinau* lots, my informant received his *tabinau* share in a heap. He then, as did every other *tabinau* head in the village, subdivided the *tabinau* share into portions appropriate to the size of each nuclear family in the *tabinau*. He set a small portion aside for himself, another of equal size for his daughter, and a larger portion for his brother's son and brother's son's wife. The brother's son's wife sidled up and quickly took up the portion set aside for her husband. The son himself should have come up and with proper words of deference courteously accepted his share from his father's hand, but he would not go so near, and so sent his wife in his stead. On other formal occasions when my informant, representing his *tabinau*, assembled shell valuables to contribute to a village exchange, the brother's son's wife brought them and discreetly dropped them near the old man's house. After she left he emerged, collected them into one basket along with his own contribution, and delivered the lot as the share of his *tabinau*.

I asked my informant why he did not disinherit the son, and he explained that it would only make trouble, and then there would be two *tabinau* instead of one. It was, he said, a very bad thing to make two *tabinau* when all along there had been only one. Now, when there was some task for all the *tabinau* to attend to in the village, they would do it, and do it properly. If "that boy" were the head of his own *tabinau* people could not rely on him. How would fish be distributed properly? Who could depend on him to contribute valuables to an exchange?

When the old man died, his brother's son inherited all the land held in the man's name. I asked others why he had never disinherited his son and learned from other informants that in the beginning he had made fierce public statements threatening to do so, but that he had soon dropped the matter and never spoke of it again.

Other cases fell roughly into the same pattern. Interpersonal relations among *tabinau* members may be severely strained, but since *tabinau* splits do more harm to village affairs than help to the parties to the split, *tabinau* stay together even when inter-personal relations are almost completely disrupted.

In sum, the sanction of disinheriting or evicting a disobedient son or younger brother from the land was probably never used very often and is today rarely exercised to my knowledge.[5] It is certainly used as a verbal threat, but one which is about as rarely carried out now as it probably was during the period of Yap's maximum population. To say that sons and brothers now own land in their own names, and that this happened only rarely in the past, is probably incorrect. Although a larger proportion of sons and younger brothers now own land in their own names than was formerly the case, the difference probably is not great, since the rate depends primarily on the size of the *tabinau*. Since *tabinau* are probably only slightly larger now (depopulation reduced the total number of *tabinau* rather than reducing the size of each *tabinau* very much) the inheritance situation probably has changed little.

It therefore seems most unlikely that the character and degree of authority of the father over his son, or of the elder brother over his younger brother, or of the head of the *tabinau* over its members, are very different now from what they were during the period of Yap's maximum population. It is the very high value placed on the political unity of the *tabinau* which inhibits splitting more than any other factor, and I would guess that this situation obtained in the past as well.

With depopulation the locus of change is thus not in the formal organization of the *tabinau* as a land holding and inheriting unit, nor in its constitution as an element in the organization of the village. The locus of change is neither in the definition of the

[5] It must be remembered that by "today" I mean 1947–48. From the work of Labby, Lingenfelter, Kirkpatrick, and Broder (1968 to 1974) there is some reason to believe that this generalization does not hold as well as it used to, although it still holds in the main. That is, eviction from some specific plots (although not from the whole estate) by the *m'fen* (father's sister and her matriline) is somewhat more common now than previously was the case, according to the results of more recent research.

roles of its members nor in the rules by which they are supposed to govern their relations with one another. The rules of inheritance are followed with no exceptions that I was able to discover on Rumung or in the short time I was in Gacepar in Gagil. The actual distribution of land holdings is perfectly predictable from the rules of inheritance.

I cannot say with confidence that there has been no change in any of the patterns for action since the period of maximum population, for while it is possible to count house platforms, to map land, and to draw inferences about the past from such evidence, it is not easy to do this with the patterns for action. On the other hand, I think it fair to say that in the light of the material presented it is unlikely that there has been change at the cultural level of the *tabinau*, its definition, and the patterns for its organization.

References Cited

Schneider, David M.
    1953 Yap Kinship Terminology and Kin Groups. American Anthropologist 55 (2) : 215–236.
    1955 Abortion and Depopulation on a Pacific Island. *In* Health, Culture, and Community. Benjamin Paul, ed. New York: Russell Sage Foundation. Pp. 211–235.
    1957 Political Organization, Supernatural Sanctions and the Punishment of Incest on Yap. American Anthropologist 59 (5) : 791–800.
    1962 Double Descent on Yap. Journal of the Polynesian Society 71 (1) : 1–24.

4. Recitation of Patrilineages among the Akha[1]

JANE R. HANKS

Phondoe, an old woman of the Chemy patriclan, and wife of the village priest (*dzoema*), died one morning in the Akha village of Saen Caj. The usual funeral rites to separate her from her living clan mates and to send her "soul" to the afterworld began immediately and lasted several days. Several times during the extensive ceremonies, a spirit doctor (*pima*) recited her patrilineage: starting with Phondoe's name, he called the name of her long-deceased father, then of her father's father, and so on, back step by step through fifty-five generations to Sumio, progenitor and culture-hero of the Akha, and founder of the tribe.

[1] The data given here were recorded in 1964 in the Akha village of Saen Caj in Chiengrai Province, Thailand. About 12,000 Akha live in Thailand, the bulk of their numbers being in Yünnan, Shan State in Burma, and Laos. For the opportunity to carry out this field work I wish to thank the National Science Foundation of Washington, D.C., which financed the Bennington-Cornell Survey of Hill Tribes in North Thailand. I am also deeply grateful to the National Research Council of Thailand, the Thai Department of Public Welfare, and the Overseas Missionary Fellowship for generous help. For corrections, valuable additions to my data, and criticism, I am indebted to the Reverend Paul Lewis, formerly of the Baptist Mission, Kengtung, Burma, now in Chiengmai, Thailand, and to my husband, Lucien M. Hanks.
The phonetics used in this paper, developed prior to Reverend Lewis's Akha-English dictionary, are based on the Haas system for Thai, but are only approximate, especially since no tonal indications are given here. I wish to thank Dr. R. B. Jones of Cornell University for help in this context. "g" is a velar fricative; capital "J" (underlined) as in English "John," whether initial or medial; "on," nasalized, as in French "son."

Nine more names he traced "not of human beings but of spirits who lived in Sumio's time," and at the end came M'ma, the Sky God, coupled with M'g'on, the Earth Spirit, sometimes seen as M'ma's female spouse, sometimes as his brother. At other times the patrilineage was recited in reverse, from Sumio to the present. At least once the names of Phondoe's last four deceased female ancestors (the spouses of her patriline—her M, FM, FFM, and FFFM) were given. Such recitations and rites are given for every married man, woman, and legitimate child who dies under peaceful circumstances within the village gates. They may be conducted by the village priest or even the headman if no spirit doctor is available.

The funeral rites assisted Phondoe's soul to depart, to "find its way" to a "river" which had to be crossed. In fact, the spirit doctor "escorted" her part of the way to the afterworld. On the farther bank of the river she would find all her deceased clan mates awaiting her en masse, to escort her to the Chemy clan spirit village where she would henceforth live. The recitations of the patrilineage from the first ancestor down to the latest had served to invite her entire personal ancestry to come to the earthly village, to welcome her into their ranks, to feast, and to take charge of her soul as it returned with them to the afterworld. Being her close kinsmen and elders, they were the ones who could appeal most strongly and whom she would obey. All knew that she, like every human being, would be reluctant to leave her beloved village, kin, and friends. When the recitation proceeded from Phondoe up the line, the object was to assist her to address correctly by name each of these deceased kinsmen whom she would meet in that order, beginning with her father, her closest relative. The immediacy of the presence of these ancestral spirits was apparent. By day, they were called into the village for the ceremonies, but at night they were sent to wait outside the village gates, for after all, they were spirits, in whose presence people felt uneasy.

The inclusion of the four nonclan females' names further illuminates the picture of this afterworld. Spouses at death are separated: a wife is thought to return to live in her clan spirit village, a husband in his. But it is said that Akha spouses, especially if long married, wish to be reunited, to live together as before with their children, and children are seen as longing to be reunited with their parents. There are two ways to effect this: an old widow herself may perform a costly ceremony (*jajae m-oe*) to rejoin her deceased husband; or one or more of her sons may at any time pay a sum of silver and a pig to the mother's brother "to pay for the milk drunk at their mother's breast." Either of these steps reimburses the mother's clan for their services and so releases the woman from her clan spirit village, thus permitting her to move after her death to the spirit village of her husband. In this manner the conjugal family is reconstituted. When the children die, they meet and live with both their parents, to be joined by their spouses through the same rituals. Recitation of these female names confirms that the wives are present and enables the soul properly to address them, too. Only the first four ascending generations of wives are ever included in the funeral recitation. The rest are allowed to be forgotten.

The purpose of these recitations within the rites, then, was clear: the spirit doctor saw to it that the newly disembodied and uneasy spirit of Phondoe was dispatched to her clan spirit village. He called in her elder, deceased, personal kinsmen to take custody of her spirit and facilitated the introductions. They could comfort her and explain the transformation. In the end she was safely installed in her new world; the living were restored and protected in theirs.

The recitation of the lineage also occurs in other contexts and is always a move to protect human beings. During marriage arrangements, the lineage may be sketched in to insure clan exogamy and avoid incest.

Its recitation is also necessary to retain the protection of tutelary ancestral spirits, without which no household can exist. The big patrilocal Akha household, comprising a nuclear family and the families of its married sons, is watched over by resident ancestral spirits (*aphimijae*), in particular those of the last four generations of the patriline and their spouses. The latter, we now see, are the four nonclan female ancestors given special attention in the recitation. Among the innumerable spirits of the world, ancestral spirits alone have direct interest in the health and welfare of their living descendants. This interest must be sustained by household feasting rites, nine per year, performed by the head of the house, the oldest male. In the course of these rites he recites the patrilineage, thus enlisting in behalf of the eight or more resident spirits the support of the entire gamut of ancestors who have watched over his line's successive households from the time of Sumio to the present. The father knows that he himself in time will play this role. In fact, one year after Phondoe's death, a ceremony will be conducted to invite her to come back and take her place as one of the household spirits.

When a household becomes overcrowded to the point of friction, the father may give one of the sons permission to move out with his family to sleep and perhaps to cook in an adjacent house. However, this son is not independent; he must return to his father's house to participate in the familial rites. He may cut the bonds to his father's house only when he has been given paternal permission, and when he is able to conduct his own household rites. These rites include the recitation of his lineage. Only then may he move, if he wishes, to another village, or lead a group of followers off to found a new village. Since no one is considered competent to recite his lineage until about the age of thirty, this is the age of full maturity and adulthood, and with it comes the possibility of household independence. Only then is he able to assume responsibility for protecting the members of his own household.

Finally, and very dramatically, the lineage recitation is a personal recourse to an Akha in dire need of help wherever he may be. An Akha told the Reverend Paul Lewis of a time when he was caught and beaten by Shans, then left alone, tied to a tree with his hands behind him. Needing supernatural strength and magical power to confuse the enemy and escape, he recounted his lineage aloud, starting with Sumio, so as to call on all the spirits of his ancestors. He ended with "Come, help me now!" At this point "his plea was answered and his bonds were miraculously released." It transpired that a nearby Shan who witnessed the event came up and ordered his release. The Akha saw this action as the work of his ancestors.

More frequently the Akha are concerned with public dangers. Spirit doctors and shamans together with the village priest are responsible for protection of the entire village against the innumerable dangerous spirits who wander in the forest and streams and who "hunt human beings just as human beings hunt animals" (Lewis n.d.). Two kinds of spirits live in the known world: inimical spirits, and those of deceased human beings, the protecting ancestors. The village of the living can survive the onslaughts of the inimical spirits only with the help of these ancestors. The village itself is a haven, clearly separated from the outside world by two ceremonial gates, surrounded with symbolic figures calculated to frighten off menacing spirits. Nevertheless, evil spirits sometimes find their way in, causing sickness and such catastrophes as the birth of twins. Since human beings are expected to bear but one child at a time, at least one if not both of a pair of twins must contain a malignant spirit who has come to the village by stealth. Consequently twins are both put to death at once.

So that the spirits of any or all households may be called on to drive out spirit intruders, or to mass defensively at the gates, the patriline of every resident in the village must be known. Consequently, when a family, a group of families, or even a whole village under a headman, asks the privilege of coming to live in another village under the latter's headman, some identification of the lineages involved must be presented. Later, the entire roster of individual lineages of the immigrants must be taught to the spirit doctor and the village priest, "so that at death these new members may be properly buried." The conducting of a funeral is a public concern, for without proper rites the deceased human spirit may turn inimical. The entire village may be endangered if the spirit of the deceased is not led away. The spirits of those who die under violent or tragic circumstances such as by accident, murder, smallpox, and the like are the most dangerous. Special rites at enormous cost of sacrificial animals are necessary to deflect their impact.

Acting as a repository of tribal history as revealed by the layout of the entire tribal genealogy, the higher spirit doctors learn as much as possible of the great branching tree of patrilines which defines the tribe as a unified whole, as one "genetic" family. As an Akha said, "Clans are dividing all the time, but all go back to an original group." Some of these splits are of ethnohistoric interest, for it appears that the major regional and social (phratry, clan, subclan) divisions of the tribe originate there, with the ancestors at these points in the lineages figuring as clan and subclan eponyms. Through the genealogies the Akha see themselves as able to keep track of their scattered members across mountains, jungles, and national boundaries despite their seminomadic way of life, and feel oriented to places as well as to people. When a man is visiting a strange village, or meets a stranger, he may give his lineage in abbreviated form for identification. Such meetings may be quite lively, as they check out their relationships to each other, or even determine their last common ancestor. Ascertaining what clans are represented in the stranger's home village, a man may send a greeting to a clan mate or connection, even if the individual is not known to him personally. Since some of the lineages are associated with certain areas, such as Doi Tung (a mountain on the Thai-Burman border), Laumi (north of Kengtung), or the Sibsongpanna, one can to some extent also trace a village's or a person's provenience.

To these private and public ends we find that every mature man in the tribe must know his own patrilineage. All the sons are taught by the father, but if the latter dies, the oldest son has the responsibility of teaching his younger brothers. If a father dies before any son has reliably memorized the list, relatives or the spirit doctor continue the drilling. Instruction starts informally when a little boy hears his elders recite. Though this knowledge is not consciously taught to women because it is not their province, still it is not secret. Women and children hear it being rehearsed, and many a little girl on her grandfather's lap has been heard repeating portions of it. Moreover, husbands must know their wives' patriline. Recitation is usually quiet, even matter-of-fact, yet one ebullient informant gave his line with obvious excitement and pride, shouting out his name joyfully at the end.

The continuity of the living with the dead, as well as the distinction between the two states, is by now clear. It is further indicated in naming. Men and women each have two names: a formal, spirit name, always the one in the recitation, and a personal name only partly linked (or not at all) to the other (cf. Lewis 1968:359). The latter is the name used by the villagers in addressing each other. Either name, and especially the spirit name, has a magnetic, magical force, to a considerable extent compelling. To name someone allocates status and condition to its bearer. Thus although a man's lineage may be recited by another while he is alive, his formal name must never be included at the end, for, as Lewis reports, it would categorize him with the dead, and so even cause death. However, a man may give his own spirit name. This may be changed for therapeutic reasons, to honor someone, or to augment auspicious influences.

The importance of names was illustrated during our trips to the Akha villages. In the census taken in 1969, village headmen listed the members of the constituent households, giving without hesitation the names of husband, wife, and innumerable children, no mean feat in a village of forty roofs, with new babies all the time. In addition, migration routes associated with the ancestors are learned. Some villages like Saen Caj can trace their paths through twenty-five areas in Burma and China, back to "Mu'u, where Sumio lives." Most spectacular is a spirit doctor's recitation of his "apostolic succession," that is, the successive custodians of the curing powers he now possesses, handed down as a professional technique from Jonphonhau, their supernatural originator, then from doctor to doctor, as teacher to disciple, to the present day. One of these series comprised one hundred and eighty-seven names, three times the length of a lineage. Names in the lineages cropped up in this list of spirit doctors.

The lineage is linked to the myth of the division between man, together with his ancestral spirits, and the evil spirits. Here is one version of the events when human beings and spirits lived adjacently in peace: In the beginning, the supreme being was Apoemijae, who created the sky, M'ma (male); the earth, M'g'on (female); and nine primeval spirits. M'g'on had a child, Sumio, the first human being and the first Akha. Human beings were different from spirits, for they had two breasts in front, whereas spirits had nine breasts on their backs. Nevertheless, they lived and worked in amity. Sumio was establishing the Akha way for the living. He and the spirits had agreed that there should be no birth or death. Consequently, fifteen generations of human beings were not born but created, and lived contemporaneously. Theirs are the first fifteen names after Sumio in the lineages. Then came Thonphonmon, who wrought evil. One day, when some human beings went to get water, a dead monkey fell from above to Sumio's feet, proof that the agreement had been violated. Wrapping the monkey in a cloth and pretending that it was a child, Sumio, evil in turn, showed it to the spirits. "Look!" he cried, "This is my child, and it is dead! You have broken our agreement!" Discovering that the cloth contained a monkey, the spirits felt they too had been deceived. Angered, they resolved never again to live with human beings. Before parting it was decided that men should live on earth, spirits in the world underneath. Spirits retained the capacity to see human beings, but humans lost the ability to see spirits. Both lost the power to speak to each other. Thonphonmon became the leader of the inimical spirit world and thereafter set about to plague the living. Evil was let loose on the land, and human beings with their ancestors had to defend themselves against spirits.

Fifteen generations down from Sumio occurs the name of the enigmatic Thonphonmon. In Kengtung, Lewis reports that patrilineal recitation often proceeds upward only as far as this Thonphonmon. In vivid image of the soul's journey to find its spirit village, it was said, "Thonphonmon was the first ancestor who was bad, thus all his descendants are bad. Since all above him are good, their names need not be given, for the soul will have no trouble finding its way."

Deceit on both sides created not only two separate worlds, but birth and death. For protection. Sumio set up ceremonies and decreed that every village should build two great gates, flanked by copulating male and female figures, both called Thonphonmon, and adorned with such symbols of wealth as money, jugs, and today even airplanes, for wealth and sex, seen as the essential human attributes, are "feared" by spirits. Since spirits have no sexual intercourse, the copulating image of Thonphonmon seems to point a finger at some sexual transgression from which may have issued as progeny the tormenting evil spirits of the world. Here may be found the origin of birth.

Let us sum up the meaning of recitation of the patrilineage among the Akha. Their world exists in two parts: an earthly world of being, fraught with inimical spirits; and an afterworld to which the living go at death to reside in ultimate security with their ancestors in their respective clan villages. These ancestors are allied solidly with their living kinsmen and are always ready to come to their call if proper relations have been observed. Communication with them is not limited to the spirit doctor or other particular officials. Accessible to all is the compelling power of the called name, which binds the ancestors into the present.

The tribe is always united, whether living in scattered localities or dead, with no sense of people gone or disappeared. The panoply of lineages, renewed with each recitation, confirms the

Akha conviction that they are a unique and homogeneous entity. The recitation may be one of the devices that has retarded absorption not only into powerful and numerous peoples like the Lisu, Miao, and Shan, but into the prestigious and magnetic vortex of Chinese culture.

A final note on the lineages themselves is desirable.[2] The Akha are only one of the Asian groups which maintain lengthy lineages orally or in writing. The Chinese with their tablets in clan temples immediately come to mind. As to other speakers of Tibeto-

---

[2] Here we present as an example the complete patriline of Phondze, a distinguished headman who though now resident in Thailand had previously lived in Shan State in Burma. Lewis (1968:360) also gives a lineage recorded in Kengtung.

Phondze's Patriline

M'ma (the Sky God), M'g'on (often coupled with M'ma, sometimes as "Sky and Earth," sometimes as husband and wife, or as "brothers"), G'onzau (note the telescoping of two spirits' names: G'onne and Nezau, cf. Lewis 1968:360), Zauzy (a spirit), Zytho (a spirit), Thoma (a spirit), Majau (a spirit), Jaunae (a spirit), Naebae (a spirit,) Baesu (a spirit), Sumio (the first Akha and first human being), Otoeloe, Toeloecum, Cummojae, Mojaeca, Caetisi, Tisili, Liphobae, Phobae'u, Unjula, Njag'acau, Caumo'oe, Mo'oeJe, Jethonphon (he had six sons, and here occurs the first great branching):

Thonphonju (from whom the Bochae clan descends)

Thonphonboe (from whom the Akhy clan descends)

Thonphonce ("in Burma")

Thonphonzoe ("in Burma")

Thonphonshon (a rather aberrant line)

Thonphonmon (the evil one, from whom many of the Akha in Thailand, including Phondze, descend) The patriline continues:

Moxauthon, XauthonJe, Jelenjau, Njauchila, Lathonboe, Thonboesu, Boesulae (an important personage, almost a second culture hero, who had three sons [Laelumbo, Laelumbjau, and Laelaci] from each of whom lines descend making up important tribal divisions; from three grandsons of Laelumbo other major tribal divisions derive; Phondze descends from Laelaci), Laelaci, Cilanae, Naesauma, Saumazy, Zycae, Caebjm, Bjmcoe, Coethau, Thau'oe, Oecu, Cutsae, Tsaebo, Phicoe, Coe'i, Imja, Mjacoe, Coedon, Donlo, Lomja, Mjadzon, Chidzoe, Dzoedzy, Dzytsa, Tsady, Dylau, Lauma, Masau, Saujae, Jaela, Ladzon, Dzonshau, ShauJa, Japhon, Phondze. One may note the two breaks in the linkage pattern: between Tsaebo and Phicoe, and between Mjadzon and Chidzoe, presumably for reasons noted in the text on page 125.

Burman languages in southeast Asia, a Kachin above Bhamo "reeled off his [family history] for the past forty generations, tracing his ancestors' migration from the north of the Triangle [the territory north of the juncture of the Mali-hka and Nmai-hka rivers in northern Burma] down slowly and by easy stages to their present home, where they had already resided for seven generations. Allowing as little as fifteen years for a generation, this amounts to 600 years" (Metford 1935:41). Lo (1945, 1949) cites lineages from the Burmese Moriya Dynasty, Achit, Moso (= Nakhi), Lolo, Woni, Nan-chao princes, and Min-kia (= Po-tseu), as has Rock (1947:66–153), from the Nakhi. The predilection may have traveled out from the Asian coast on the boats of the Polynesians, there to flower in the great genealogies that go back to Maui.

Patronymic linkage, a repeated syllable in the naming system, creates a mnemonic device which facilitates learning the lineages. Lo (1945:349) points out that in southeast Asia it is character-istic only of Tibeto-Burman speakers. By this device, the first syllable of a child's name is always the terminal syllable of its father's name. The pattern is *ab/bc/cd;* for example, the chil-dren of Bjau*dzoe* were *Dzoe*don and *Dzoe*bau. In three-syllable names, usually the last two syllables are repeated (*abc/bcd*). This mnemonic resource is not available to the long list of holders of a spirit doctor's powers, for only occasionally are disciples the sons of their teachers.

Are the lineages accurate enough to be treated as bona fide historical resources? Though the primeval names are usually learned letter-perfect, errors occur in the later sections. A treach-erous reef on which to founder is unconscious abridgment: the sequence "Bjoemondzon, Dzoncoe, Coeg'oe, G'oecae" was tele-scoped into "Bjoemondzon, Dzong'oe, G'oecae." Elsewhere this leapfrogging compressed eight names into three.

The sociological implications of errors are interesting. When names are temporarily forgotten, the gap may be filled in with what in one case appears to be fabrication, perfectly fitted into the linkage system. Small blocks of names from one lineage have been found cropping up in another, as if someone were making capital out of prestigious names. One man inserted into his own lineage a block belonging to the headman and the dominant clan of his village. Elsewhere the sequence "Jeshau, Shaucoe" and also "Joebau, Baulau, Lody" turn up in strange contexts. Jeshau and Joebau were both clan founders with whom one could pridefully associate. In fact one lineage contained so many well-known names all linked in proper linkage that one wonders if the reciter might be a non-Akha or his descendant who put together an acceptable lineage.

Some aberrancies in the perfect flow of this naming system—for instance in the sequence "Lota, Tahan, Salo" (*ab/bc/de*)—are explained in other ways. We have already noted that spirit names may be changed. Whenever all the older sons die and the remaining son is ill, a name is taken from some healthy person and given to the sick child to assure his survival. The new name is not linked patronymically. Lewis contributes additional explanations from Kengtung: once, to honor the spirit doctor who had cured a certain boy, the latter's name was changed from "Casa" to "Pisa" (from the word *pima,* meaning "spirit doctor"). Also, if a man dies a violent death (from smallpox, drowning, or tiger attack, for example), his name is stricken from his lineage and that of his wife is henceforth inserted in its place. His name is not recited because the souls of his descendants, on their way to the afterworld, will not, or must not, meet him. His spirit will become a vicious being, living in a special hell for those dying in this fashion. However, the terminal syllable of his name is not stricken from his children's names. Finally, the tragedy of a twin birth leaves its trace in the name list. The twins are put to death nameless, but the names of all children born subsequently to the unfortunate parents are not permitted to enjoy the usual *ab/bc* linkage with their father.

Nevertheless, the historic reliability of the lists often seems great. A case in point concerned on the one hand some Monpho

Akha, long residents of the Sibsongpanna in Yünnan, who emigrated in 1957, spent five years in Burma and six months in Laos, then came in 1963 to Thailand to live in the village of Phami; and on the other, a woman who came in 1961 to Saen Caj's village about ten miles from Phami. Married in the Myang Tung-Myang Khwan district of Shan State twenty-five years before, the woman had also lived for many years on the Thai-Burman border. Her lineage, recited by her husband, was identical to that of one of the Monpho, even phonically, down to a common ancestor who lived thirteen generations ago. Thus genealogies give one clues for tracing tribal movements.

These lineages, usually recited in hushed tones at lightning speed, mainly bind together the living and the dead. The dead are friendly spirits who do not punish the living for their misdemeanors, and in their presence friendly contacts take place between the living who share some common names, if they are Akha at all. These names foster harmony, rather than differentiate privileged from unprivileged. No patriline seems to be superior to another. The descendants of Chemy respect, and are respected as much as, the descendants of Lechy, Amaw, or any other ancestor. Such an emphasis united Akha vis-à-vis inimical or possibly inimical spirits and human beings who are not Akha. In this sense it pronounces that all Akha are brothers.

References Cited

Lewis, Paul
    n.d.   Unpublished notes at the Human Relations Area Files. New Haven, Conn.
    1968 Akha-English Dictionary. Ithaca, N.Y.: Southeast Asia Program Data Paper No. 70, Cornell University.
Lo, Tchang-pei
    1945 The Genealogical Patronymic Linkage System of the Tibeto-Burman Speaking Tribes. Harvard Journal of Asiatic Studies 8:349–363.

1949 Nouvelles remarques sur le lien généalogique du patronyme chez les tribus de langue Tibeto-Birmane. Han-Hieu: Bulletin du Centre d'Etudes Sinologiques de Pekin 2 (4) :347–351.

Metford, Beatrix
1935 Where China Meets Burma. London and Glasgow: Blackie and Son.

Rock, Joseph F.
1947 The Ancient Na-Khi Kingdom of Southwest China. Cambridge: Harvard University Press.

5. Marriage and Adoption in Northern Taiwan

ARTHUR P. WOLF

The aim of this essay is to describe the various forms of marriage and adoption recognized by customary law in northern Taiwan in the first two decades of this century. By "customary law" I mean the law acknowledged in the beliefs and practices of the farmers and shopkeepers who made up the great majority of the population of northern Taiwan. This law is similar in principle but often differs in detail from the law recognized by the Chinese authorities who ruled Taiwan before 1895 and by the Japanese colonial government that succeeded them. To avoid confusing the three I have purposely built my analysis on evidence from documents drawn up outside of the courts, from interviews, and, to a large extent, from an analysis of mourning dress, kinship terminology, and the rites of ancestor worship.

Of the various forms of marriage I discuss, one stands out as the model in terms of which others are evaluated and negotiated. This type of marriage is spoken of as *tūa-chūa*.[1] *Tūa* means "big" and implies "great" and "grand"; *chūa* is the verb for the act by which a man takes a wife or a family a daughter-in-law. I try to catch the native sense of the term by referring to these marriages as major marriages.

A major marriage is initiated by a betrothal known as *sàng-tīa:* and proceeds through several stages to *cùe-khěq*, the formal

---

[1] My romanization of Hokkien terms follows the orthography outlined in Nicholas C. Bodman's *Spoken Amoy Hokkien*. Chinese terms are italicized and marked for tone on first occurrence only.

visit the bride and groom pay to her parents three days after the wedding. Although the ceremonies performed at each stage of the marriage are revealing, their content is not as important as their occurrence. All other forms of marriage lack a distinctive procedure and are only ritualized insofar as the rites of the major marriage can be appropriately followed. The major form of marriage embodies an ideal and at the same time provides a model for negotiating easily intelligible alternatives. That most families do not choose the major form of marriage when they have a choice does not affect its importance as a legal and social point of reference. The native views the alternative forms of marriage as compromises made to accommodate social and economic reality.

The parties to a major marriage are, on one side, the groom and his father's line of descent, and, on the other, the bride and her father's line of descent. The line of which a man is the head by virtue of being its eldest living member consists of his sons and grandsons, the ancestors named on his altar, and, in theory, all those men who will someday trace their descent from him. In northern Taiwan, as in China generally, this group is the basic property-owning corporation and the social unit responsible for the rites of ancestor worship. Males are recruited to lines by being recognized as a son of a member and with recognition acquire rights in the line's estate. Women are associated with lines by birth and by marriage but can never become members of lines and are therefore excluded from property rights.

The status of women with respect to lines is evident in ancestor worship. Where a married woman has a right to have her tablet placed on her husband's altar, an unmarried woman has no such right with respect to her father's altar. The small sachet of incense ashes that substitutes for the usual tablet is either placed in a basket and hung in a back room of the house, or is sent to a *kô-niu-biōu* (maiden's temple) where it becomes part of a collective spirit worshiped by prostitutes and other female entertainers. Women are not members of their father's line and only come to be treated as though they were members of any line by marrying. I say "as though they were members" because marriage does not make a woman a full-fledged member of her husband's line. A married woman has a right to support in this life and the next, but she does not have a right to inherit a share of her husband's line's estate. A widow can only claim a share of the estate if she has a son who takes his descent from her deceased husband. The small parcels of property given to some elderly women as *lău-pùn* (capital for the elderly) is not inheritance. The land is only granted for the woman's use in recognition of the obligation that a line has to provide support for the wife of a member.

In analyzing the legal transaction involved in major marriages I have followed E. R. Leach's example (1961:107–108) and simply listed the rights and duties assigned to each of the parties. It is important to note that I have listed as the husband's rights only those rights that he alone can exercise. After his father's death the rights assigned to the husband's line fall to the husband himself, but until then they are exercised by his father or grandfather as head of the line.

A. To the husband's line, the right to determine the descent of the children.
B. To the husband's line, the right to exercise control of the wife's labor services.
C. To the husband, the right to a monopoly of his wife's sexuality.
D. To the husband, the right to be regarded as the legal father of all children not sold to other lines.
E. To the wife, the right to support from her husband's line in this world and the next.
F. To the wife, the right to be regarded as a legal mother of all her husband's children.
G. To the wife's line, the right to see that she is properly treated by her husband and her husband's line.
H. To the two lines, the right to expect the other to attend to requests for favors and amply reciprocate favors granted.

Item A explains the absence of any reference to the rights of the children. Children acquire their rights through lines and not as the offspring of particular people. Item A allows the head of the husband's line to dispose of the children in any one of several ways. A male child may be accepted as a member of his father's line, assigned to the line of a collateral agnate, or sold outright to another family. A female child may be committed in marriage at an early age or sold as a servant-slave (*cā-bô-kàn*). An important but as yet unresolved question is the age at which a male child is no longer subject to Item A. Interviews conducted in 1901 by members of the Taiwan Kanshū Kenkyūkai (1901:46) indicate that after age sixteen a boy is entitled to have an ancestral tablet erected in the event of his death. The close association between the rites of ancestor worship and the rights of descent suggest that this is the legal limit of Item A, but the evidence is equivocal. At the time I was writing this essay Emily Ahern was in Taiwan and kindly inquired into several matters that puzzled me.[2] She was unable to find any age beyond which a son cannot be adopted out. "People say that one would not sell a child old enough to find his real parents again unless he were a willing partner to the transaction. But they refuse to say that it is his *right* not to be sold out. It is just that unless he is willing, there is no use trying to arrange it."

The pivotal importance of Item A is also apparent in the contingencies implied by Items D and F. The rights of the parents *qua* parents are only effective with respect to children assigned to the husband's line of descent. They do not include a right to challenge a decision to sell a child. The right to decide descent belongs to the line as a corporate body and can be rightfully exercised by only the head of the line.

Items E and G assign responsibility for the welfare of the wife. The husband's line has the duty to provide for her material and spiritual needs, and her father's line has the right (and the re-

[2] The evidence attributed to Ahern is quoted with her permission from personal correspondence.

sponsibility) to see that this duty is fulfilled. The marriage transaction gives them the right to judge the treatment received by
the woman in her husband's home, and the right to complain if
she is not provided for or is subjected to unreasonable abuse.
When a woman dies her husband or her sons must immediately
inform her natal family and cannot seal the coffin until one of
her brothers has been given an opportunity to inspect the body
for evidence of suicide or homicide. Many of my informants
claim that a woman's brothers also have the right to inspect her
husband's body. They argue that because a man's death affects
his wife's welfare, her brothers must ascertain the cause of his
death.

Item F also provides security for a woman whose marriage
places her among strangers. It allows her to claim the rights of a
mother with respect to all of her husband's children. This includes adopted children, the children of concubines, and even
the children of a second wife taken after her death. The most
striking consequence of this provision occurs when a woman who
has been committed in marriage dies before the union is consum-
mated. Her intended husband's parents must accept her tablet
and later assign one of their grandsons the duty of worshiping
this tablet as the tablet of a mother. This does not interfere with
the rights of the boy's natal mother because the rights of a mother
are not necessarily exclusive rights. The children of concubines
are expected to perform filial duties toward both their mother
and their father's primary wife.

It is important to note that the rights granted by E and F are
contingent on the wife's continued association with her husband's
line. A woman who divorces her husband or insists on marrying
out of his family if widowed surrenders her rights in her children
and any land she holds as lau-pun. In the case of a widow who
remarries, this is not a consequence of her marrying. She can
remarry and retain these rights if her second husband marries
into her first husband's family. She only forfeits her rights by be-

coming party to a transaction that negates the rights of her first husband's line.

As evidence for these points consider two cases taken from my field notes. In the first case, a young widow remarried and left her one son with her husband's brother's family. Her son did not attend his mother's funeral and does not worship her as an ancestor.[3] In the second case, a woman's husband's parents "called in" a second husband after their son (the woman's first husband) died. When the woman died, her tablet was placed next to her first husband's tablet on the main family altar where her sons make offerings on her deathday and major calendar holidays. Her second husband retained his own surname and so does not qualify for a place on the family altar. His tablet is on a little shelf in a back room where it is tended by a daughter who took his surname.

Although the issues are too complex to consider in detail, I must at least note that Item G glosses over a controversy. Although no one denies that a major marriage creates bonds of affinity between two lines, there is almost total disagreement as to the relative status of the lines bonded by marriage. In an important essay on marriage rites, Maurice Freedman (1970:185) takes the view that marrying off a daughter puts the girl's family "ritually and socially in a relationship of inferiority with the

---

[3] Although he was probably unaware of it, the son had precedence on his side in refusing to attend his divorced mother's funeral. Giles (1915:116–117) writes: "He [T'an Kung, a writer of the third and fourth centuries B.C.] tells how the son of Tzu-ssu, the grandson of Confucius, who had divorced his wife, refused to attend the funeral of his divorced mother, and how his father was interrogated by one of his own disciples, saying, 'Did not *your* father attend *his* divorced mother's funeral (alluding to the divorced wife of Confucius), and if so, why cannot you make your son do likewise.' 'My grandfather,' replied Tzu-ssu, 'was a man of complete virtue. With him, whatever was, was right. I cannot aspire to his level. For me, so long as the deceased was my wife, she was my son's mother. When she ceased to be my wife, she ceased also to be his mother.' From that time forth, it became the rule among the descendants of Confucius not to attend the funeral of a divorced mother."

boy's." Ahern (1974) argues that the transfer of a woman creates a debt that puts the girl's family in a position of ritual and social superiority. My own view, for which I have provided some evidence elsewhere, is that marriage creates equality rather than inequality. "One family may be wealthier or more powerful than the other, but in the realm of kinship they stand on the same plane" (Wolf 1970b: 198–199).

I must make one further point concerning the legal consequences of major marriages. In a recent essay Myron Cohen (1970:22) suggests that marriage effects an important change in the groom's relationship with his father and his father's line. After noting that the term *fang* is sometimes used "to designate the conjugal unit consisting of husband, wife, and children," he writes: "In many, if not most, cases the marriage that established the *fang* also made it an autonomous unit with respect to property rights and economic resources. In theory, the bride had exclusive rights over parts of her dowry, which might have included cash; this confirmed her as an independent property-holder. In fact, her husband as well as she might use these rights to develop an economic subsystem on a *fang* basis distinct from the larger system of the *chia*." Toward the end of the same essay Cohen (1970:34) adds this observation: "Before marriage, paternal authority might in itself be sufficient to ensure that a young man working outside faithfully remit home a portion of his earnings. . . . After marriage, the situation would be somewhat different. The person working outside was now in a position to assert his own rights to the estate."

I agree that marriage sometimes establishes the wife as an independent property-holder.[4] I also agree that on marriage most men begin to seek a greater degree of independence from their father's authority. But I think Cohen exaggerates the consequences of marriage by not noting that a man's rights in his father's estate are acquired as a child when he is accepted as a

[4] Women can hold such property as they acquire as individuals because they are not members of lines.

member of his father's line and that these rights are in no way contingent on his marrying. Indeed, we will see later that these rights exist even if the boy dies as a child. Moreover, I do not believe that rights that exist before marriage are enhanced by marriage. A married man with children consumes a larger share of the income from his line's estate, but this is granted on the basis of greater need rather than on the basis of greater right. By marrying, a man does not acquire the right to demand division of his father's estate, and, if division does occur, married men are not entitled to larger shares than their unmarried brothers.

I turn now to the alternatives to the major form of marriage. The first point to note is that all except one of the eight provisions listed above are sometimes qualified and occasionally set aside. The one exception is Item C. In China there is no form of marriage in which anyone except the husband acquires rights in the wife's sexuality. Because this is the only constant in a widely varying array of arrangements, marriage is best defined as a legal agreement that grants a man a monopoly of a woman's sexuality.[5]

The simplest alternative to the major marriage is what is known in northern Taiwan as *ciŏu-zĭp-chŭa-chût*. *Ciŏu-zĭp* refers to the husband and means "called in"; *chŭa-chût* refers to the wife and means "taken out." The husband and his line agree to provide some financial support for the wife's parents but otherwise retain all of the rights granted by a major marriage. This is one of the means by which an elderly or disabled man whose only sons are very young can use an adult daughter to add to his family's income.

A second relatively simple alternative departs from the major marriage model in another direction. All of the provisions of the major marriage apply except that the bride is handed over only on the condition that one of her children be assigned to her father's line. A child so "adopted" is spoken of as a *tĭ-bû-sùe;*

---

[5] This supports Ward H. Goodenough's (1970:12–13) contention that "a definition of marriage that includes other than considerations of sex and reproduction cannot be applied universally."

literally, "the tax on a sow." His mother is the "sow"; the child, the "tax." My informants explain that farmers sometimes give a sow to a neighbor with the understanding that he will return the favor by giving the animal's original owner all or part of its next litter.

These two types of marriage are generally conducted as though they were major marriages and are usually accepted as such by the community. The more noticeable departures from the major marriage model are those that involve a reversal of the usual residence rule. Because these institutions differ from those Freedman (1957:122–123) found among Chinese in Singapore, it is worth quoting his analysis at length. The comparison between Taiwan and Singapore practice helps clarify the issues involved.

In Singapore men who marry into their wives' households fall analytically in several categories. One extreme category embraces husbands who, from a structural point of view may be considered as male brides. Their functions, that is to say, approximate to those of a woman; they produce children to the surname of the household. This is the perpetuation of a well-known Chinese institution in which the patrilineal system is held intact by reversing the sex of the incoming partner. Such a husband is said, harshly, to *bōe-tōa-teng,* "sell the great lantern," for he resigns his proper place under the house-lantern which bears his own surname and goes out to beget children who will take the surname of his father-in-law. He does not become a son to his wife's parents; he is rather a sort of male daughter-in-law. His status is inferior. (If, however, he has been brought in, not for a daughter, but a *sim-pū-kiaⁿ*, a prospective daughter-in-law, his position vis-à-vis his wife may not be so low.) The expression *chio-jîpkiaⁿ-sài,* "called-in son-in-law," sometimes covers this kind of arrangement, but also extends to versions of in-marriage where the shameful abdication of rights is mitigated by provisions that one or more of the sons born of the union shall revert to the surname of their father. At the time of marriage, for example, the agreement may be that only the first-born son shall take his mother's surname, leaving the other children to acquire their descent in the normal way.

It should be clear that what I am loosely calling matrilocal marriage sometimes entails not merely a variation in the rule of residence, but also a conventional distortion of the principle of patrilineal descent. At the other extreme of the categories I am discussing residence alone is affected. What is often called *chìn-tsòe* is a custom by which a man goes on marriage to live with his wife's people without prejudice to his rights as a father. This may not be an invention of the Nan-yang, but it is an institution which figures predominantly in the older settlements of Chinese in Malaya, and seems to have been favoured by earlier conditions of immigration in which the unattached *sin-kheh,* newcomer, found himself a comfortable berth along with a wife. The systematic continuance of the institution in places such as Penang means that a "permanent" variation in the rule of residence and the position of women as wives and daughters has taken place. *Chìn-tsòe* marriage does not imply that the in-marrying husband is of low status. He may be thought of as enjoying a position of some privilege.

Between the two extreme categories of matrilocal marriage lies another in which the husband, while, as in the case of *chìn-tsòe,* having full rights over his children, is committed to definite economic obligations towards his parents-in-law. The term *ióng-lāu-sài* sometimes covers such a husband. He receives his bride on the understanding that he will live in her parents' household and support them as long as they live.

The first arrangement Freedman describes has no counterpart in northern Taiwan. Although there are marriages that remove the husband from his natal line and assign all of his children to his wife's father's line, these unions always involve an additional legal act that gives the husband the status of a son with respect to his wife's father. In fact, I find it difficult to believe that any Chinese male would agree to resign from his line and surrender his children without this provision. He would be left without any hope of an inheritance and without children obligated to worship him after his death. I must question Freedman's characterization of this arrangement as "the perpetuation of a well-known Chinese institution." It appears to me to be a complete negation of Chinese institutions.[6]

The second custom discussed by Freedman is commonplace in northern Taiwan. The husband goes to live with his wife's family and agrees that some but not all of his children will take their descent from his wife's father. One common arrangement is to assign the first-born son to the wife's father's line; another is to alternate the descent of the children without regard to sex. In either case the result is a household and a sibling set split between two lines of descent. The household acts as one unit in community affairs and worship of the tutelary deities, but is two distinct units as regards property rights and the rites of ancestor worship. The children assigned to the husband's line inherit from their father and worship his ancestors; those assigned to their mother's father's line inherit from him and worship his ancestors.

In a household created by this type marriage the jural independence of the two lines is expressed by the location of their ancestral tablets. Where the wife's father's tablets are always found on the primary altar in the main hall, the husband's tablets are usually located on a subsidiary altar in a back room of the house. And when they are allowed on the primary altar in the hall, they are always placed on the inferior (right) side and are commonly separated from the wife's father's tablets by a small wooden partition. More importantly, no matter where the two sets of tablets are located in relation to one another, they are always served by individual incense burners. An incense burner and the ashes it contains are the ultimate symbol of the line. Its burner represents a line as a corporate body and for this reason can never serve ancestors who belong to other lines.

This class of uxorilocal marriages illustrates the need for the distinction I have drawn between the right to decide descent

[6] The fact that I disagree with Freedman on this and other issues should not be allowed to conceal the debt owed him. This paper was inspired by his work and incorporates points he made after reading my first draft.

(Item A) and the right of a man to be regarded as the legal father of all his children (Item B). These arrangements affect only the first of these rights. The husband is the legal father of all his children, regardless of where they take their descent. As father, he can command their respect and obedience, but he cannot expect them all to treat him as an ascendant and worship him as an ancestor. Those of his sons who take their descent from him must accompany his coffin to the grave and are obligated to worship him as an ancestor. Those who take their descent from their mother's father should wear mourning for their father but need not accompany his coffin and are not obligated to worship him. The obligation of ancestor worship (but not necessarily the performance of it) follows descent.

The treatment accorded a woman whose children take their descent from two different lines does not vary in this way. Instead, the woman is divided between the two lines. Suppose her husband is surnamed Ong and her father Lim. In this case, those of her sons who take their descent from her husband worship her as Ong Ma, "Ancestress Ong"; while those who take their descent from her father worship her as Lim Ma, "Ancestress Lim." A woman married in this fashion is a wife of her father's line as well as a wife of her husband's line and therefore has the right to be treated as an ancestor by both lines.

Freedman's suggestion that chin-tsoe is an invention of the Nan-yang is probably correct. At least I can say that marriages of this type do not occur in northern Taiwan. Although a man may go on marriage "to live with his wife's people without prejudice to his rights as a father," he is always looked down on by his wife's neighbors who take his marriage as evidence that he is an inferior man. The extent of personal disapprobation varies with the circumstances attending the marriage and the social class of the parties, but I have never encountered a case in which an uxorilocally married man was thought of "as enjoying a position of some privilege."

To the best of my knowledge, the term iong-lau-sai is not used in northern Taiwan, but marriages similar to those Freedman describes are common. The only difference is that the man who goes to live with his wife's parents, taking on definite economic obligations toward them without at the same time surrendering some of his children, does not usually remain in their household until they die. If the wife's father does not have sons of his own, he usually insists on claiming one of his daughter's children for his line. An agreement that involves economic obligations but not descent occurs only when the wife's father has sons but needs someone to help him support his family for a few years. He is often an elderly man whose only male children were born late in his life. He therefore foregoes the bride-price he could obtain for his daughter in return for an agreement by which his son-in-law joins his family and works for him until his own sons are old enough to cope. At that point the son-in-law is free to take his wife and reside where he will.

The one marital arrangement that occurs in northern Taiwan but apparently not in Singapore is that which makes the husband a son with respect to his wife's parents. From a jural point of view, these are dual transactions: the husband is adopted and then marries his father's daughter.[7] Often the two phases of the transaction occur simultaneously, but this is not always the case. The man may assume the status of a son a few months and even a few years before the marriage. One cannot draw a clear distinction between adoption and adoption *cum* marriage.

In these transactions the adoption is the prior act legally as well as temporally. It excludes the possibility of normal affinal ties and determines the extent to which the husband retains any ties at all with his natal family. He may remain a son with respect to his natural parents, or he may break off all ties with his parents "the same if he had been sold." It depends on the type

[7] In the village of Kao Yao in Yünnan the bride-to-be was expelled from her own family a few days before the wedding in order to be married into it again as the wife of her parents' newly adopted son (Osgood 1963:285).

of adoption involved. We must examine the three forms of adoption practiced in northern Taiwan before we can understand the adoption of sons-in-law.

In the first case the child who is the subject of the adoption is referred to as *kè-pāng-kìa:*. *Kìa:* means "child"—in this context, a male child; *kĕ* is the verb "to cross." The basic meaning of the term *páng* is "house," but it is extended to refer to the branches of a line or a lineage. Asked to explain the term ke-pang-kia:, some informants take the first meaning of the term pang, some the second. The former point to the large U-shaped compounds in which most farm families live and say that a ke-pang-kia: is a child who crosses from one wing of the house to another. The latter draw a genealogical chart and show that a ke-pang-kia: is a child transferred from one branch to another. The first interpretation reflects the fact that the parties to these transactions are usually brothers who live in the same house; the second, the fact that while the parties are not always brothers, they are always agnates.

The circumstances of this form of adoption vary. If a man dies without descendants, one of his brothers usually assigns a son to carry on the dead man's line. This boy is then entitled to whatever share of the estate the dead man would have inherited. Thus, if the head of the line had three sons, the ke-pang-kia: inherits one-third of the property, the representatives of lines being equal regardless of their generational status. One result is that if one of three brothers dies without heirs, each of the survivors will usually give him a son as ke-pang-kia:. This is the only way one can prevent the other from assuming effective control of two-thirds of the estate.

Adopting a ke-pang-kia: is also one of the alternatives open to a man who fails to produce children of his own. Usually he appeals to his brothers to give him one of their male children, but the term applies to any child adopted from a recognized agnate. The legal status of the child adopted by a living man is the same as that of a child given to a dead man. The difference is that the boy adopted by a living man changes his residence and grows up under the authority of his foster father.

In an article comparing adoption in Eurasian and African societies, Jack Goody (1969:58) argues that the term should be reserved for those instances in which the subject is ranked as the child of its adopter and ceases to be regarded as the child of its parents. By this definition a transaction involving a ke-pang-kia: is not adoption at all. Regardless of the circumstances of the adoption, a ke-pang-kia: retains his ties with his natural parents. The boy simply acquires a second set of parents and a second set of rights and duties. A case cited by the Taiwan Kanshū Kenkyūkai (1901:39–40) indicates that Ch'ing courts on Taiwan would not allow a ke-pang-kia: to claim a share of his natural father's estate, but by custom he remained a member of his natal line while becoming a member of another line. Thus, he was entitled to inherit twice. As my informants sometimes put it, *Tī-â-kìa: cǐaq sān-bû-lǐeng;* "The little pig sucks from two tits."

The only institution in northern Taiwan that qualifies as adoption under Goody's usage is that by which a boy is adopted as a *bǐeng-lǐeng-kìa:.* The term catches the essence of the institution. A *bǐeng-lǐèng* is a kind of insect that is said to lay its eggs and leave them for another species to hatch. A bieng-lieng-kia: breaks all ties with his natural parents and becomes the exclusive property of the adopter's line of descent. The adoption is essentially a business transaction in which all rights in the child are sold. In fact, according to Ahern, many people do not know the term bieng-lieng-kia: and use instead the term *khĭt-e,* "purchased."

Although the parties to a transaction involving a bieng-lieng-kia: are sometimes known to each other, this is the exception rather than the rule. A man who wishes to "buy" a bieng-lieng-kia: usually travels to a distant part of the island to make his purchase or takes a child offered by a dealer who guarantees that the boy will never be able to find his real parents. We thus find two types of male adoption correlated with two types of social relations. On the one hand, there is the ke-pang-kia: who is always a child of an agnate; on the other, the bieng-lieng-kia: who is usually a child of a complete stranger. Logic alone suggests that Taiwanese custom should recognize a third category of male adoption to accommodate transactions involving families related by marriage. My informants tell me that such adoptions occur but do not know what the child is called or anything about the terms of the transaction. The only information I have is from an early article by Santaro Okamatsu (1901:1[9]3). One of his informants noted that a child taken from an affinally related family is called *ciēng-kìa:*, a "gift child." The term fits the situation so perfectly that it must be right. The exchange of gifts at such events as weddings and birthdays is the most characteristic aspect of affinal relationships.

Men who are adopted as young adults and then marry a daughter or adopted daughter are seldom spoken of as ke-pang-kia: or bieng-lieng-kia:, but they are referred to by these terms in both the household registers and native genealogies. More importantly, their legal status is the same as that of men who are taken in as small children. Regardless of whether he is the son of an agnate or a stranger, the man who is adopted to marry a daughter becomes a member of his father-in-law's line and is thereby entitled to inherit. The only difference is that where the son of an agnate retains his ties with his natal family, the son of a stranger must break all ties when he is adopted. I once asked a man who had married his daughter to a man adopted from an unrelated family if his son-in-law worshiped his natural parents. He answered: "No, he couldn't do that. We bought him. So far as his parents are concerned, it is the same as if he had died."

The fact that deviations from the major marriage model often involve uxorilocal residence should not lead the reader to conclude that there is an intrinsic relationship between residence and the various rights and duties assigned by marriage. We have already seen that a man who resides uxorilocally may or may not retain the right to assign some of his children to his natal line, and the same is true of a woman who goes at marriage to live with her husband's family. Although the great majority of these marriages give the husband's line full rights in all the children, this is not always the case. A woman who is the last living representative of a line may bring her tablets with her on marriage and assign at least one of her children to that line. The result is a household with much the same composition as that created when a man marries uxorilocally and surrenders some but not all of his children to his wife's father. The children assigned to the line introduced by the wife inherit its land and must worship its deceased members; those assigned to the husband's line inherit from their father and must worship him and his forebears.

The other provisions of marriage also vary independently of residence and of one another. A man who takes on economic obligations toward his wife's parents may or may not reside with them, and he may or may not compromise the rights of his line with respect to the children of the marriage. Women are sometimes given out in marriage on the condition that one child is returned as ti-bu-sue, and the same condition is occasionally applied to uxorilocal marriages that make the husband a son of his wife's father. I have recorded two cases in which a man was "sold" to his wife's parents on the condition that he return his first-born son to his childless older brother. The general point to be stressed is that except for major marriages, there are no clusters of rights and duties that can be said to constitute forms of marriage. People do not choose between two or three recognized forms of marriage each of which entails a generally accepted set of legal consequences. Instead, those whose needs would not be served by a major marriage negotiate exceptions, compromising cultural ideals in order to achieve specific goals.

One consequence of this is that the terms used to refer to marriages that deviate from the major marriage model are not applied strictly. In northern Taiwan as in Singapore one finds the same term used in several ways and with varying degrees of generality (Freedman 1957:123). For example, the term *ciou-e* (called-in) is sometimes used to refer to any man who resides uxorilocally, but it is also used in opposition to the term khit-e (bought) to refer to men who marry uxorilocally but retain their own surnames. Some people apply the term *pùa: ciŏu-e* (half-called-in) to men who agree to reside uxorilocally and support their wives' parents but retain full rights over their children. Others use this term to refer to a man who remains in his parents' home but agrees to assign one or more of his children to a line represented by his wife. In my view, the alternatives to the major form of marriage lack generally accepted names because they are only *ad hoc* arrangements and not institutions.

A second consequence of the *ad hoc* character of alternatives to the major form of marriage is the need for marriage contracts. With reference to "matrilocal marriages" in Singapore, Freedman (1957:123) writes: "I should perhaps stress that its deviance from ideal norms is reflected in the practice of drawing up documents at the time of marriage setting out the conditions which vary it from the patrilineal standard." The point applies equally well to Taiwanese practice. Although contracts are sometimes written for major marriages, it is only in the case of an alternative arrangement that the economic obligations of the husband and the descent of the children are specified.[8] The provisions of the major form of marriage are understood to apply unless there is notice to the contrary. When exceptions are to be made these must be formulated in writing because there are no alternative institutions with generally understood sets of rights and duties.

What I call minor marriages appear to be exceptions to this generalization but in fact are not. They are regarded as socially inferior and affect the wife's status but do not create exceptions to the provisions itemized above. Legally if not socially, they are major marriages. But we must leave this point until we have discussed female adoption, since this type of marriage introduces the

[8] For examples see Rinji Taiwan Kyūkan Chōsakai, Chōsa Dai-san Hōkokusho (1910–11:Vol. 2, pt. 2, Appendix).

bride into her husband's family as a small child. Again Freedman's (1957:65) analysis of Singapore practices provides us with
a helpful point of departure. He notes the existence of two distinct forms of female adoption:

> In the old days among Malayan Chinese the institution of *mui
> tsai* (a Cantonese term used in official parlance for which the
> Hokkien is *tsa-bō-kán*) was common among well-to-do Chinese;
> young girls were taken from poor homes to be unpaid skivvies. Their
> social sphere was the kitchen and they were treated with some
> severity. However, they were not slaves and their subjection did not
> normally last beyond the age of marriage, for their adopters were
> obliged to find them husbands. It is not an exaggeration to call the
> *mui tsai* system a form of female adoption, for, however lowly their
> status, the girls were allotted a kinship position as daughters and
> sisters, and after their departure in marriage their relations with
> their adoptive parents and siblings, although still couched in an
> idiom of inferiority, were modelled on those of genuine children.
> Colonial administration in the last twenty years has made an assault
> on this system, and while *mui tsai* still certainly exist in a few cases,
> there is a very general carefulness on the part of Chinese to steer
> clear of the penal sanctions against the practice.
>
> There is, on the other hand, nothing to prevent people having
> *sim-pū-kia*ⁿ, "little daughters-in-law," who, while they are in theory
> young girls brought into a household in prospective marriage, may
> actually occupy a status something like that of a domestic servant.
> But this possible ambiguity apart, there is another reason why the
> institution of *sim-pū-kia*ⁿ can be looked upon as a form of adoption
> as distinct from a form of marriage. Again in theory, prospective
> daughters-in-law are taken for a particular son of the house, but in
> fact even if such a stipulation is made it does not seem to follow that
> this marriage must take place. Should the son of the house die or the
> marriage be impossible, for example, because, as sometimes happens,
> the son refuses to accept the girl as a wife, then the *sim-pū-kia*ⁿ can
> be treated as a daughter and be married off to an outsider or have a
> married-in husband provided for her. The category *sim-pū-kia*ⁿ
> certainly is not a precise one and a number of different statuses may
> be sheltering under one label. However, most "little daughters-in-

law" have this in common, that, in accepting a bride-price for them, their parents largely abandon them to their "adopters" and refrain from interfering with them. In other words, the relations between parents and the daughter they give away in this system (despite its terminological assimilation to marriage) are not those between parents and married daughter.

Until the Japanese colonial administration put an end to the practice, wealthy families in northern Taiwan also took in female children (ca-bo-kan) to work as unpaid servants. Sophie Sa Winckler's important study of merchant families in the older sections of Taipei City indicates that these girls were taken in at five or six years of age and commonly left by marriage a few years after puberty.[9] To this extent, the Taiwan institution resembles Freedman's account of Singapore practice, but beyond this there are important differences. The evidence from Taiwan indicates that ca-bo-kan were not assimilated to a kinship status. They were slaves and were treated like property. Okamatsu (1901:1[9]15) notes that on taking shares out of an estate the heirs divided the family's ca-bo-kan on a *per stirpes* basis the same as they divided landed property. To this, Ahern adds the fact that ca-bo-kan did not have the right to marry. Many did marry but only as an allowance on the part of the family that had purchased rights over the girl's person. One informant said that if a ca-bo-kan ran away and married without the family's consent "she would be dragged back and severely beaten." Another informant claimed that many ca-bo-kan did not marry and spent their lives as servant-slaves. "When they died their bodies were taken out through the back door and buried like dogs."

The question of the status of the *sīm-pûà* (sim-pu-kia) is more complex. In northern Taiwan as in Singapore many sim-pua do not marry a son of their foster parents. The intended husband sometimes dies as a child or refuses to go through with the match as an adult. More commonly, the girl's foster parents do not even

[9] The first report of this study will take the form of a doctoral dissertation submitted to the Department of Sociology, Harvard University.

have a son. Of all the girls adopted into six villages in northern Taiwan in the years 1906–1925, approximately 40 per cent were taken by people who did not have a son at the time. The belief that bringing in a female child will increase a woman's chances of bearing a male child encourages people to adopt girls in the hope of obtaining sons. The girl so adopted is said to *ciŏu-siôu-tĩ*, "to call in a younger brother," or, in the view of those who have a better command of native metaphysics, "to restore the (mother's) flower tree and save the white blossoms (representing sons)."[10]

Sim-pua taken as wives for particular men are described as *ŭ thāu-tŭi*, "matched"; those for whom a husband is not named at the time of the adoption are spoken of as *bōu thāu-tŭi*, "unmatched." This distinction appears to confirm Freedman's suspicion that the label sim-pua shelters different statuses, but this is not in fact the case. Although the conditions and consequences of the two types of adoption differ significantly, the legal status of u thau-tui and bou thau-tui is essentially the same. Both are sim-pua and thus eligible to marry a foster brother. Whether or not they actually marry a foster brother depends, not on their legal status, but on their foster family's fortunes in bearing and rearing sons. If her intended husband dies as a child, the u thau-tui must marry out or call in a husband. Should she be successful in "leading a son into the family," the bou thau-tui may become his wife. People see nothing wrong with marrying a bou thau-tui to one of their later-born sons.

Freedman classifies the act of taking a sim-pua as "adoption" rather than "marriage" because the girl does not necessarily marry her foster brother and "can be treated as a daughter and be married off to an outsider or have a married-in husband provided for her." Without further evidence I cannot question Freedman's interpretation of the Singapore institution, but it is definitely not applicable to the situation in northern Taiwan. A

[10] For further details see Doolittle (1865:Vol. 1, 113–114).

sim-pua's status is closer to that of a daughter than is the status of a woman married in the major fashion, but her status is not the same as that of a daughter. For one thing, the girl's foster parents may call in as her husband a man of the same lineage, a marriage that would be incestuous for a daughter. For another, the sim-pua who marries uxorilocally does not thereby become a daughter. The terms children of uxorilocally married women use in addressing their mother's brothers indicate that no matter how a sim-pua marries she remains a daughter-in-law. Where the children of an uxorilocally married daughter address her brothers as *ā-kū*, "mother's brother," the children of an uxorilocally married sim-pua use the agnatic terms *ā-pĕq* and *ā-cĭĕk*, "father's older brother" and "father's younger brother." Address can only be made to conform to descent when the mother is not considered a child of the line and therefore not a full sibling of her children's uncles.

But the fact that sim-pua do not become daughters is not a good reason for withholding the label "adoption." Only a very ethnocentric interpretation of the term would insist that to qualify the child must become the precise legal equivalent of a daughter. I prefer to view the taking of a sim-pua as the first step toward a marriage because this is the way the Chinese view it. Whether she is taken as u thau-tui or bou thau-tui, a sim-pua's removal from her natal home is always treated as marriage. The token sum of money given the girl's parents is referred to as *phièng-kīm* (betrothal money), and even as an infant a sim-pua always comes to her new home dressed in red "because that is what all brides wore in the old days." That there is a sense in which a sim-pua is married as a result is made strikingly evident if she should die before entering a conjugal relationship. Where the soul of an unmarried daughter is represented at her funeral by a small sachet of incense ashes that is later relegated to a back room or removed from the house, the soul of a sim-pua is represented by an ancestral tablet that is accorded a place on the family altar where it becomes the object of regular offerings. A sim-pua who marries out of her foster family even runs the risk of being castigated as a twice-married woman. Gossips count her entry into her foster family as one marriage and her departure as a young adult as the second.

In my view a sim-pua is married to precisely the same degree as a woman who has passed through the sang-tia: stage of the major form of marriage. In both cases the family taking the bride must accept her ancestral tablet in the event of death and must appoint a junior member of their line to serve as her descendant. The only difference is that where the woman marrying in the major fashion is committed to a particular man, the sim-pua is committed to marrying within a particular line. A sim-pua's foster parents are not free to marry her to any man of their choice any more than the parents-in-law of a woman marrying in the major fashion are free to substitute another man for their son. To arrange a marriage that would hand the girl over to a third line, they must have the consent of her parents or her brothers. The fact that this is considered a formality should not be taken to indicate that a sim-pua's natal line surrenders all rights in the girl at the point of adoption. They have a continuing right (and responsibility) to see that she is properly treated in her new home. Contrary to the situation Freedman describes for Singapore, the relations between a sim-pua and her natural parents are the same as those between parents and a married daughter. Although it is a right that is not frequently exercised, they can insist on reclaiming the girl if she is abused by her foster parents.

The transfer of a sim-pua and the sang-tia: stage of a major marriage also resemble one another in the extent to which they activate affinal ties. Ahern's description of the partial ties that exist between a sim-pua's parents and foster parents applies equally well to the relations between the parents of a couple who have passed the sang-tia: stage of a major marriage but are not yet wedded: "From the point of adoption the two families address each other as *chin-kê* and *cī:-m̂,* invite each other to feasts, exchange birthday presents, etc. Up until the marriage, if they attend funerals of the other family, they wear only the costume of a friend, usually only a paper flower. More often than not they do not attend one another's funerals. After the marriage, the girl's natal family wears the full affinal costume and plays the usual role at the funeral of her husband or her parents-in-law."

These parallels between the manner in which sim-pua and brides leave their natal homes and their status in the interim before marriage demand the conclusion that the act of taking a sim-pua is the first step of marriage. However, it does not follow that major and minor marriages are precise equivalents. They are equivalent in regard to all the items listed above, but there are also differences. A sim-pua is not a daughter, but she is more like a daughter than a daughter-in-law acquired by means of a major marriage. When a woman marries in the major fashion her relationship with her husband's parents endures only as long as she continues to perform her role as a daughter-in-law. If she divorces her husband or insists on marrying out of his family as a widow, her ties with his parents are automatically dissolved. But this is not the case with a sim-pua. The household registers from the Japanese period contain instances in which a sim-pua's foster parents call in a husband for her after she has been divorced from their son, and Okamatsu (1901:1[9]17) notes that a sim-pua who marries out of her foster family is expected to mourn for her foster parents the same as a daughter. A sim-pua's ties with her foster parents are strong enough to support regular affinal ties. If a girl who was raised as a sim-pua marries out of her foster family, the marriage creates affinal ties between her husband's family and her foster family as well as between her husband's family and her natal family. This is one of the reasons many people do not want to take another family's sim-pua as a daughter-in-law. They say it is a burden to have two sets of affines. "You spend all of your time running here and there to weddings and funerals."

One consequence of this partial assimilation of the sim-pua

to the status of daughter is weaker affinal ties. Although both Ahern and I have recorded numerous cases in which the ties accompanying minor marriages are every bit as effective as those resulting from major marriages, I have also encountered many cases in which the ties created by minor marriages lack substance. The two families acknowledge the relationship when the matter is raised but do not exchange gifts and invitations and do not depend on one another as kinsmen. Whether this is a result of the very different personal relations created by the two forms of marriage or a socially expected consequence, I cannot say. All I am confident of is that minor marriages are less likely to create strong affinal ties than major marriages.

One further difference between major and minor marriages must be noted. Like all marriages that depart from the major marriage model, minor marriages are conducted with a minimum of ritual elaboration. A sim-pua is dressed in red the day she is transported to her future husband's home, but there is no procession and no festivities to mark the occasion of her arrival. And this lack of ritual attention is not made up for when she finally marries her foster brother ten to fifteen years later. Because she is already a member of her husband's family and a daughter-in-law, the wedding is viewed as a domestic event that does not require public recognition. In most cases the couple are made husband and wife on the eve of the lunar New Year when by custom every family holds a small feast for its members. Often the only formality is an announcement by the head of the household to the effect that the boy and girl will henceforth share the same bed. Their reaction is suggested by the colloquial way of referring to this final act in the marriage process. It is generally spoken of as sàq-cùe-tûi, "shoving (them) together" (Wolf 1970a).

I turn now to what I call second and secondary marriages. A second marriage, as compared with a first marriage, is a union involving a previously married person. The defining feature of secondary marriages is that one of the partners is currently married. As legal arrangements, Taiwanese second marriages are as varied as first marriages, ranging over all of the possibilities already discussed. Secondary marriages, on the other hand, are all of a kind. The bride goes to live with her husband and his first wife, and bears children all of whom take their descent from their father.

Chinese custom draws a sharp distinction between second marriages in which the wife is widowed or divorced and those in which she is marrying for the first time. If a man who has been previously married takes as his second wife a previously unmarried woman, the marriage can be conducted as though it were a major marriage. But if the wife has been previously married, the union is usually given a minimum of public attention, regardless of the husband's marital history. One of my elderly informants told me that in the old days a union of this kind would not be given any ritual recognition. "The man would just go and get the woman and help her carry her things to his house." Another informant claimed that the wife would come to her new home at night, "so no one would see her in the street."

The arrangements made in second marriages depend in part on the nature of the partners' previous unions and the means by which they were dissolved. The simplest and most common case is that in which a widower takes as his second wife a previously unmarried woman. A marriage negotiated under these conditions usually follows the same legal format as a major marriage. The only difference is that sometimes the second wife assumes the role of the first wife in relation to her natal family. By paying a cue-kheq visit to the first wife's family she enters into what is known as a *ciâp-khă-cî-bē* relationship with her predecessor. *Ciâp-khā* means "to continue" or "to carry on"; *cî-bē* simply means "sisters" or "sisterhood." Thus, a second wife who enters into such a relationship with her husband's first wife becomes what we might call her "sister substitute." She is expected to address her predecessor's parents as "father" and "mother" and to mourn for them as a daughter when they die.

Although only a minority of all second wives enter into a ciap-kha-ci-be relationship, there is a feeling that the first wife has a right to expect this of her successor. When a second wife falls ill people often say it is because she has failed to fulfill her duty to her predecessor. I attribute this to the fact that a second wife acquires most of the rights of a mother with respect to a first wife's children. She is thereby indebted to the first wife and should reciprocate by fulfilling the first wife's filial duties.

It is also interesting to note that when a sim-pua dies before marriage and her foster family adopts a replacement, the second girl may be placed in a ciap-kha-ci-be relationship with the first. She is then obliged to treat her predecessor's natal family as though it were her own, the same as a second wife who enters into this type of relationship with her husband's first wife's family. This argues, on the one hand, that sim-pua do not sever all ties with their natal families, and, on the other, that their status is essentially the same as that of married women.

To the best of my knowledge, previously married women are not encouraged to enter into ciap-kha-ci-be relations with their predecessors. But when a woman has been previously married there are other matters that demand attention. If her first marriage was dissolved by divorce, the fate of her children will have been decided. But if she is a widow with children, decisions must be made when she remarries. What is decided depends in large part on the nature of her first marriage. Except in the rare case in which her first husband's line allows her second husband to adopt one or more of the children, the woman whose first marriage was a major marriage must give up all rights in her children to remarry. But if her first marriage assigned one or more of her children to some line of descent other than her husband's, she may have the right to take some of her children with her when she leaves her first husband's home. It occasionally happens that the second husband adopts these children as his own, but more often than not they are the sole representatives of other lines and must retain their own descent.

All that has been said up to this point assumes that the woman is divorced or that she remarries of her own volition, an act that is the legal equivalent of divorce. In either case she loses all rights in those children assigned to her first husband's line. But as I have already noted in discussing the legal provisions of the major form of marriage, this is not the inevitable consequence of a woman's remarrying. In northern Taiwan a woman's parents-in-law commonly call in a second husband for her in the event of her first husband's death, and in this case the second marriage does not alter the rights created by the first marriage. Often the second marriage is arranged as a means of continuing the first husband's line. If the first husband died before producing children or after producing only female children, the in-marrying second husband is usually given his wife on the condition that one or more of his children take their descent from his predecessor. The fact that the other children take their descent from their father does not affect the wife's rights with respect to her first husband's line. A woman may even marry virilocally without giving up these rights if her husband's death leaves her as the sole surviving adult member of his household. The crucial point is that so long as a woman continues to perform the duties of a wife and mother with respect to a line, she retains her rights vis-à-vis that line. Her remarrying does not necessarily affect these rights and may even be viewed as performance of the duties she undertook on marrying into the line.

What is true of a woman marrying for the second time is also true of a man. If an uxorilocally married son-in-law insists on marrying out of his wife's family after her death, he must leave behind those children who took their descent from his wife's father and give up his right to cultivate land held by this line. But this is not a consequence of his remarrying per se; it is a result of his abandoning the role he assumed on marrying into his first wife's family. So long as the man remains with his first wife's family and continues to perform his duties as a son-in-law, his first wife's parents are obliged to provide him with a second wife to replace their daughter. He then retains his rights as a father and continues to derive his living from his father-in-law's land.

One of the curious aspects of second marriages in northern Taiwan is the surprising frequency with which parents and children marry simultaneously. A man takes a second wife and at the same time marries his son to her daughter or his daughter to her son. If the couple's children are not old enough to enter into a conjugal relationship at the same time as their parents, the same effect is sometimes achieved by having the husband or the wife adopt one of the other's daughters as a sim-pua. This girl is then raised as the future wife of her stepfather's or stepmother's son.

These marriages save the expense of a dowry and bride-price for the junior generation, but this is not the only reason they are popular. Examination of the arrangements made indicates that the junior marriage is often undertaken as a solution to a problem that the senior marriage cannot solve. Consider the case of a woman who is responsible for perpetuating her first husband's line and whose only child is a daughter. She may be too old to be confident of bearing a son for her first husband, or her second husband may have only one son himself and insist on claiming all the children they produce. One solution would be to marry the woman's daughter to her second husband's son on the condition that one of the children be assigned to carry on her first husband's line. The arrangement would be attractive to the second husband because it would assure him of a wife for his son and to the woman because it would allow her to fulfill her responsibility to her first husband.

Double marriages of this kind illustrate what I take to be the essential character of second marriages. Like all marriages that do not follow the major marriage model, they are negotiable unions undertaken in response to particular sets of circumstances. The relative frequency of the various agreements reached reflects the fact that some circumstancs occur more frequently than others. People do not choose between two or three culturally defined alternatives; they negotiate compromises that provide reasonably satisfactory solutions to their problems.

Secondary marriages are easier to describe because they adhere closely to the major marriage model. Indeed, they are major marriages in all respects but one. The rights and duties allocated to the four parties are essentially the same as those assigned by a major marriage, and often the wedding is carried out as an only slightly less pompous version of a wedding in the major fashion. The one critical difference between the two forms of marriage is that the first wife and her family have a right to take precedence over the second wife and her family. In her husband's house the second wife must always defer to the first wife, and at such public occasions as funerals the second wife's family must allow the other family to play the leading role. Because both families are regarded as the husband's affines, both must attend his funeral and wear the appropriate mourning costume. In Ahern's words, the difference is that "the family of the first wife takes the principal role and acts as the representative of the other families."

The last institution we need note is what is known in northern Taiwan as *tōng-kû,* "living together." The characteristic feature of tong-ku is that it is not a legal union, but this does not mean that it is not governed by clearly understood norms. A couple described as tong-ku are understood as having entered into a relationship with clearly prescribed rights and duties. The man is expected to provide support for the woman and her dependent children, and in return she is expected to provide labor and sexual services. There is also the clear expectation that the relationship is an enduring one. A couple are not spoken of as tong-ku until they have lived together for some time and appear likely to remain together in the future. Like a common-law union a tong-ku relationship is tested by time; the difference is that it does not in time become the legal equivalent of marriage.

The term tong-ku is applied to a variety of relationships. So far as I can judge on the basis of the cases described in my field notes, the most common form involves a widowed woman and a man who has never married or has lost all of his family. The man usually takes up residence in the widow's former husband's home and replaces him by providing for her and her children. In another common form of tong-ku union the couple are a married man and an unmarried woman whose position is something like that of a mistress. The man spends part of his time with his wife and part with his mistress for whom he provides a house and support. I have also encountered a few examples of tong-ku unions in which neither the man nor the woman had ever been married. The two cases I know best involve women whose parents insisted on an uxorilocal marriage and men who refused to marry into their wives' families. The result is that they have lived together all of their lives without being formally married.

The one feature all of these unions have in common is that the children take their descent from the woman's line. If she is a widow, as in the first case noted above, the children are assigned to the line of her former husband. If, on the other hand, she is unmarried, as in the second and third cases, they take their descent from her father. A man who enters into a tong-ku relationship can make no claim on the children he begets. The children of tong-ku unions do sometimes end up as members of their father's line but only after he has adopted them as bieng-lieng-kia: or sim-pua. Rights over the children reside with the line that controls the woman and must be transferred to the man who is their natural father.

So far as rights in children are concerned, a tong-ku union is no different than a casual relationship with a prostitute. The difference is that tong-ku unions endure and in time create strong feelings of obligation between the partners and their children. The most striking evidence of this is the fact that the woman and her children often worship the man as an ancestor. It was an inquiry about ancestor worship that first made me aware of the strength of the bonds created by tong-ku unions. I one day noted at the side of a domestic ancestral altar a small red sachet and asked what it was. My informant kindly explained that "it is the same as an ancestral tablet." "My husband's mother lived for a long time with another man after her husband died. He helped her raise her children and was very good to her. He had no children when he died, and so we felt that we had to take care of him."

This essay has concentrated on the legal aspects of marriage and adoption to the total neglect of the behavior of the people who were faced with choosing one form of marriage or adoption rather than another. This approach was taken by choice, not out of necessity. Any investigator who has the patience and skill to make use of the magnificient sources available on Taiwan can find in them data to test a plethora of hypotheses about the Chinese family. These data give us a rare opportunity to examine the circumstances under which people chose one alternative over another and an ever rarer opportunity to see something of the consequences of those decisions.

References Cited

Ahern, Emily
    1974 Affines and the Rituals of Kinship. *In* Religion and Ritual in Chinese Society. Arthur P. Wolf, ed. Stanford Calif.: Stanford University Press.
Bodman, Nicholas C.
    1955 Spoken Amoy Hokkien. Kuala Lumpur: Grenier and Son. 2 vols.
Cohen, Myron
    1970 Developmental Process in the Chinese Domestic Group. *In* Family and Kinship in Chinese Society. Maurice Freedman, ed. Stanford, California: Stanford University Press. Pp. 21–36.
Doolittle, Rev. Justus
    1965 Social Life of the Chinese. New York: Harper. 2 vols.
Freedman, Maurice
    1957 Chinese Family and Marriage in Singapore. Colonial Re-

search Study No. 20. London: Her Majesty's Stationery Office. Quotations are reprinted with the permission of the Controller of Her Britannic Majesty's Stationary Office.

1970 Ritual Aspects of Kinship and Marriage. *In* Family and Kinship in Chinese Society. Maurice Freedman, ed. Stanford, Calif.: Stanford University Press. Pp. 163–187.

Giles, Herbert A.

1915 Confucianism and Its Rivals. London: Williams and Norgate.

Goodenough, Ward H.

1970 Description and Comparison in Cultural Anthropology. Chicago: Aldine.

Goody, Jack

1969 Adoption in Cross-Cultural Perspective. Comparative Studies in Society and History 11:55–78.

Leach, E. R.

1961 Polyandry, Inheritance and the Definition of Marriage: With Special Reference to Sinhalese Customary Law. *In* E. R. Leach, Rethinking Anthropology. London: University of London, Athlone Press, Pp. 105–113.

Okamatsu, Santaro

1901 Shinzoku Sōzoku (Descent and Inheritance). Taiwan Kanshū Kiji 1 (4) :25–33; 1 (8) :12–24; 1 (9) :1–28; 1 (10) :18–37.

Osgood, Cornelius

1963 Village Life in Old China. New York: Ronald Press.

Rinji Taiwan Kyūkan Chōsakai, Chōsa Dai-san Kai Hōkokusho

1910–11 Taiwan Shihō (Private Law in Taiwan). Tokyo and Kobe: Rinji Taiwan Kyūkan Chōsakai. 13 vols.

Taiwan Kanshū Kenkyūkai

1901 Mondō (Interview). Taiwan Kanshū Kiji 1 (11) :38–48.

Wolf, Arthur P.

1970a Childhood Association and Sexual Attraction: A Further Test of the Westermarck Hypothesis. American Anthropologist 72:503–515.

1970b Chinese Kinship and Mourning Dress. *In* Family and Kinship in Chinese Society. Maurice Freedman, ed. Stanford, Calif.: Stanford University Press. Pp. 189–207.

6. The Relevance of Family Patterns in the Process of Modernization in East Asia

CHARLES MADGE

Population densities in Southeast Asia are, except for Java, well below those of several major Asian countries, though no simple difference in climate or terrain explains this. Wet rice is, and has been for centuries, the major or elite crop in all these countries. Estimates of population in the historical past are, of course, subject to error, but it is quite clear that some hundreds of years ago the contrast in population density between India, and Japan on the one hand and Thailand, Burma, and Indonesia on the other was even greater than it is today. In the early nineteenth century Java had a population of only about 4.5 million, whereas Japan already had about 30 million. In the mid-nineteenth century Thailand has been estimated to have had a population of 4.5 to 6 million, and Burma about the same (Skinner 1957:68–70; Riggs 1966:16).

The bulk of these populations, past and present, has consisted of families farming on a small scale. Although most of them have been basically subsistence farmers, they have also produced enough to pay taxes, in money or in kind, which have supported some sort of apparatus of state. Nor have they all subsisted at a uniform level; there have been rich farmers and poor farmers, and in many cases a more complex social division of labor, a growth of cities, markets, and administration, has arisen. What is nowadays called "development" has been going on for a very long time, and in the past as now its pace has been set partly by the initiative of ruling groups, partly by the industry and foresight of individual families. The principal form of development in the past has been the extension of the cultivated area, the increase of the population, and in some instances the improvement of crop yields by various methods including irrigation systems. Ancient manuals of statecraft like the *Arthasastra* and the *Book of Lord Shang* show full awareness of the ruler's role in promoting such development, and history has many examples of compulsory or semicompulsory emigration and settlement. But quite probably the economic necessity and interest of individual families, and their willingness to make present sacrifices for future gains, have played at least as important a part in the opening up of new lands. How much importance should we attach to the motives of rulers, and how much to those of peasants, in the promotion of development, and how if at all are the two levels of motivation related? In what ways, if at all, have variations in these motivations set the scene for present-day potentiality for development in the modern sense? Without providing full or final answers, this paper will pose questions of this kind in the context of Southeast Asian societies, with those of India, China, and Japan briefly sketched in for comparison.

The material for a historical sociodemography of India is, in any case, extremely scanty. Davis (1951:24) and Clark (1967: 75) accept the conjectures of Nath (1929:122) and Moreland (1920:9–22), who suggest a population of 100–140 million in the second century B.C. and one of 100 million in the early seventeenth century A.D. Clark agrees with Davis in raising the figure given by the first census under British rule in 1871 to 255 million, which would imply something like a doubling of the population over the preceding hundred years. Subsequent and increasingly accurate decennial censuses show a slow fluctuating growth after that until 1921. Since then the population has grown at a steadily increasing rate.

We can form a general if speculative impression of the way

in which Hinduism and the caste system accompanied the spread of settled agriculture over the subcontinent (O'Malley 1941:2; Kosambi 1956:31). With all the abundant variation that now exists among regions and subcastes, there are substantial uniformities in the pattern of family organization, both in theory and practice. It is patrilineal, authoritarian, and religious. On the side of political history, we can appreciate Moreland's (1944: 34) characterization of India as "parcelled out among a number of kingdoms of varying size and importance . . . frequently at war among themselves, as well as with the tribes on their borders, except for the limited intervals when peace was imposed by the authority of a transient paramount power." We can also accept the dictum that: "It is not in the political sphere that the society finds its unity, but in the social regime of castes" (Dumont 1962: 66).

The history of population growth in China is far clearer than that of India. China has an ancient tradition of registration of households, and figures exist for periods as far back as 1000 B.C. The difficulty lies in their interpretation. According to one authority, China had a population that for the first thousand years of our era was fluctuating around 50 million (Durand 1960). By the beginning of the twelfth century, under the Sung dynasty, it increased to more than 100 million. In the eighteenth century, which under Manchu rule was a period of unusual prosperity and order, there was a prolonged phase of population increase. By 1751 the population was more than 200 million, by 1851 it was more than 400 million. The nineteenth century, however, was a period of mounting disorder which continued until the end of the civil war in 1949. In 1953 the first census of approximately modern type to be taken in China gave a population of 583 million, far higher than most of the accepted estimates up to that time.

Unlike India, China has been politically as well as culturally unified over most of its recorded history. There is abundant evidence of the development policies of Chinese rulers, from the earliest time onward. Population changes can be related to these policies, to changes in agricultural technology, and to other economic and political factors, internal and external (Ho 1959:169).

Family organization in China, as in India, has for centuries been both patrilineal and authoritarian. All authorities are agreed that family loyalty has been the overriding motive in Chinese life at every social level to an extent generally considered to have few if any parallels.

For the premodern history of population growth in Japan and its relation to various political, economic, and social factors, we have two excellent chapters in the standard work on the population of Japan (Taeuber 1958:3–34). We find that by the late twelfth century the Japanese economy supported from six to nine million people; in the middle of the nineteenth century it supported more than 30 million. The population seems to have changed irregularly but with a general upward movement from the thirteenth until the sixteenth century. It is believed to have increased rapidly in the seventeenth (a period of peace and stability after centuries of internal warfare), changing little from the early eighteenth century until the mid-nineteenth century.

Japanese rulers from the earliest times pursued conscious policies of development based on Chinese models, but evolving characteristic institutions of their own. Only a small proportion of their mountainous islands are cultivable. Here there soon appeared relatively dense agrarian populations and an exceptional growth of towns and cities, including the three great cities of Edo, Osaka, and Kyoto. The civil wars from the twelfth to the early seventeenth century did not stop the increase of population and may even have stimulated the growth of towns (Taeuber 1958:20). The long period of internal peace which followed, in which conservative-minded rulers attempted to maintain the status quo by policies restrictive of mobility and change, saw yet greater urbanization, the spread of a money economy, and, for some sections of the population, the development of education.

The Taika Reform of 645 A.D. included a household code; and

a Japanese version of Confucian patrilineal familism was established, at first in the upper strata and finally, by the late nineteenth century, among the people as a whole. During the period of civil war, family authority was consolidated, women and children were more strictly subordinated, and the role of the family head was more strongly emphasized (Taeuber 1958:17). At this stage, nevertheless, peasant practices continued to be more permissive and the status of women less inferior to that of men; village endogamy was the norm. All this changed with the extension, in modern times, of upper-class norms to the whole population, both in custom and in law (Taeuber 1958:207).

What India, China, and Japan have in common, then, are long-established high agrarian population densities, and authoritarian patrilineal norms emanating from elite groups and diffusing to the population as a whole. They also share traditions of statecraft in which peasant numbers and productivity are deliberately developed and encouraged. While one cannot be sure how much the growth of populations owed to this encouragement, one can reasonably suppose that it helped the process to gain momentum and to become self-propelling.

The value systems of India, China, and Japan differ markedly, as does their historical evolution in the period leading up to modern times. To trace these differences in detail is, of course, an absorbing task, but here the aim is rather to draw a broad contrast between three societies which have long been populous and patrilineal and other societies, in Southeast Asia, where the population has either remained small or has only grown to any notable extent since about 1800 and where family institutions are predominantly cognatic (Murdock 1960:2). It is not suggested that there is necessarily a direct causal link between non-unilineality and low population density, but rather that there are indirect links which have been important in the past and which may contribute toward a distinctive pattern of modern development in these societies.

In a discussion by Taeuber (1958:15) of the early stages of

population growth in Japan we read: "Once people had increased in number, there was a strong compulsion to extend the cultivation of the soil and so secure the increased amount of subsistence essential to the survival of the greater number of people. The growing number of people whose survival was permitted by agriculture thus stimulated the further development of agriculture." This important insight is treated at booklength by Boserup (1965). Whereas population growth is often regarded as the dependent variable, determined by preceding changes in agricultural productivity, this author argues that the main line of causation is in the opposite direction. She believes that population growth is the independent variable which in its turn is a major factor determining agricultural developments.

Before population pressure compels the adoption of more productive techniques, there persists what she calls the vicious circle of sparse population and primitive techniques. "A population which is small in relation to the total territory it commands cannot owing to this very smallness get into a process of economic and cultural development" (Boserup 1965:73). It will not start on that process until agriculture has become more intensive and numbers have increased. But apart from the cultural backwardness and poor communications of such a population, its members have a natural or rational-economic resistance to more intensive methods, since it can be shown that these yield lower output per man-hour (Boserup 1965:43–55; Clark and Hasswell 1964:86, 115). This is true of each successive form of intensification. To simplify her analysis, Boserup distinguishes among five main types of land use, in order of increasing intensity: (1) forest-fallow cultivation, with a fallow period of some twenty to twenty-five years; (2) bush-fallow, with a shorter fallow period, not long enough for true forest to be re-established; (3) short-fallow, with a fallow period of one or two years only, during which nothing but wild grasses have time to grow; (4) annual cropping, in which the land is uncultivated between the harvesting of one crop and the planting of the next; (5) multicropping, in which the same plot bears two or more successive crops in one year, and there is virtually no fallow period.

Under the pressure of increasing population, she points out, there has been a shift in recent decades from more extensive to more intensive systems of land use all over the world. But this shift has in fact been going on gradually over a very long period. For example, there was a gradual shortening of fallow in western Europe during and after the Middle Ages ending in the change to annual cropping in the second half of the eighteenth century.

Until recently rates of population growth were low or very low in most pre-industrial communities and from time to time the size of the population would be reduced by wars, famines or epidemics. Thus, we should expect the rate of technological change in agriculture to have been slow and interrupted by periods of stagnation or even regression of techniques; before intensive systems of land use had time to be applied over the whole territory of a given village or region, a set-back to population growth might often have occurred and the process of change would be interrupted. Thus the slowly penetrating systems of land use and techniques would be expected to co-exist for long periods with older systems within the same village or in different villages within the same region [Boserup 1965:56].

Microanalysis at the community level can show how the statistical concept of "population pressure" is the result of different amounts of pressure on families of different types and sizes with differing resources. Macroanalysis at the societal level can show whether the density of the population is sufficient to support centralized political institutions. Of course, neither the families at the community level nor the elite groups at the societal level are inexorably controlled by numbers or techniques. Normative standards and institutional structures can intervene, can in fact change or be altered over time, by diffusion, by missionary effort, by ideological propaganda, and so on. What in the title of this paper are inclusively called "family patterns" have potential significance both at the community level, where the multitude of decisions affecting the size and activity of the families constituting the "population" are made, and at the societal level, where they will enter into the motives and plans of elite groups and individuals strategically placed to modify the historical development of the society.[1]

Unilineal institutions in large societies are unlikely to have the same force in all parts of the society or at all times in its history. Their strength in any given time or place may be interpreted as in part a community-level response to local circumstances and in part an effect of a centrally sponsored ideology. In India and China, unilineal institutions were extended, consolidated, remolded in both these ways, both from above and below as it were, over many centuries. In Japan they were introduced from above and gradually spread throughout the society. Unilineal institutions can hardly be maintained without a supporting ideology. No special ideology, however, is needed to maintain the *absence* of unilineal institutions, which is in effect what is meant by "cognatic" kinship systems.

In making comparisons we should not forget, however, that for the peasant populations of Burma, Thailand, Indonesia, and other countries in this part of the world, family institutions are no less than elsewhere a universal reality; households and pooled ownership involving a group of kin wider than the nuclear family

[1] Something of the complexity and also of the logic of these interrelations comes to light in the writings of social historians who study the "process of economic and cultural development" regionally and locally, taking into account, where data exist, the interplay of ecological, demographic, and sociological factors. To take an example from western Europe, in the course of an impressively detailed and at the same time analytical account of the region of Languedoc, we read that after the Black Death had brought to an end a prolonged period of population increase and extension of the cultivated area, there was between 1350 and 1500 a remarkable development of extended family institutions, reflected in legal documents. These the historian interprets as means by which families mobilized their diminished demographic resources to carry out agrarian tasks and to regain internally the sense of security which state and feudal institutions were failing to provide (Le Roy Ladurie 1966:162–168). There was a comparable revival of the lineage in tenth-century Burgundy (Duby 1953:263–281).

are common. The status of men *is* marginally (but not emphatically) higher than that of women. Young people *usually* choose their own mates, and sheer proximity makes it *likely* that these will be in their own village. There are few if any complications about divorce and remarriage. Until the recent past there have been no surnames to fix a continuing family identity. Easygoing, permissive, cooperative—these are the frequently ascribed attributes of both family life and working life among the peasants of Southeast Asia.

The traditional political pattern of this part of Asia has been of fragmentation into petty kingdoms, warring with one another like those of India rather than unified in bureaucratic empires like that of China. Even small kingdoms presumably could not exist without some concentration of population based on settled cultivation, but the area of such cultivation seems not to have been systematically extended (or not as a rule; there are some historical exceptions) as was the case in India, China, and Japan. It may be significant that the dynasties ruling the petty kingdoms normally had Hindu affiliations and institutions; though there was minimal family continuity at the base of these societies, there was at least some dynastic continuity at the top. In Malaya and Indonesia, hereditary Muslim rulers followed. To take one example only, we may recall the fifty "classical" kingdoms, Hindu *and* Muslim, shown on Schrieke's map of Java, mostly developing around areas in the interior of the island peculiarly suited to wet rice (Schrieke 1957:end papers; Geertz 1963a:43).

Java is now densely populated and part of a large state, but there are still countries in Southeast Asia where something like the "classical" political pattern is still to be found. In Laos, one of the least urbanized areas of the world, "prior to French rule the Lao were organized in a series of petty kingdoms with small towns as their ritual and market centres" (Halpern 1964:83) —a situation which also prevailed over most of Thailand when the early Thai dynasties embarked on what is probably the most politically successful project for unification in the region. The rulers exercised in exaggerated form the parental authority which was unstressed in the peasant family. They were Lords of Life and Death, and extreme deference was paid them. Of Laos a recent observer writes that the only part of this small country where "a significant feudal arrangement" obtains is the immediate vicinity of the royal capital of Luang Prabang, limited to a few villages where the royal family continues to have extensive holdings (Halpern 1964:83). To most Lao villagers, however, the same auther has written, "the government system is not very clear" and the non-Lao groups are often unaware that they have a king (Halpern 1958:128).

Petty kingdoms with only small peasant concentrations of a few villages to support them cannot exert much influence on the scattered outlying population. There were, of course, in the history of Southeast Asia many instances of a "petty" kingdom developing into a more politically substantial structure, with a sizable capital city, an extensive territory under direct rule, and beyond that tributary states or tribes. Thus, before the first independent Thai dynasty in A.D. 1238; "There were numerous T'ai settlements known as Mueng, each ruled by their own *Chao* (Ruling Prince), all were under Khmer suzerainty, but Khmer rule was not at all times so strict or rigid. Communication was difficult and the muengs were scattered over a wide area and interspersed by thick tropical jungle. . . . Under this loosely knitted Khmer domination, the T'ai chaos came to realize that it was in their interest to unite and mould themselves into large principalities, and finally into a kingdom" (Chakrabongse 1960: 21, and see Riggs 1966:83).

Even when a substantial kingdom was built up, as in Thailand, population density remained low by comparison with that of Mauryan India, Han China, or Japan at the time of the Taika Reform. Vast tracts of territory remained under shifting cultivation—the "forest fallow" and "bush fallow" of Boserup's fivefold scheme. Although topography may account partly for the continuing low density in Laos, it can hardly be the explanation for Southeast Asia as a whole. Malaria and other diseases may have been a deterrent to settlement over much of the region, as it was in the southern provinces of China, but persistent settlers overcame these hazards elsewhere. In fact, malaria is mentioned as an "ancient and a widespread disease" in Japan (Taeuber 1958: 51). Wars such as those between Thailand and Burma no doubt helped to retard population growth, but invasions and internal wars also affected the populations of India and China, and as we have seen, four centuries of civil war in Japan did not stop Japanese population increase (Skinner 1957:30; Taeuber 1958: 20; Sansom 1946:438–439).

It seems more plausible to suppose that the process of economic and cultural development took a characteristically and systematically different course in Southeast Asia from that taken in the countries where populations early became dense. Yet the political or politicoreligious *theories* of rulers and elite groups in the region were broadly similar—in fact Southeast Asia took these theories mainly from India. It was not the theory that was different, but the practical result. Is it possible that the factor absent in most of Southeast Asia but present in India, China, and Japan—the lineage with its associated institutions of parental authority—was responsible for the greater tendency to population increase in the latter countries? Was it due to the effect of family-centered, parent-controlled, continuity-seeking institutions and ideologies on the whole complex interaction of state policies and popular responses?

A crucial aspect of this interaction is the point at which families decide to extend or intensify their agricultural activity. It is always in the interest of rulers that they should do so. It may also be in their own interest, but whether they see it that way may depend partly on how much of their increased production is taken off by taxes, rents, and so on, partly on the amount of additional hard work involved and the nature of the practical difficulties, and partly on prevailing norms of family aspiration and loyalty.

On the side of rulers, techniques of getting peasants to produce more have varied over a whole spectrum of approaches and devices. Let us take only one example from Mogul India. Orders issued under Aurangzeb in 1665–1666 set forth his development policy: "Extension of cultivation comes first, then increase in the area under high-class crops, then the repair and construction of wells for irrigation. Peasants who cooperated actively in carrying out this policy were to be treated with consideration, and their reasonable requests for assistance were to be met; but the idea of cultivation as a duty owed to the State was still paramount, and flogging was specifically authorized in cases where this duty was neglected" (Moreland 1929:134). At this date, according to Moreland (1929:147), the problem was not the shortage of land but of peasants, who had been driven away from their settlements by oppressive government.

We will consider below in more detail another means by which a peasant population could balk its rulers in their quest for additional production, besides withholding labor or running away. They could deliberately limit their own numbers. Our focus of concern here is not with the problems of rulers with already large peasant populations but with the more or less chronic "under-development," until recent times, of large areas of Southeast Asia. In the contemporary world, these problems can be illustrated from the present situation in Laos. Here too the difficulty is more one of underpopulation than of a shortage of land suitable for intensive cultivation.

Even in the river valleys and particularly in northern Laos, extra rice land is usually available to those who can clear the land. This takes considerable time and labor, especially in terracing and irrigation works. A poor Lao farmer with a small family cannot clear land by himself, and to invite others to help necessitates incurring the expense of their labor, or at least a feast.

Most villages are only semi-permanent, and forest land is still available. The irrigated rice fields, or *na,* have become fragmented because their yields are more reliable than those of the *hai* [plots cleared by slash-and-burn cultivation]. However the creation of new *na* involves the extension of irrigation ditches and a major investment of labor. This labor, if not hired, must be supplied by the family itself, and this implies existing fluid capital or a large extended family containing a number of able-bodied workers. Neither of these situations commonly occurs among Lao peasants [Halpern 1963:85, 86].

The absence of suitable social organization and motivation is retarding the speed of transition from shifting cultivation to wet-rice cultivation, and helping to keep numbers low and families small.

It appears that in fact Lao villages are rather small and the average number of people per household is rather low. Of the non-Lao people, the Khmu (or Ka) have even smaller villages. The Meo (or Miao) villages are smaller still, but the number of people per household is larger. Halpern (1958:9) observes that this is due to Meo social structure. Unlike the Lao or Khmu, the Meo have a definite patriarchal type of social organization with the extended family. With large households each separate Meo group can function more readily as an independent economic unit than can the smaller households of the Lao and Khmu (Ruey 1960:145). Social structure is one aspect of the small size of Lao households; also to be borne in mind is the effect of very high rates of fetal mortality, infantile mortality, and childhood mortality: "No statistics exist on fetal mortality for Laos but I would estimate them to be about like this: fifty percent of pregnancies do not go to completion. Of one hundred babies conceived, only fifty will be born alive. Of these fifty, twenty will die during infancy, from smallpox, cholera, malnutrition, whooping cough or pneumonia. Of the thirty left, ten will die during childhood from malaria, trauma, or dysentery" (Halpern 1958: 98, quoting Dooley 1958:90).

These figures are conjecture, of course, but prenatal and postnatal mortalities of this order are needed to explain the stationary populations of primitive or near-primitive social groups. Accord-

ing to Colin Clark, the lowest survival rates known with reasonable accuracy are those for Stone Age man (55 per cent mortality before the age of fourteen), Bronze Age man (50 per cent
mortality), and the Sambura of East Africa, "a very primitive
pastoral tribe inhabiting arid country," among whom somewhat
less than 50 per cent die before the age of fourteen. Clark
(1967:46) comments that with this rate of survival the biological
maximum of reproductivity only just suffices to maintain the
population.

The Meo of Laos are said to have come south into Laos from
Yünnan in the last 150 years; they "inhabit literally the tops of
the mountains," according to Halpern, and prefer virgin forest
for their shifting cultivation. In other words they are true "forest-
fallow" cultivators, whereas the Khmu "return to forest clearings
which have remained fallow for several years." There is a
gradient in type of cultivation from Meo to Khmu to Lao, with
corresponding increase in population density. Whereas for the
Khmu swidden cultivation is the norm, and working paddy fields
an innovation, the majority of Lao farmers have permanent rice
fields and only cultivate swiddens as second best (Halpern
1958:28–31).

The Lao people of northeast Thailand have at the present time
moved even further toward wet-rice cultivation as their main
subsistence activity. The population densities of the provinces of
northeast Thailand are far higher than those of Laos and are
rapidly increasing, but this population growth is very recent.
Densities and conditions in general which now obtain in Laos can
serve as reminders of the demographic and ecological pattern
that prevailed over nearly the whole of Southeast Asia until
around 1900. Even those parts of Thailand which are now most
agriculturally productive and densely populated were relatively
"underdeveloped" at the time when the Jakkri dynasty moved
the capital from Ayudhya to Bangkok.

It has been implied above, following Halpern's suggestion, that
the size of the Lao household is relatively small as a result of

"of social structure," and moreover that this small size is a definite handicap when it becomes necessary to clear forest and make new rice fields. But it should be emphasized that neither Lao nor Thai villagers have any systematic prejudice in favor of small households. They are in most cases simply unable to raise large families, primarily because of high prenatal and postnatal mortalities; and the "social structure" does not prescribe as its ideal the kind of corporate family arrangements which have made it possible for at least a portion of families in other peasant societies to reach a size more favorable to agroeconomic development.[2]

[2] Southeast Asian peasant society includes many small households but also a substantial number of larger households. A group of households in the village of Pa-ao in northeast Thailand comprised 32 families consisting of parents and children only, with an average size of 5.5 persons per household; 18 other families in which to this nucleus were added unmarried blood relatives, such as nephews and nieces; and 25 households which included a male relative by marriage, usually a son-in-law. The effect of this is to produce a two-tier household, which includes some of the grandchildren as well as the children of the original parental couple. Many permutations are possible, and other relatives may be added. The average size of the two-tier households was 8.5 persons. From an agricultural point of view, of course, the number of persons in the household is not what counts, but the number of able-bodied adults. The two most prosperous households in this group consisted of 9 persons aged thirteen and upward and 7 children, and 13 persons aged thirteen and upward and 6 children, respectively. Among the poorest households were four who suffered from having a small amount of unproductive land on which to grow food for a fairly large family (Madge 1954: 15, 23).

Of 94 households in Nondwin, an "ordinary village of dry zone Burma," 53 were of parents and children, sometimes with secondary relatives as satellite residents; 32 comprised an "extended conjugal family, in which a son or daughter has formed a conjugal family and is coresident with the father and mother and jurally subordinate to the father-mother family"; and 5 comprised a "joint conjugal family, in which relatives such as siblings or cousins or in-laws live in the same compound, with coordinate jural status between or among the families." "The joint and the extended families are those having the land base to support more than a single family and to utilize the labor of more than a single family. This follows the observation that the rich families tend to be the extended families; the poorer families tend to be simple conjugal ones. It is only the very

The larger households of Thailand are *ad hoc* arrangements, useful from the agricultural point of view but not based on ideas of long-term continuity of the family, long-term extension and improvement of its collective assets, or disciplined acceptance of the authority and responsibility of the family head. Such ideas are not totally absent but they are much more weakly present than in communities with unilineal institutions. There are also cooperative working groups for specific tasks such as harvesting, house building, well digging, and so on, as in other peasant communities, but they too are less highly organized and motivated than those of China or Japan. A full comparative treatment of such groups and their significance for the process of economic and cultural development would require too much space to be included here.

Another important difference between the unilineal and cognatic systems is that the former incorporates in far stronger form the idea that size of family and the numbers of male and female children can be manipulated and controlled. For many families in unilineal systems this implies a restriction of numbers rather than maximization. For the very poorest, restriction on increase in number is involuntary; the poorest men cannot obtain wives, or if they do their wives are particularly prone to miscarriages and stillbirths and their children tend to die in infancy or childhood (Crook and Crook 1959:5; Yang 1959:18). At a somewhat higher level of prosperity, economic pressure may lead to deliberate restriction of numbers by abortion or infanticide, especially female infanticide. One may recall the British efforts in India to eliminate female infanticide (Minturn and Hitchcock 1966:45, 78), the historical evidence for the persistence of this practice in China (Ho 1959:58), and the strong suspicion of

---

rich who can hold on to their sons and have the sons' families live in the same compound and under the authority of the father and mother. The small number, nine, of extended conjugal families through a male line indicates that this is a rare event, as rare as the big rich in Nondwin" (Nash 1965:44–45, 49).

Geddes, when he revisited in 1956 the village of K'aihsienkung, previously surveyed by Fei in 1936, that infanticide was still being practiced under communism (Fei 1939:33–34; Geddes 1963: 17). Buck (1937) noted the very marked relationship between the crop area of the farms in his survey and the mean size of family. Most Chinese rural families, he says, had about as many members as the farm could support, and he quotes the proverbial verse (1937:371):

> To feed a family of five
> A farmer must work like an animal,
> But to feed a family of six
> Even a flogged animal will not work.

The tendency to restrict numbers is all the more striking in view of the strong preference for a large number of children as the ideal, a preference by no means due only to cultural and religious considerations but based on practical experience of the economic and political advantages of a large household. Naturally, rulers were always opposed to infanticide or any other method by which peasants restricted their numbers, and sometimes they punished such practices severely. The very widespread practice of infanticide in eighteenth-century Japan, and the efforts of the government to stop it, have often been described (Taeuber 1958:16–34, 272).

In the societies with unilineal institutions, the ideal number of children and the ideal size of household are large. Smaller households aspire to become large ones and to reap the advantages of size. Large households have sought to remain large and to postpone the inevitable process of fission. Even when numbers are restricted, the practice is seen as a necessary evil rather than a good in itself: it constitutes, one might say, a policy of *reculer pour mieux sauter*. For a family with a small crop area to have more children than the area can support is to condemn itself to the prospect of ceaseless hard work and grinding poverty. If, however, it can increase its assets in land and livestock, it will welcome more children, and if these are not forthcoming within the family, a solution may be sought through adoption or similar means, or (in traditional China) through the taking of a concubine. The crucial feature, from a demographic and economic standpoint, is the implicit belief that family numbers can be managed in the interests of family fortunes.

Turing to Southeast Asia, we find, as we might expect, a less deliberate kind of motivation. On Thailand, we have the statement by deYoung (1955:49):

Children are wanted and have a high position in the peasant's cultural and economic values, and attempts to prevent conception are rare. Village families in modern Thailand, however, are not large: surveys in the 1930's showed an average family size of five members, and recent studies of Thai villages reveal that the size of family has not changed appreciably since then. In north Thailand, the average family has about five members, and in central Thailand about five and a half members, with ordinarily only two children younger than fourteen in each household. Compared with the peasantry of other countries of Asia, Thai village families have a remarkably small number of children, a situation brought about by a relatively low fertility rate which unquestionably is linked with health and nutritional patterns, and a high infant-mortality rate. Deliberate abortion is not common in rural Thailand even though methods to induce it are known. Specific information about abortion is hard to obtain in any peasant area, but it may be assumed that since birth control is not practiced, any deliberate limitation of family size must be in the hands of women, and that abortion is practiced occasionally. Thai women, particularly midwives, know the abortifacient value of certain local drugs, especially quinine, which is used for this purpose throughout Southeast Asia. In north and northeast Thailand, where malaria is an endemic recurrent disease, continual dosage of quinine may well be the cause of some unintentional miscarriages. Infanticide is so unthinkable by Thai Buddhist standards that anyone who committed it would be judged insane. The high cultural value attached to bearing children is shown by the belief that sterility is sinful, since a sterile woman has not been "blessed by Buddha."

Whether or not Buddhism is a factor in this context, we have the following report by Fraser (1960:193) from a Malay Muslim fishing village in southern Thailand:

Almost without exception, families in Rusembilan desire children, and pregnancy is considered a happy and fortunate event. There is no preference as to the sex of the child, unless one sex is overwhelmingly represented in the family already. On the rare occasions when family economic pressures make the arrival of a child undesirable, the villagers practice a method of birth control which they say usually proves effective. This method involves the use of a certain root, a decoction of which must be taken with rice morning and evening for two months following the birth of a child in order to prevent becoming pregnant again. How long this treatment remains effective is not certain. Its effect would appear to be only temporary, however, as it is again prescribed when the woman becomes pregnant. At this stage in the treatment, the decoction is taken until abortion occurs.

Nash (1965:256) writes of a Burmese village near Mandalay:

Women and men do not, when married, try in any way to restrict the possibility of having children. Coitus interruptus or reservatus is apparently unknown and unpracticed. There is a vague knowledge that women may be more or less fertile at different times during the month, but this is not a guide to frequency or timing of intercourse. Married couples will not practice the several methods of abortion that villagers know, nor is there any contraceptive device in use. . . . When pressed, women will say that three (live) children is a good size family, but they do not begin to complain about the burdens of childbearing until they have six children, and then one may hear from the woman herself and from her neighbors expressions of commiseration about how much work and trouble child-rearing is. But, given the fearsome child waste in Burma (infant mortality is the second highest in the world), the problems of restricting family

size loom less large than the hazards of bringing infants into childhood.

Finally, Koentjaraningrat (1960:103) writes of south central
Java in the 1950's: "Most Javanese desire a large family because
of the general belief that many children are a blessing and contribute a *slamet* [a state of emotional calm] within the household.
There is, in addition, the very practical consideration that children can take care of their parents in old age. A couple without
children usually consult a physician or, in rural areas, a *dukun*
[traditional midwife], who is a specialist in supernatural methods
of inducing impregnation as well as in midwifery. Birth control
is absolutely unknown in rural areas, and the urban population,
though usually possessing some knowledge of contraceptive devices, rarely utilizes them."

These statements by careful observers in different areas of
Southeast Asia, while not necessarily generalizable to the region
as a whole, are suggestively unanimous about the value attached
to children and the rare recourse to the restricting of numbers.
There is no suggestion here that small family size, where it occurs
in the region, must be deliberate. It is more likely to result from
environmental factors leading to high mortality rates. A change
in these factors has certainly led to very rapid increase in numbers, earlier in Java and more recently in Thailand and elsewhere
in the region.

Lorimer (1954) discussed at considerable length "the relation
of cultural conditions to fertility in non-industrial and transitional
societies." Given the immense complexity of the topic and the
lack of accurate comparative data, it is not surprising that he
was unable to provide a theory that could explain all, or anything like all, the observed variability. But his survey is in many
ways a masterly one, raising many pertinent questions and arriving at some interesting if tentative conclusions. With African
material mainly in mind, he suggests this general principle: "Corporate unilateral kinship groups and the related emphasis on
mother rights or father rights in social organization tend to gen-

erate strong motivations for high fertility." And again: "Corporate clans and lineages (with closed membership, a system of
authority, and continuity through successive generations) are
widely prevalent among the dominant tribal societies in areas of
intense competition for resources among tribal societies. They
are a common, though not universal, characteristic of societies in
such situations." But, he says, the function of corporate kinship
groups is not limited to situations of actual or potential conflict.
They "promote orderly adjustment of peaceful economic activities" (Lorimer 1954:90, 92, 93).

Lorimer points out that many of the great agricultural civilizations rose through gradual transitions from tribal societies with
patrilineal descent and corporate clans and lineage groups. He
cites the Chinese and Roman civilizations, and both the early
Aryan and the later Muslim migrations into India. He then ar-
rives at two complementary hypotheses he describes as:

appropriate to the family patterns and related values of some
Asiatic agrarian societies—neither of which affords a wholly adequate
basis of interpretation apart from the other:
   1. The structure and values of the prevalent agnatic group-family
relations emerged as adaptations of forms of kinship relation that
had major functional value in relatively mobile tribal societies in
competitive relation with other societies. They are, in part, sustained
by the persistence of principles formed in this context.
   2. Some stable patterns of group life are essential to the orderly
life of any society and to the well-being and security of its members.
The patterns of family life in agrarian societies have the function of
meeting this ever-present need. They are, in part, maintained and
constantly adapted as responses to this need [Lorimer 1954:154].

The second of the hypotheses is unexceptionable to the point of
being almost platitudinous. The first may well have been true
of, say, the Vedic period in India as it seems to be true of a more
recent historical period in Africa. But it will have become clear
from the earlier part of this paper that Lorimer's hypotheses,
sound in themselves, need supplementing to explain both the

early growth of very dense agrarian populations in India, China, and Japan and the absence of this growth over the greater part of Southeast Asia, to which he barely refers. In this paper I suggest that the explanation lies in the interaction between two factors: (a) the type of family structure, and (b) the encouragement given by rulers to the development of agriculture, to the extension of the cultivated area, to the increase of crop yields, and so on. Perhaps the traditional rulers of Southeast Asia were just as anxious as those of India, China, and Japan to fill their territories with productive peasants and their treasuries with the resulting tax yields. I suggest that they were seldom so successful because the family patterns of Southeast Asia made their populations less amenable to this kind of encouragement.

So far we have been concerned with possible explanations for differences in the buildup of agrarian populations in the fairly remote past, a period of protodevelopment which long preceded the sort of development with which all modern societies, including all Asian societies, are currently preoccupied. I propose to consider briefly the possible effects of variations in the protodevelopment phase between one society and another on its present potentialities for development in the modern economic sense. We cannot assume that the constellation of factors which delayed, for example, the protodevelopment of land and population in Thailand will now be adverse either to the growth of population or of its productivity. Let us take some preliminary soundings on the differential predisposition to economic effort of some of the cultures concerned. First, Swift (1963) discussing Malay peasants:

Every human society is confronted with an economic problem, for wants exceed the means available to meet them, and even to achieve the level of want satisfaction which has become normal or customary requires some definite effort. Therefore every society will give some positive valuation to economic effort, to industry, thrift, enterprise and so on. This will mean that the verbally expressed values of societies will tend to be very similar, and this is, in fact, what a comparison between the Chinese, who are regarded as models of economic virtue, and the Malays, who are not, reveals. It is not a case of one race saying that hard work is a virtue, and the other denying it; or of one race maintaining that wealth is highly desirable and important, while the other says that it is not. Nor, to reverse the matter, is here any disagreement over propositions such as "wealth alone cannot bring happiness," or that sufficiency and an easy heart is a more desirable state than great wealth with all its attendant fears and worries. I have often heard such platitudes from both Chinese and Malays, and I have no doubt that they were sincerely enough meant. Where the difference comes is in the interpretation of these maxims, which are part of the material from which we can hope to study values and attitudes, are given in behavior [Swift 1963:241].

The Malay case shows time and time again enterprising individuals attempting to increase their wealth, and failing, and cooperative ventures among the peasantry also failing. A study of these examples raises the question of whether there are not other important factors apart from individual motivation. One of these is the ability to organize. One important advantage which the Chinese have is the presence of traditional organization forms and groupings which can be used for economic purposes. Clan and surname associations, dialect associations, district associations are all used for business purposes. The tight corporate organization of the family, with its clear and effective allocation of authority, is also of great value in business. Malay society has nothing comparable, and this is at least a part explanation of the small size of Malay business [Swift 1963:243]

Dewey (1964:237, 240) draws a similar contrast between Chinese and Javanese:

Javanese social structure has no clans, castes, age-grades or groupings of the kind which bind large numbers of people together. The kinship system is bilateral and the kindred has no clearly defined limits and no existence as a group. . . . Within the various Chinese groupings . . . ties of kinship, common nationality and co-membership in various types of associations reinforce commercial relationships and are reinforced by them. The result is a series of closely-knit inter-connected Chinese communities extending all over Java and often beyond. Social ties are used as a basis for extending commercial relations beyond the nuclear family and the local group. Thus Chinese social structure tends to encourage larger commercial units, while Javanese social structure gives no basis for extending cooperation beyond a small circle.

These contrasts are suggestive. But the classic texts in this connection are undoubtedly the two full-scale studies by Skinner (1957, 1958) of the Chinese in Thailand. There is room here to draw on only a few of the main points that emerge. Modern Thailand owes much of its prosperity and stability to the kings of the Jakkri dynasty. Their new capital, Bangkok, was founded on the site of the Chinese port and trading center which had developed during the 1770's, and thus had from the beginning a strong Chinese element. There was also, from the first, an extensive Chinese strain in the Jakkri royal family, "one which, through reinforcement, continued strong to the twentieth century" and which the kings themselves acknowledged (Skinner 1957:24, 27).

The first two Jakkri kings developed state trading and royal monopoly to an unprecedented degree. In order to increase production for export and provide crews for their royal ships, they encouraged Chinese immigration. Bangkok remained the chief center of Chinese concentration and the Chinese "probably constituted over half the population in the capital throughout the first half of the nineteenth century" (Skinner 1957:81).

Skinner analyzes the ethnic division of labor within the Thai economy that developed during the nineteenth and twentieth centuries: "The Thai have consistently preferred agriculture, governmental service, and self-employment in general to other occupations, while Chinese immigrants and their descendants have shown an equally strong preference for commercial activities of all kinds, industry, finance, mining, and wage labor in general" (Skinner 1957:91).

Skinner looks for significant contrasts in the village life or rural culture of south China and Thailand to explain this:

Of primary importance perhaps is the fact that the south Chinese lived in a grimly Malthusian setting where thrift and industry were essential for survival. Characteristics that may have arisen from necessity through the centuries came, in time, to be cultural imperatives. The Thai peasant . . . lived in an underpopulated and fertile land where the requirements for subsistence were modest and easily obtained. In premodern times, moreover, he could be (and was) more self-sufficient economically than his Chinese counterpart. Under these circumstances, thrift as such was of limited value and work for its own sake simply senseless. . . . But this is only part of the picture, for the industriousness and thrift of the Chinese peasant served cultural goals absent in Thai rural culture. The Chinese peasant had a definite place in a temporal continuum of kin. Within the extended kin groups—dead, living, and yet to be born—he looked to the past as well as to the future: he was not only grateful to his ancestors for what his immediate family had, but was responsible to them for what he did to further the fortune of his family and lineage. His world view was, thus, historical and kin-centered, and in this context his industriousness and thrift served ends transcending his individual life. His primary goal was not individual salvation, but lineage survival and advancement [Skinner 1957:92].

For reasons of space I must abbreviate this highly pertinent analysis, and also the historical account of the way in which Chinese entrepreneurs strengthened their position in the Thai economy during the one hundred years from 1810 to 1910, the crucial period of economic modernization. "The expansion of the Thai economy must, in the first instance, be attributed to Western example, innovation, and enterprise, but in general Chinese entrepreneurs outdid Westerners in exploiting the new opportunities" (Skinner 1957:109). The Thais themselves (apart from the royal family) took no direct part in the changes.

Moreover, while for the first two-thirds of the nineteenth century, the merchant-entrepreneur was the type par excellence of the Chinese immigrant, the expansion of the Thai economy after 1855 greatly increased the demand for manual workers and eventually led to the recruitment of Chinese peasants for coolie labor and to the mass migration which began in 1880's. Furthermore, "for a period of at least fifty years, during which Siam achieved a modern government, a thriving economy, and entered the world economy and family of nations, almost half of the government's revenues was derived directly or indirectly from the comparatively small Chinese minority. On fiscal grounds alone, the Chinese contribution to Siam's achievement must be given considerable weight" (Skinner 1957:125). And during the three decades following 1919, Chinese provided between 60 and 75 per cent of all skilled and unskilled nonagricultural labor in Thailand (Skinner 1957:217, 302).

In recent decades, increasing Thai nationalism has led to a government program of "economic Thai-ification," but in the event, on Skinner's analysis, this led to an intensified Sino-Thai alliance, "with Chinese supplying the capital and entrepreneurial skill and Thai officials supplying 'protection' for the Chinese, official privileges, and in some cases government contracts" (Skinner 1957:360).[3]

There is no need to labor the part played by cultural, ethnic, and religious minorities in the economies of Southeast Asia. But most countries of this region have now become populous, with

[3] This is analyzed further, in great detail, by Skinner (1958). Writing in 1956, he predicted that the top-level Sino-Thai business alliance would remain a permanent feature of Thailand's socioeconomic structure. According to informed opinion in Bangkok in 1967 the alliance had in fact become even stronger. If the Thai economy is at present booming (Wilson 1967; Klatt 1967), while this is no doubt due in part to American involvement in Southeast Asia, it is also very largely due to Chinese entrepreneurial activity. Credit is also due the Thai government for having made use of the entrepreneurial aptitudes of the Chinese for the promotion of the economy, while encouraging their cultural assimilation into Thai society.

relatively good communications and fairly advanced governmental and educational institutions. Is the lag in economic motivation and aptitude of the cultural majorities of the region about to be broken? Are new indigenous entrepreneurial groups emerging? With some possible exceptions, it would seem in general that they are not.[4] This might, of course, be due to some continuing psychological side effect of their nonunilineal family institutions.[5] But to end this paper on a more strictly sociological note, there

[4] Geertz (1963a:116–123) cites a study done by Schrieke in 1928 (1955:83–166) on the Minangkabau region of west central Sumatra. Dating from 1908–1912, according to Schrieke, shifting cultivators have turned to cash crop production with conspicuous success. "Here we have to do with a revolution in spirit similar to that of the early capitalist period in Europe as indicated by Max Weber and Sombart. The 'economic mentality' has made its entry upon the scene" (Schrieke 1955:98–106; cited in Geertz 1963a:120). According to Geertz, Minangkabau culture is "an unusual fusion of Islamism, matrilineality, and gnomic moralism." It might possibly be significant that the Minangkabaus, being unilineal (in this case matrilineal) depart from the prevailing Southeast Asian cognatic family patterns. Their development recalls that of the indigenous matrilineal cocoa farmers of Ghana.

In Indonesia the indigenous but culturally and religiously distinct *Santri* community of traders also deserves mention. But according to Geertz (1963b:28), although they lack neither capital nor the equivalent of a Protestant ethic, "They lack the capacity to form efficient economic institutions: they are entrepreneurs without enterprises."

[5] It would be legitimate and interesting to bring in at this point the question of differences in child-rearing practices, their effect on achievement orientation, and so forth. Great progress has been made in comparative studies on these lines in recent years. McClelland (1961:381) quotes data collected by Fraser on Indian school children which show a clear-cut connection between the caste occupation of their fathers and their level of achievement motivation. Minturn and Hitchcock (1966:130) remark on the lack of self-reliance training in a Rajput community and connect this with "the apparent lack of self-reliance in both adults and children." Notable also is the work of Phillips (1965) on "modal personality" in a Thai village. Hall and Beardsley (1965:368) include a chapter on "personality psychology" in Japan, and give a large number of references. But while I am sure that psychological studies will eventually throw much new light on the problems discussed in this paper, I hesitate to build upon the slender evidence as yet available.

is another aspect of the contrast between Southeast Asia and some other Asian countries (especially Japan) which might enter into the explanation of a continuing lag, and to which it seems worthwhile to draw attention. In the twentieth century, and in some cases in the nineteenth century, population in Southeast Asia, after centuries of stagnation, began increasing rapidly. By comparison with Japan (and possibly India and China too), however, there has been no equivalent increase in urbanization. Geertz notes that in Java, in spite of rapid population growth after 1830, urbanization was retarded, towns and cities growing much less rapidly than total population. Over the same period in Japan, urbanization was accelerated, particularly after the Restoration of 1868. Towns and cities grew much more rapidly than total population (Geertz 1963a:138).

In Thailand, towns outside Bangkok have remained small, and Bangkok, as we have seen, has always been a largely Chinese city. Since early times, on the other hand, Japan has been notable for the number of its large cities. The great population concentrations of modern Japan were already developed in the seventeenth century. This is in accordance with the two important general tendencies noted, as Colin Clark (1967:286) points out, by Lösch (1954): first, that regions already densely populated and growing attract still more industry and population; second, that such tendencies are only reversed extremely slowly. Thus the present distribution of industrial population in western Europe can be seen to be largely controlled by the pattern of population densities which had already been established in the agricultural society of the eighteenth century.

This would seem to imply that modern economic development will tend to take place where population concentration has been going on for centuries, at first on a mainly rural and agricultural, then increasingly on an urban and industrial, basis. The countries of Southeast Asia have no such centuries-old history of population growth. The absence of indigenous drives toward urbanization and industrialization in these countries, and their reliance on outside stimuli and minority cultural groups to provide these, may be another effect of this long period of underpopulation and a relatively short period of population growth.[6]

[6] Compare Kuznets (1964:129): "China and India (and to a lesser extent Japan) managed to attain effective social cohesiveness, and often political unity, over past centuries—with population masses far larger than those in the rest of the world (including presently advanced Europe and North America). Such notable achievements were made possible by the social and technological innovations enjoyed by these areas for a long time before the rest of the world. After all, the ECAFE [Economic Commission for Asia and the Far East] region is the locus of the old Sinic and Indic civilizations which, in many respects, particularly in the ability to organize large population masses into cohesive and viable social units, were for centuries in the vanguard. And the effects of these past advances and achievements, modified and even distorted, to be sure, by contact with western countries in recent centuries, may still persist.

"Insofar as they do persist, they must be taken into account in any analysis of recent demographic and economic trends in the region. If, in China, the administration of a large population over a wide area required a standardized non-phonetic language, a centralized bureaucracy, and many other appurtenances of a 'hydraulic empire,' this language, and some of the established patterns of relation between the governors and governed are still in use. If, in India, the caste system and a common religion were effective means of social organization and economic operation over the pre-modern centuries, some of the effects of these institutions are still being felt. In short, low income, large population, and high population density are, in large part, consequences of past achievements and the effects of the technological and social innovations by which these past achievements were attained may still persist. Consequently, in considering the demographic and economic growth problems stemming from low income, large population, and high population density, we must take account also of the effects of the past on the social and economic behavior patterns of the societies in the region."

Following up this line of argument in the light of the comparative analysis attempted in this paper, one might argue that India and China had paid too heavy an institutional price for their priority in high population density and that they had correspondingly great difficulty later on in developing their economies. The Southeast Asian societies may not have had enough population density, India and China may have had too much. Japan may be the only country where population increase was a sufficient stimulus without being an excessive burden and which therefore was destined to be the first Asian country to industrialize.

Postscript

Since writing this paper I have read Chie Nakane's *Kinship and Economic Organization in Rural Japan,* in which she argues that Japanese peasant society was not patrilineal, that locality rather than kinship is the basis of corporate organization, and that "Such forms as *ie* and *dozoku, in which a strongly male-centred principle operates, are institutions historically developed in the absence of a unilineal descent system,* and are not a survival from a unilineal descent system" (1967:170, Nakane's italics). On this showing, the special predisposition of Japan toward early urbanization and industrialization might be connected with its being neither unilineal, like India and China, nor bilateral *without* a "strongly male-centred principle," like the Southeast Asian societies. The unique Japanese development might be interpreted in terms of the transplanting of unilineal ideology to a nonunilineal society.

Smith (1962a, 1962b) has pointed out that Japanese kinship terminology, as first recorded in the tenth century A.D., was and remains bilateral. He has also made (Smith 1972) the very interesting suggestion that Japanese bilateral kinship terminology, among other features of the traditional system, facilitated the transition to an urban-industrial way of life.

References Cited

Boserup, Ester
  1965 The Conditions of Agricultural Growth. London: Allen and Unwin.
Buck, J. Lossing
  1937 Land Utilization in China. Chicago: University of Chicago Press.
Chakrabongse, *Prince* Chula
  1960 Lords of Life. London: Alvin Redman.

Clark, Colin
1967 Population Growth and Land Use. London: Macmillan.
Clark, Colin, and M. R. Haswell
1964 The Economics of Subsistence Agriculture. London: Macmillan.
Crook, David, and Isabel Crook
1959 Revolution in a Chinese Village: Ten Mile Inn. London: Routledge & Kegan Paul.
Davis, Kingsley
1951 The Population of India and Pakistan. Princeton: Princeton University Press.
Dewey, Alice
1964 Capital, Credit and Saving in Javanese Marketing. *In* Capital, Saving and Credit in Peasant Societies. Raymond Firth and B. S. Yamey, eds. London: Allen and Unwin. Pp. 230–255. Quotations are reprinted by permission of the publisher.
deYoung, John E.
1955 Village Life in Modern Thailand. Berkeley: University of California Press.
Dooley, Thomas A.
1958 The Edge of Tomorrow. New York: Farrar, Straus and Cudahy.
Duby, G.
1953 La société au XI° et XII° siècles dans la région maconnaise. Paris: Librairie Armand Colin.
Dumont, Louis
1962 The Conception of Kingship in Ancient India. Contributions to Indian Sociology 6:48–77.
Durand, John D.
1960 The Population Statistics of China, A.D. 2–1953. Population Studies 13 (3):209–256.
Fei, Hsiao-Tung
1939 Peasant Life in China. London: Routledge & Kegan Paul.
Fraser, Thomas M.
1960 Rusembilan: A Malay Fishing Village in Southern Thailand. Ithaca, N.Y.: Cornell University Press.

Geddes, William R.
1963 Peasant Life in Communist China. Society for Applied Anthropology, Monograph No. 5

Geertz, Clifford
1963a Agricultural Involution: The Processes of Ecological Change in Indonesia. Berkeley: University of California Press.
1963b Peddlers and Princes: Social Development and Economic Change in Two Indonesian Towns. Chicago: University of Chicago Press.

Hall, John W., and Richard K. Beardsley
1965 Twelve Doors to Japan. New York: McGraw-Hill.

Halpern, Joel M.
1958 Aspects of Village Life and Cultural Change in Laos. New York: Council on Economic and Cultural Affairs.
1964 Capital, Saving and Credit among Lao Peasants. In Capital, Saving and Credit in Peasant Societies. Raymond Firth and B. S. Yamey, eds. London: Allen and Unwin. pp. 82–103.

Ho, Ping-Ti
1959 Studies on the Population of China, 1368–1953. Cambridge: Harvard University Press.

Klatt, Werner
1967 *Khaaw* Spells Prosperity. The Times (London), August 8.

Koentjaraningrat, R. M.
1960 The Javanese of South Central Java. In Social Structure in Southeast Asia. George Peter Murdock, ed. Chicago: Quadrangle Books. pp. 88–115. Originally published by the Wenner-Gren Foundation for Anthropological Research, Inc. Quotations are reprinted by permission of the original publisher and the author.

Kosambi, Damodar D.
1956 An Introduction to the Study of Indian History. Bombay: Popular Book Depot.

Kuznets, Simon
1964 Growth and Structure of National Product, Countries in the ECAFE Region, 1950–1961. In Asian Population Conference 1963, New Delhi. Report of the Asian Population Conference and Selected Papers, United Nations, New York: pp. 128–142. Quotations are reprinted by permission of Unesco.

Le Roy Ladurie, Emmanuel
1966 Les paysans de Languedoc. Paris: S.E.V.P.E.N.
Lorimer, Frank
1954 Culture and Human Fertility. Paris: Unesco. Quotations are reprinted by permission of Unesco. © Unesco 1958.
Lösch, August
1954 The Economics of Location. New Haven: Yale University Press.
Madge, Charles
1954 Village Communities in Northeast Thailand: Report on a Preliminary Survey for the Thailand-UNESCO Fundamental Education Centre (TUFEC). Ubon: TUFEC. Mimeographed.
McClelland, David C.
1961 The Achieving Society. New York: Van Nostrand.
Minturn, Leigh, and John T. Hitchcock
1966 The Rajputs of Khalapur, India. New York: John Wiley.
Moreland, William H.
1920 India at the Death of Akbar. London: Macmillan.
1929 The Agrarian System of Moslem India. Cambridge: Heffer.
1944 A Short History of India. London: Longmans, Green.
Murdock, George Peter
1960 Cognatic Forms of Social Organization. In Social Structure in Southeast Asia. George Peter Murdock, ed. Chicago: Quadrangle Books. Pp. 1–14.
Nakane, Chie
1967 Kinship and Economic Organization in Rural Japan. London: Athlone.
Nash, Manning
1965 The Golden Road to Modernity: Village Life in Contemporary Burma. New York: John Wiley.
Nath, Pran
1929 A Study in the Economic Conditions of Ancient India. London: Royal Asiatic Society.
O'Malley, Lewis S. S.
1941 Modern India and the West. London: Oxford University Press.

Phillips, Herbert P.
1965 Thai Peasant Personality. Berkeley: University of California Press.
Riggs, Fred W.
1966 Thailand: The Modernization of a Bureaucratic Polity. Honolulu: East-West Center Press.
Ruey, Yih-Fu
1960 The Magpie Miao of Southern Szechuan. *In* Social Structure in Southeast Asia. George Peter Murdock, ed. Chicago: Quadrangle Books. Pp. 143–155.
Sansom, *Sir* George B.
1946 Japan: A Short Cultural History. London: Cresset. Rev. ed.
Schrieke, Bertram J. O.
1955 Indonesian Sociological Studies: Part I. The Hague: W. van Hoeve.
1957 Indonesian Sociological Studies: Part II. The Hague: W. van Hoeve.
Skinner, G. William
1957 Chinese Society in Thailand: An Analytical History. Ithaca, N.Y.: Cornell University Press.
1958 Leadership and Power in the Chinese Community in Thailand. Ithaca, N.Y.: Cornell University Press.
Smith, Robert J.
1962a Stability in Japanese Kinship Terminology: The Historical Evidence. *In* Japanese Culture: Its Development and Characteristics. Robert J. Smith and Richard K. Beardsley, eds. Chicago: Aldine. Pp. 25–32.
1962b Japanese Kinship Terminology: The History of a Nomenclature. Ethnology 1 (3) : 349–359.
1972 Small Families, Small Households, and Residential Instability: Town and City in "Pre-Modern" Japan. *In* Household and Family in Past Time. Peter Laslett, ed. Cambridge: Cambridge University Press. Pp. 429–472.
Swift, Michael G.
1963 Malay Peasants. *In* The Role of Savings and Wealth in Southern Asia and the West. Richard D. Lambert and Bert F. Hoselitz, eds. Paris: Unesco. Pp. 219–244. Quotations are reprinted by permission of Unesco. © Unesco 1963.

Taeuber, Irene
  1958 The Population of Japan. Princeton: Princeton University
  Press.
Wilson, Dick
  1967 Land of Booming Industry. The Times (London), August 8.
Yang, C. K.
  1959 A Chinese Village in Early Communist Transition. Cambridge: Harvard University Press.

7. Applied Anthropology in the Mountain Province, Philippines[1]

FRED EGGAN

Applied anthropology, as a self-conscious profession with a journal and a code of ethics, is a recent phenomenon, dating in the United States from just before World War II. Part of its development took place in Africa where British administrators faced with difficult problems called in anthropologists to work cooperatively with them.[2] In such situations the anthropologist had no hand in formulating policy with regard to African tribes. His task was to assist the administrator by securing basic data needed for the adequate development of policy, helping to carry it out, investigating the "trouble" spots that developed, and making recommendations for handling them. In the United States the Bureau of American Ethnology was established as early as 1879, but anthropologists were not utilized by the Bureau of Indian Affairs until the 1930's, and then not very effectively, though one of them, John Provinse, remained to become an Assistant Commissioner in the postwar period.

In the Philippines anthropological viewpoints and knowledge were applied to the solution of administrative problems long before applied anthropology was recognized as a profession. In fact the first applied anthropologists, in the sense of persons with

[1] This paper, in briefer form, was presented at the Eighth Pacific Science Congress held in Manila in 1953.

[2] See, for example, Brown and Hutt (1935) for a pioneer account of cooperation between an anthropologist (Brown) and an administrator (Hutt).

anthropological training who were faced with practical problems, may well have been those active in the Philippines during the first decade of this century. I have particular reference to David P. Barrows, who with Merton L. Miller and Albert E. Jenks organized the Bureau of Non-Christian Tribes and later the Ethnological Survey, and laid the foundations for the administration of the Mountain Province and the Moslem areas. Barrows and Miller had taken their doctorates in anthropology in 1897 at the then new University of Chicago under the direction of Frederick Starr, Barrows' thesis being on the ethnobotany of the Cahuilla, and Miller's on a study of Taos Pueblo. Jenks took his degree two years later at the University of Wisconsin with an economic study of the wild-rice gatherers of the upper Great Lakes.[3]

They had a remarkable sponsor in Dean C. Worcester, a zoologist from the University of Michigan who had done extensive work in the Philippines in the late Spanish period and who served as Secretary of the Interior in the Islands from 1901 to 1913. Worcester took an active interest in the peoples and cultures of the Mountain Province and assembled an outstanding group of administrators from among army officers, teachers, and the constabulary. The rapid development of the Mountain Province which took place before World War I was in large measure due to their skill in utilizing local culture patterns and custom law in the solution of the problems that faced them.

The instructions prepared for the Second Philippine Commission by Elihu Root and presented to them by President William A. McKinley in April 1900 noted that "the commission should bear in mind that the government which they were establishing is designed not for our satisfaction, or for the expression of our theoretical views, but for the happiness, peace and prosperity of the people of the Philippine Islands, and the measures adopted should be made to conform to their customs, their habits, and even their prejudices, to the fullest extent consistent with the accomplishment of the indispensable requisites of just and effective

[3] See Barrows (1900), Miller (1898), and Jenks (1900).

government" (Worcester 1930:271). This enlightened point of view found its most successful expression in the organization and administration of the Mountain Province.

In the Philippines at the beginning of this century the problems with regard to the non-Christian peoples were particularly acute, and at the same time the essential information regarding them was scanty and unreliable. The Mountain Province then had a population of around 200,000 in an area of some 5,000 square miles, but the Spanish administrattion had pacified only a few areas and the religious orders had converted only some of the marginal groups. Even these accomplishments were swept away in the revolutionary activities of 1898–1900, and the native peoples had reverted to their previous condition. The collection of basic ethnological information had to proceed at the same time that order was being re-established and new governmental structures evolved.

This task initially fell to Barrows, who was appointed chief of the newly founded Bureau of Non-Christian Tribes which was organized under the Department of the Interior in October 1901. Barrows had taught briefly at a teacher's college in San Diego after taking his degree, and in 1900 had received an offer from the U.S. government to engage in educational work in the Philippines. On his arrival he found himself superintendent of schools for Manila, a task which helped prepare him for the larger job of director of education which he assumed three years later. In the meantime he had come to Worcester's attention, with the resulting appointment as chief of the Bureau of Non-Christian Tribes.

In his first annual report, dated September 1, 1902, Barrows reviewed what was then known of Philippine ethnology and summarized the work of the Bureau. With regard to the peoples of the Philippines he concluded that "the variety of problems they present is equally great for the ethnologist and the statesman, and nowhere, it may be asserted, must the constructive work of administration be so dependent for information and guidance upon the researches of the expert student. . . . In the establishment of order in these islands the government is attempting to rear a new standard of relationship between the white man and the Malay. The success of this effort, so full of possibilities for the future of life and intercourse in the Far East, will depend in a large measure on our correct understanding and scientific grasp of the peoples whose problems we are facing" (1902:681).

One of Barrows' first tasks was to visit the United States to examine at first hand the Indian reservations and schools and to engage additional personnel. On the recommendation of W. J. McGee, he hired Jenks as assistant chief of the Bureau, but his survey convinced him that the reservation system was unsuitable for the Philippines—except temporarily for some of the Negrito groups. In the case of the Mountain Province tribes he recommended that "governmental efforts should tend to encourage admixture rather than to maintain isolation" (Barrows 1902:684). He was also critical of the boarding schools, whose curriculum bore no relation to the life the Indian must of necessity lead, and he thought that the reservation schools were a better model for the Philippines. After the teaching of English, the major objective should be a practical industrial school, planned to meet the needs of each tribe.

But the most important work of the Bureau, as Barrows saw it, was in the field. In his unpublished memoirs (Barrows n.d.) he describes at length his reconnaissance of the various groups of the Mountain Province and his more detailed study of the Benguet Igorots. For the eight or nine ethnic and linguistic units which occupied distinct regions in the mountains, Barrows (n.d.: 82) adopted the term "culture areas," borrowed as he remembers from the German term *Kultur gebiet*. One of the first published descriptions of a culture area is Jenks's (1905) chapter on "The Bontoc Culture Area," with an accompanying sketch map, in his pioneer study, one of the earliest technical uses of this later widespread concept.

During this early period Barrows came to know and respect the mountain peoples and to develop some definite ideas about how they should be governed. He aided in the establishment of the subprovinces of the Mountain Province, but Worcester for some reason never appointed him as an administrator, possibly because he was still under thirty years of age or perhaps because of Worcester's own intense anthropological interest in these non-Christian tribes.

In 1903, Governor-General William Howard Taft unexpectedly appointed Barrows as General Superintendent of Education for the Philippines with the task of organizing "a system of public instruction in the Philippines that would meet the popular need and realize the objectives of the American government" (Barrows n.d.:99). Before leaving the Bureau of Non-Christian Tribes, Barrows prepared a history of the Philippine population and a revised classification of the non-Christian groups for the 1903 census volumes, and also prepared a short history of the Philippines. The latter volume, which was critical of the work of the religious orders during the Spanish regime, was severely attacked by the Catholic Church, an event that ultimately blocked Barrows' appointment to the Philippine Commission. In addition, the Christian Filipinos resented the special attention given to the non-Christian groups and the resulting image of Filipinos as headhunters in G-strings, and as they gained greater control over their internal affairs they reduced the anthropological program of the Bureau and ultimately changed its name to the Ethnological Survey, putting it under the Bureau of Education.

Barrows accepted a professorship in education at the University of California in 1909, after establishing the educational system of the Philippines on a firm basis, and later shifted to political science before becoming president of the university a decade later. In the meantime Jenks and Miller carried on the Ethnological Survey for a few years, but its research and publication programs were greatly curtailed, and they also soon returned to the United States.

The next two decades saw a different kind of development with respect to anthropology in the Philippines. There were few professional anthropologists who even visited the Islands, but among the large number of teachers brought over to staff the new Philippine school system were a number who became interested in Filipino life and culture and remained to study it. Both H. Otley Beyer and R. F. Barton arrived as prospective teachers in 1905–1906 and both were soon in the Mountain Province. Beyer was sent by Barrows to begin a study of the Ifugao at Banaue, preparatory to establishing an industrial school, but he left to pursue graduate work at Harvard under Roland B. Dixon and on his return in 1910 was appointed ethnologist in the Bureau of Science. He was thus enabled to continue his researches in the Mountain Province and elsewhere until the establishment of the University of the Philippines, which he joined as an instructor in 1914, remaining until his retirement in 1954. His recent death in 1966 ended a career of more than sixty years devoted to Philippine anthropology, and during much of his professional lifetime he was the only anthropologist resident in the Philippines.[4]

R. F. Barton was likewise assigned as a supervising teacher among the Ifugao of Kiangan, where he remained for almost a decade. Here he not only learned the language but developed a remarkable command of the culture as well, and particularly the custom law. His *Ifugao Law* (1919), published while he was at the University of California, was soon recognized as a classic, and his later *The Half-Way Sun* (1930) gave an intimate view of the Ifugao under American rule. Except for a decade in Russia, Barton spent much of his life studying the Ifugao and Kalinga in the Mountain Province.

Neither Barton nor Beyer regarded himself as an applied anthropologist, but they had an important influence on the administration of the Mountain Province and other areas of the Philip-

[4] Of particular interest in this connection are the biographical chapters in Zamora, ed. (1967).

pines. Barton's detailed studies of Ifugao and Kalinga customary law showed the inadequacies of the earlier surveys and led to informal involvement in the decision-making processes of the government at both the local and the provincial level. In 1926, the then governor of the Mountain Province, John C. Early, recommended detailed study of native customary law after the model provided by Barton and other anthropologists, but no funds were forthcoming from the central government. Beyer, in the meantime, had begun his systematic collection of Philippine ethnography, including some ten volumes of manuscripts on Philippine customary law selected by F. D. Holleman, a specialist on Indonesian customary law. As Professor Beyer's students increased in number and entered the government they frequently consulted him on policies and appointments, not only on the Mountain Province but for Mindanao and the Moslem areas as well.

Anthropological research on a larger scale did not get underway until the early 1930's when Felix M. and Marie Keesing were invited by the Philippine Council of the Institute of Pacific Relations to make a study in the Philippines. The Keesings were pioneers in the study of social and cultural change and their *Taming Philippine Headhunters: A Study of Government and Cultural Change in Northern Luzon* (1934), in which they viewed the developments and modifications of life in the Mountain Province in the broader context of the Philippines, was an admirable survey. After a historical introduction they discuss the problems of governmental administration, justice and public order, subsistence and commerce, missions, public health and education, on each of which they have important things to say. This is a volume which every administrator in the Mountain Province should read and utilize, but its unfortunate title (added by the publisher), and the transition to Commonwealth status which occurred in 1935, has led to its almost complete neglect in the Philippines.

The initial phase of Mountain Province administration involved the establishment of peace and order, the cessation of headhunting and attendant feuds, and the construction of roads and trails throughout the region. Here the American administrators were highly successful. They developed an excellent native constabulary, settled disputes in terms of native conceptions, and utilized the native system of "peace pacts" to establish law and order over a wider area. Though some of their methods were questionable by modern standards, these early administrators won the esteem and affection of the mountain peoples, and were able to govern and control them with relatively small constabulary forces. Dean C. Worcester's annual visits were occasions for great congregations of native peoples during which the settlement of disputes, tug-of-war and other contests, and large-scale feasting took place between formerly hostile communities.

The second phase of Mountain Province administration involved acculturation on a larger scale, principally through the agencies of the mission, the school, and the public health services. Here the problems were more difficult and the knowledge required more profound, and the earlier administrators were generally inadequate to the new tasks and were gradually replaced by a new group with different training and objectives. Progress during this period was considerably slower but ultimately more effective.

Both Protestant and Catholic missions were established in the Mountain Province, the Belgian Fathers taking over the Catholic mission from the Spanish orders. Many of the Belgian fathers have contributed to anthropological studies and Keesing quotes one of them as follows: "One great principle of our Mission is never to forbid anything without giving something to take its place. We ask them to change rather than to do away with their feasts and customs" (Keesing and Keesing 1934:230). And Protestant missionaries, such as C. R. Moss (1920a, 1920b) have contributed to our knowledge of Nabaloi and Kankanay ceremonies and customary law.

The school is a major acculturating mechanism and American administrators have given special attention to education in the

Mountain Province, but so far the school has not been as effective as it might be. Instruction was initially in English, with considerable success, but more recently the national language (Pilipino) has come to be more important, and there is considerable experimentation with the use of local dialects in the early grades. The superior attitudes of lowland teachers have also complicated the situation but the increasing number of qualified mountaineers is ameliorating this problem.[5]

The field of health, because of wartime developments, shows promise of advances in the mountain areas of the Philippines. In addition to the reduction in epidemic diseases it is now possible to eradicate malaria from the foothill zones, where it was endemic, and thus open up considerable areas to resettlement. The increase in Mountain Province population is clear evidence for the effectiveness of the Public Health Service, but so far the scientific understanding of the causes of disease and sickness have not penetrated very deeply.

During the period of American control of the Philippines the basic policy was one of partial separation of the Mountain Province from the lowland regions for the purpose of bringing the mountain peoples to the level of development of the Filipinos generally. Fears have been expressed that without special protection the mountain peoples would be submerged in the surrounding Ilocano milieu, particularly as Filipino policy has been one of equal treatment, looking toward ultimate assimilation.

As a result of the war and of postwar experiences, however, the feared submergence has not occurred. During World War II the mountain peoples found that they could stand on their own feet in their own environment. Just as the earlier Spanish and American occupations forged the bonds of Filipino unity, so did

---

[5] Perhaps the most important task in connection with the mountain people is to bring about a change in the attitudes of the lowlanders toward them. The term Igorot was long used by lowlanders as an epithet, but the mountain people are gradually restoring it to its original meaning, "dwellers in the mountains."

the Japanese occupation bring about a new feeling of unity and common problems in the mountain area. The slogan "The Mountain Province for the mountain people" is now a part of general thinking, rather than the property of a few educated individuals. This new attitude is being reflected in the election campaigns for representatives to the legislature, and for local offices. In 1932, Keesing noted that there are "no politics in the Mountain Province"; in 1949 candidates for the legislature were campaigning all over the area. (That one of the winners depended heavily on the large number of "peace pacts" that he held with former enemy towns illustrates the adaptation of older patterns of relationship to modern uses.)

More recently the unity of the Mountain Province has been threatened by a new development. The drive for regional autonomy, first proposed by H. A. Kamora (1932) with reference to the subprovince of Benguet, has now resulted in the division of the Mountain Province into four separate provinces, based largely on ethnolinguistic considerations. While this represents a dramatic "coming of age" so far as political developments are concerned, it re-establishes older ethnic divisions and rivalries which had been partially submerged in the larger unity. It remains to be seen whether these new rivalries will enhance or slow down political and cultural integration.

One of the recommendations offered by the Keesings was that the government might employ an ethnologist to assist in the administration of the Mountain Province, a recommendation which echoed earlier ones by Barrows and others. Philippine politicians, in their drive for independence, cut off funds for the study of non-Christian peoples on the grounds that such studies were a hindrance to the sought-for goal. But now that independence is in hand it seems foolish to continue that policy. The Philippine government utilizes experts in other fields and now that it is responsible for its own minority groups it needs all the help it can find.

In the postwar period the pagan and Moslem populations of

Mindanao and Sulu have felt the brunt of population expansion and resettlement from the Luzon and Bisayan regions, and the focus of interest in cultural minorities has shifted to the south. The Report on Problems of Philippine Cultural Minorities, prepared by the Philippine Senate Committee on National Minorities in 1963, has given new life to the Commission on National Integration which was created in 1959 to aid the advancement of cultural minorities and "to render real, complete and permanent the integration of all said cultural minorities into the body politic" (Philippines, Laws and Resolutions 1958: 45). This is a return in part to the objectives of the Bureau of Non-Christian Tribes. The Commission has been of considerable assistance in terms of providing scholarships, better health facilities, and protection of lands, but has been given only ten years; and as Father Rahmann (1967:453) points out, "Four hundred years have not seen any significant progress towards the goal of integration and there is no likelihood that ten years can see much more."[6]

The last decade has seen the development of a small group of trained Filipino social scientists, however, and these may be destined to play an important role in the applications of scientific knowledge to social problems. Such anthropologists as Mario D. Zamora, F. Landa Jocano, E. Arsenio Manuel, Juan Francisco, Marcelino Maceda, Moises Bello, Alfredo Evangelista, David Baradas, and Timoteo Oracion, along with their colleagues in other social-science disciplines, are now available, and, indeed, are already being put to use by the government. Filipino anthropologists have the great advantage of the basic knowledge of language and culture which comes of growing up in a particular society, and once they have developed the detached perspective which comes from comparative study they can become invaluable to their country as well as to their discipline.

[6] This article deals generally with applied anthropology, and in some detail with cultural minorities and with assistance and integrative programs in the Philippines, as well as with the role of applied anthropology in the solution of community welfare problems.

In the Philippines, applied anthropology has come full circle, beginning with the early anthropologists who were perhaps the first "applied" anthropologists in the sense of professionally trained scholars applying their anthropological knowledge to administrative problems, through a period in which anthropological rescarch was discouraged, to the present period where Filipino scholars are in a position to apply their special knowledge in more sophisticated ways. Filipino anthropologists will be particularly helpful in evaluating the problems involved in reorienting social institutions and basic cultural beliefs as industrialization proceeds and population continues to expand. With regard to the cultural minorities they might also prevent the application of policies which may have costly effects. As Father Rahmann (1967:459) notes:

The assistance of anthropologists is not enough in itself to insure the success of any program of assistance for the improvement of the welfare of the cultural minorities, but it can prevent to a considerable degree disastrous consequences by averting the formulations of measures and reforms which clash with the attitudes deeply rooted in these cultures . . . it is the responsibility of the anthropologist who is working on community welfare problems to bring about change in a less painful way by providing basic facts, concepts and perspectives which shed light on the perennial problems of minority groups in order that proper measures may be formulated for the solutions to these problems.[7]

Here is the challenge to the Filipino anthropologists and social scientists—and to those of other countries of Southeast Asia as well.

[7] Father Rahmann's article became available only after I had written much of my paper. Hence I have not utilized it as extensively as it deserves. The same is true for several additional articles in Zamora, ed. (1967), particularly those by Milton Barnett, Moises Bello, Isao Fujimoto, and Timoteo S. Oracion.

References Cited

Barrows, David P.
1900 Ethnobotany of the Cahuilla. Chicago: University of Chicago Press.
1902 Report of the Bureau of Non-Christian Tribes of the Philippine Islands for the Year Ended August 31, 1902. Washington, D.C.: Report of the Philippine Commission, Bureau of Insular Affairs, War Department. Appendix Q: 679–688.
n.d. Memoirs of David Prescott Barrows, 1873–1954. 247 pp. Mimeographed.
Barton, R. F.
1919 Ifugao Law. Berkeley: University of California Publications in American Archaeology and Ethnology, Vol. 15, No. 1.
1930 The Half-Way Sun. New York: Brewer and Warren.
Brown, C. G., and A. M. Hutt
1935 Anthropology in Action. London: Oxford University Press.
Jenks, Albert E.
1900 The Wild Rice Gatherers of the Upper Great Lakes: A Study in American Primitive Economics. Washington, D.C.: Nineteenth Annual Report, Bureau of American Ethnology.
1905 The Bontoc Igorot. Manila: Ethnological Survey Publications, Vol. 1.
Kamora, H. A.
1932 Why the Sub-Province of Benguet Should be Made a Separate Specially Organized Province. Manila.
Keesing, Felix M., and Marie Keesing
1934 Taming Philippine Headhunters: A Study of Government and of Cultural Change in Northern Luzon. London: Allen and Unwin.
Miller, Merton L.
1898 Taos Pueblo. Chicago: University of Chicago Press.
Moss, C. R.
1920a Nabaloi Law and Ritual. Berkeley: University of California Publications in American Archaeology and Ethnology, Vol. 15, No. 3.

1920b Kankanay Ceremonies. Berkeley: University of California Publications in American Archaeology and Ethnology, Vol. 15, No. 4.

Philippines. Laws and Resolutions 1958.
1958 Republic Act No. 1888. Manila.

Rahmann, Rudolf, *S.V.D.*
1967 Our Responsibilities toward the Cultural Minorities. *In* Studies in Philippine Anthropology. Mario D. Zamora, ed. Quezon City: Alemar-Phoenix. Pp. 443–462.

Worcester, D. C.
1930 The Philippines, Past and Present. New York: Macmillan. New ed.

Zamora, Mario D., ed.
1967 Studies in Philippine Anthropology (In Honor of H. Otley Beyer). Quezon City: Alemar-Phoenix.

8. Social Change in Commune Baw, Thailand, 1958–1967

LAURENCE C. JUDD

How do Thai villages change over time? In 1958, the author made a study in depth of Commune Baw, Mu'ang District, Nan Province, Thailand, describing fifteen aspects of community life and having three focuses: the nature of the agricultural system, the effect of the religious orientation on the rest of the culture, and the nature of the social change taking place (Judd 1961). The author, while working in Thailand during 1961–1965 and 1966–1970, revisited the area frequently and made this restudy in 1967. This essay compares the changes predicted on the basis of the 1958 study with those that had actually taken place in this particular commune by 1967.

The Natural and Social Environment

Commune Baw, a hilly area of approximately 100 square kilometers, is located twenty kilometers north of Nan Town, hereafter referred to as "town." In the commune are ten hamlets grouped by the government in four "legal hamlets." The population of the ten hamlets varies from 8 to 120 households, with an average household membership of 4.5 people. Four of the hamlets have Buddhist temples, one a Christian church, and the other five neither. The first settlement in the commune dates from about 1850, and all but one hamlet have existed since 1938 or earlier. The tribal background of the hamlets is Lu (3), Khamu (2), northern Thai (4), and Lao (1), but all now consider themselves northern Thai.

In this whole area in 1958 there was not a single *rai* (.4 acre) of paddy land. Because the agricultural orientation of all ten hamlets was subsistence swidden agriculture, we might refer to these villagers as "hill Thai." Hill Thai are not nearly so numerous as lowland (paddy-field) Thai, but villagers engaged in partial or integral swiddening in Thailand do number probably as many as a million people, and most of these consider themselves Thai.

Swidden agriculture is defined as "discontinuous cropping of particular fields which are slash cleared and burned for one or more year's crops, and then allowed to lie fallow and return to natural vegetation for at least several years before being used again" (Conklin 1957:1). The Thai term for this practice is *tham rai*. As practiced in Commune Baw (Judd 1964:34), the fields are rotated on a cycle of six or more years. The homesite is permanent. This is possible because of the low population density of 12.9 per square kilometer, and only about 30 per cent of the potential of agriculturally usable land is cultivated during the six-year cycle.

The Value Systems

Four value systems compete for the allegiance of the Commune Baw villagers: swidden, Buddhist, secular, and Christian. Some understanding of the manifestation of each of these is necessary, and the swidden values must be sketched in greatest detail.

Each aspect of swidden culture is governed by norms of varying intensities, which in turn reflect one or more fundamental values. Regarding land, hamlet ownership takes precedence over private ownership, with little concern for legal ownership and title, even of the homesite. As to materials for house construction, bamboo and grass are sufficient. The swiddener values the use of local materials for all technology, but does not resist the introduction of practical tools and artifacts that facilitate or expedite traditional practices, such as the use of cigarette lighters for lighting fires and kerosene for cotton-wick lamps. Most forms of transport are considered unnecessary. Of foods eaten, rice is the only item given absolute value, although animal foods and liquor have important instrumental value for the proper performance of ceremonies and the celebration of holidays. Condiments such as chili pepper, garlic, and salt are also highly valued.

As a way of earning a living, slash-and-burn agriculture, supplemented by forest gathering, hunting, and fishing, is preferred. This is obviously the dominant value of swidden culture. Persistence in work is valued, but not drudgery. Only during holidays is full-time loafing practiced, the nonswiddening hours at other times being used for handicraft production. Games and dances have no place in hill Thai swidden culture, but semivocational sports such as fishing and hunting are greatly enjoyed. Music is used principally for courting and carousing. Monetary wealth is alien to the swidden value system which considers rough rice as the prime form of wealth.

Showing at least verbal respect to all older than oneself is essential, and old age is honored, perhaps because so few attain it. Nevertheless, the activities in which the swiddener's life is invested require the strength of vigorous adulthood, and few tears are shed for the dead. Taking one's own life or that of another is rare and thought improper, but little attention is given to devising improved methods of sanitation or to restricting activities that might cause death. Parents love their children, but the presence of children alone is not sufficient cause to prevent separation of husband and wife. Kin beyond the family of orientation are not usually valued above other hamlet members. Mutual respect between husband and wife is common, but faithfulness to a dead spouse is not valued. There is no common pattern of preferential marriage. Male and female are equally valued and share most roles.

Social cohesiveness and helpfulness are considered obligatory, both in the swidden fields (through a work group) and in the hamlet. No villager should refuse a reasonable request from another, nor are many hesitant to ask for aid when needed—whether for material or ceremonial requirements. Everyone living in a hamlet is expected to take part in its joint activities, both those related to the hamlet's livelihood and to the world of the spirits.

Bodily cleanliness is the only important value in the area of health; to this is related the custom of keeping the floor of one's home spotless, though the walls and ceiling may be filthy. When sick, the proper place to be is in one's own home, near one's guardian spirits. Proper propitiation of one's personal guardian spirit or of the hamlet spirit, and of evil spirits that might have reason or occasion to harm one, is another fundamental value.

Formal education, or even literacy and writing ability, have no place in the swidden value system, which emphasizes only the ability to function skillfully in regard to plant and animal resources. All manifestations or facilitating aspects of formal schooling such as textbooks, teaching equipment, curricula, teaching methods, and the training of the teacher are likewise outside the swidden value system. The world beyond Commune Baw has no significance or value to the swiddener, but everything that takes place within his hamlet does. To learn about other people or cultures is not a goal, but to keep informed about one's own environment is important.

Loyalty to one's hamlet neighbors is very important, but no larger social unit is highly valued. Within the hamlet, all individuals are considered to be on a par with others of their age range. Government is increasingly negatively valued in proportion to its distance from the hamlet.

Of all these values prominent in the various aspects of hamlet life, five can be called the dominant values of integral swidden society: swidden-type agriculture, hamlet cohesiveness and ownership of land, rice as the important food and as the symbol and proper measure of wealth, satisfaction with a technology based on locally available resources, and proper spirit propitiation. One would expect the swidden value system to be traditional and conservative, as it is apt to be weakened by any changes that occur.

What is the normative attitude toward change of each of the other value systems operative in Commune Baw? Although Christianity as practiced in northern Thailand has been identified with a rather literal Biblical theology, it has never been conservative in its attitude toward social change. Having stressed the value of secular education and the use of modern medicine, and having been closely involved with western missionaries, it has been a source of many new ideas. In seeking the conversion of the populace, it naturally urged change. It is less environmentally bound than animism and less nationalistic than Thai Buddhism. Furthermore, the united Church of Christ in Thailand, through its various programs, especially since 1948, has attempted to enrich the meaning of being a Christian.

Thai Buddhism, likewise, has been undergoing a period of structural diversification and renewed scholarship that is bound to modify its value system. Traditional Buddhism in northern Nan Province, however, is yet to be affected. The only changes stressed have been efforts to encourage hamlets to enlarge or improve their local temple buildings and to recruit enough young men as novices and priests to reopen closed temples. As the established religion of the kingdom, however, Buddhism is expected to draw its adherents in the direction of the official or government-sponsored cultural system.

Secular urban-centered society is composed of two main parts, the official or government-sponsored cultural pattern and the organized but diffuse subpatterns of urban society. For both, sociocultural change is a major value. The government seeks to direct major aspects of village and urban life into forms which it has defined as ideal, modern, or "Thai." Many nongovernmental urban people have either a product or a service which they wish to sell to the villager or some crop or product that they want him

to produce and sell to them, both practices encouraging or requiring change.

In 1958 each hamlet[1] had its own mixture of value systems
(Judd 1961:335), which may be briefly described by hamlet as
follows:

Only HPH1 attempted to use the single swidden value system
and appeared to be succeeding, partly by denying hospitality to
strangers, something contrary to the other three value systems.

PK4 used the Buddhist system of values, not as a replacement
of swidden values but as an alternative or a supplementary foundation for norms. As elsewhere in the commune, Buddhist values
are segmented so that Buddhist moral values were considered
applicable primarily to those entering the Buddhist Order, but
Buddhist ceremonial values were considered applicable to all villagers. The greatest change from swidden values in PK4 comes
from the impact of the secular urban-centered value system. For
many in PK4, money had become at least a desirable instrumental value, housing had become a status symbol, and occupations
other than swiddening were favored by some.

In HY2, Buddhist values for the laity were likewise only ceremonial, but animistic practices were less frequent than in most
other hamlets; religiously, HY2 might be called predominantly
secular. Here urban values were the strongest in the commune,
due to settlement from town and frequent contact with it and
with travelers. This was seen in the slightly higher value given
to secondary education, the wider vocational interests character-

---

[1] In the original study (Judd 1961), a code for the ten hamlets in
Commune Baw was devised for ease of reading. In every case, the hamlet
is designated by the initial letters of its name plus a number, which refers
to the "Legal Hamlet" to which it has been administratively assigned.
Thus, WM1 refers throughout to Hamlet Wang Maw, one of the units of
Legal Hamlet 1. The complete list is as follows:

Wang Maw	WM1	Huai Yune	HY2	Sala	S3
Haad Pla Haeng	HPH1	Pak Ngao	PN2	Phu Wieng	PW3
Haad Pha Sing	HPS1	Rai Prai Wan	RPW2	Pha Khwang	PK4
Pang Tan	PT1				

istic of a partial swiddening system, greater participation in a money economy, a greater interest in private land ownership, and a minimum of hamlet cohesiveness.

PW3 and S3 retained all the dominant swidden society values but also honored ceremonial Buddhism to a degree more than HY2 but less than PK4. Efficient swidden techniques provided cash income from salable surpluses, but most expenditures were for ceremonial items and occasions. Children were encouraged to attend the one-teacher primary school but none were sent for further education. There was general contentment with traditional technology, hamlet social patterns, and the underlying swidden value system.

RPW2 combined a traditional swidden value system with a willing acceptance of urban values which as yet could not be supported economically. Here a limited interest in Christianity had been checked by a fear of social displeasure if they did not nominally support the HY2 temple; yet they held neither moral nor ceremonial Buddhism as a dominant value. In this hamlet, integral swiddening was giving way to partial swiddening supplemented by the planting of orange orchards and the sale of forest-gathered products.

PN2 represented an earlier denial of urban values in favor of the swidden value system while retaining a lukewarm commitment to Buddhism as a ceremonial religious system. This earlier denial of urban life was being challenged by the re-entry of urban values.

HPS1 retained most integral swidden-culture values. In accepting Christianity, its residents renounced all dependence upon *phi* (spirits), the use of liquor, and the concept of independence from society that is outside their own hamlet. They accorded significant value to secular education as a religious duty, considered prayer and Western-style medicine as more efficacious than spirit propitiation, and accepted responsibility for sharing in province-wide church activities.

PT1 included both Christians and animists. Being out of frequent contact with Buddhist hamlets, it was under no pressure to observe any Buddhist values. The Christians of PT1 were related to or working for the Christian absentee orchard owners from Phrae and had many challenges of urban values to consider.

WM1 was buffeted by both ceremonial Buddhism via PK4 and Christianity via HPS1, and received a limited amount of secular urban influence through travelers, but essentially held to swidden-culture values. Ceremonial Buddhism was only a three-day-a-year phenomenon in WM1. Having sons join the priesthood was not a goal. A few families had become Christian.

In 1959 new laws against swiddening were passed as a result of increased government cognizance of the significance of the hill tribes in terms of national security with the expansion of the Vietnamese War, and of growing concern about the effects of hillside land use on lowland agriculture and on timber resources.

Theoretical Considerations

Sharp (1953:2) has written:

It is postulated that in any society no one important element of change can be clearly understood except in relation to other elements. Biological factors—birth rates, disease, malnutrition—must be investigated in relation to the physical environment and the total culture of the society in which they occur. Functional aspects of the society—family life, economy, education, religion—must be studied in relation to each other rather than simply as isolated segments of group life.

The ideal [study of each community] is a description through time in which such different elements are treated in enough detail to permit them to be studied together as a total culture or way of life. An "adequate" description will then be concerned with the community's natural environment, human biology, technology, social structure . . . and systems of belief, ideas, and sentiments. Analysis and interpretation will then deal with those elements as part of a system—existing in the individual and between individuals—and as factors which must be taken into account when considering the possibilities of changing behavior within the culture as a whole.

Commune Baw contained not one system of belief, ideas, and sentiments, but the above described mixtures of four systems. The degree of physical isolation of each of the hamlets from town culture and from each other played a significant part in the differential distribution of value systems. Since ten hamlets exist in the commune, there are multiple bases from which change must be judged.

Types of change on which attention was focused in the 1958 study were three: technological, social, and ideological. These can be restated as changes in how the villager uses the natural resources and the cultural artifacts at his disposal, how he structures the roles performed in the society, and how he interprets or defines the meaning of his actions and of the world about him. These changes could come about by interaction between the value systems in the commune itself or as responses to outside influences on the natural and social environment of the commune. Modifying a theory proposed by Willmott (1960:303), significant motivations for change were listed (Judd 1961:350) in order of importance as imposed change, necessitated change, emergent change, and purposive change, each with specific predictions of what effect they might have on commune life.

Changes Predicted

In brief, the predictions of 1958 were:

Imposed Change: The principal source of imposed change was taken to be the national government. The following imposed changes were predicted: gradual prohibition of swiddening, increased emphasis on personal land ownership, community development under commune council sponsorship, increased observance of government-supported ceremonies, and increased schooling. It was further predicted that the Buddhist and Christian church organizations would endeavor to organize programs of lay and clerical study and witness. The possibility of communist-inspired change was noted.

Necessitated Change: Necessitated change can arise as repercussions of imposed change or can come about independently through acts of nature or other "permanent" changes in the physical or sociocultural environment. It was predicted that alternatives to and modifications of swiddening would develop partly from government pressure but more from demographic pressure and that the nature of the residential pattern would begin to change, fundamentally weakening hamlet solidarity, shared work, religious participation, and socialization patterns. Natural plant and animal life was expected to become scarcer, making hunting and fishing more difficult even to the point of impoverishment of the villagers' diet.

Emergent Change: By definition, emergent change is based on dissatisfaction with some part of the existing cultural order. It is most apt to begin with an individual, but general dissatisfaction with certain conditions or customs does spread through a hamlet and may lead to group-supported change rather than individual behavior which is considered deviant. Among the emergent changes predicted were the construction of more "permanent" housing, the greater use of manufactured goods, expansion of a cash economy, a new frame of mind challenging at least some norms of swidden culture, increased outside nongovernment aids, fundamental changes arising out of increased schooling, and greater use of milled rice.

Purposive Change: Purposive change normally involves the addition of practices, structures, artifacts, or ideas that are thought to strengthen or improve the expression of some cultural goal, and these often lead to further changes which threaten the dominant cultural system. The presence of multiple value systems in the commune and of ideological variations in the swidden practices of the various hamlets testify to some purposive change everywhere, but it was predicted that the hamlets holding less strongly to the swidden value system would be more apt to encourage purposive change. Increased schooling, wider literacy, increased availability of literature in the commune, plus the efforts of provincial religious organizations, were expected to lead to greater understanding of Buddhism or Christianity by some of their adherents. Increased orange-grove cultivation and growing of cash crops was predicted.

Communication Resources Changes: It was doubted that telephone or telegraph service would become available in the commune even though improvements of these services were linking Nan Province more closely to the rest of the nation and thus steepening the cultural gradient between town and commune. Newspapers and magazines were expected to continue to be available in coffee shops if not in the homes of villagers. The purchase of more radios was expected to bring more news into each hamlet. Improvement of the roadway to make it passable almost all year was expected to have a considerable effect, with more government officials, merchants, and travelers visiting the commune and more villagers traveling out, thus making isolation primarily a psychological rather than a physical factor.

In summary, it was predicted that "what takes place in Commune Baw during the next decade will reflect most of all the present practices in each aspect of hamlet life; secondly, responses to those sections of prohibitive and stimulative laws and policies that the district government attempts to administer; thirdly, actions arising from a synthesis of the goals of the interacting value systems already represented in the different hamlets; and lastly, those emergent and purposive changes that the villagers, individually and as groups, are able to specify and carry through" (Judd 1961:366).

Actual Changes and Their Effects

Some changes are simple in both motivation and effect, but more often change involves multiple motivations as well as unintentional effects, together affecting many elements of the culture. Little attempt is made in this brief essay to classify clearly the predominant motivation or to separate wholly the types of change. However, this report moves generally from physical to technological to social to ideological changes.

Improvement of the Roadway

The most obvious and most far-reaching change during the past ten years has been the improvement of the roadway from Nan Town all the way north to the districts of Pua and Tung Chang (Lae). Within Commune Baw this has meant the building of five concrete bridges, including a major one over the Nan River at the northern boundary of the commune, the straightening and leveling of the roadway so that ordinary passenger cars can easily travel through the commune even during the rainy season, and the realignment of the road so that it passes one kilometer to the west of the Pha Khwang (PK4) hamlet. As the Nan River Bridge was opened for use only in October 1967, the full effects of these alterations in the physical environment are still unknown but many changes are already obvious.

This roadway had been surveyed and listed for construction every year since the early 1950's, but funds were not allocated until 1965 when, owing to the desire of the Thai army to transport forces and supplies to the upper Nan Province border with Laos, funds become available. Further improvement is expected, as this will be a part of an extensive system of military roads linking all the border provinces. Construction to date has given opportunities for day labor at higher than usual rates to many Commune Baw residents, although in the long run the improved roadway will provide fewer maintenance jobs since wooden bridges will no longer have to be rebuilt after each rainy season.

The improved roadway has had considerable effect on the travel and transport habits of villagers. Since the price of a trip to town has been reduced almost 50 per cent, the villagers now almost never walk the twenty odd-kilometers. Traffic has increased to the point that three small buses come as far north as RPW2 (where the path from S3/PW3 meets the road) several times a day, and larger buses which connect Muang and Pua districts make travel possible from any of the roadside hamlets many times a day. This brings many villagers into Nan Town, which has itself seen many changes. There are now three banks, three filling stations, a new large hotel, a bus depot with regularly scheduled buses going south to Phrae and other provinces, a second movie theater, new stores, and an army camp and an airfield under construction.

Lower transport charges have made possible the growing of field corn, though the profit margin is still very low. There is less necessity to sell the orange crop to middlemen, and the contract basis has changed to price per box from a flat figure for the whole crop, set while the oranges were still on the trees. Some housewives from the four southernmost hamlets (S3/RPW2/PN2/HY2) now market vegetables in town early each morning and bring back foodstuffs from the Nan Town fresh market. There are still no markets where fresh vegetables and meat are sold in any of the Commune Baw hamlets, but once a week fresh meat is sold by a villager from PK4 who visits the other roadside hamlets by bicycle.

There is common agreement that wild animal and plant life has become scarcer. This is especially true of fish, which are trapped at the rapids south of Commune Baw and killed by illegal explosives and poison and by a new technique of electrification. Few are for sale anymore at HY2. In spite of much complaining in the commune about the scarcity of fish to eat, there has been no formal complaint made at the district office.

The types of manufactured goods for sale within Commune Baw has not noticeably changed, but there has been an increase in the sale of factory-made cloth, medicines, preserved foodstuffs, and cosmetics.

A few families derive significant income from their orange groves, with one man from PK4 receiving $4,000 (80,000 *baht*) in 1966, but the more common income from the usual small orchard is a few hundred *baht*, and many have no fruit to sell. Because practically no one is fertilizing or spraying, the trees die at an early age. The cultivation techniques used are more characteristic of swidden culture and forest gathering than they are of orchard management. A majority of the villagers claimed orchard sites and many small orchards were planted in the early 1960's, but fewer trees are being planted now than are going out of production. Some villagers will get some income from selling their orchard sites, although there seems to be no special rush to claim potential sites with easy access to the new roadway. The new right-of-way leaves the old road just south of HPH1 and cuts directly north over higher land coming eventually to a suitable point with bluffs on either side where it can cross the Nan River.

The construction of the Nan River Bridge and the relocation of the roadway to bypass PK4 is disrupting the PK4 economy. Apart from retail sales lost, the lucrative business of ferrying travelers and cars across the river has ended. This provided both an income to several families and an agreed percentage for the improvement of the local temple and the school building. The PK4 headman plans to continue to maintain the old roadway and to request bulldozer help to make a new road along the edge of the river up to the new bridge, but it is not clear how much use will be made of these by other than the villagers. The riverside road may hurt the economy again by taking a considerable part of the fertile, annually flooded garden sites out of production.

PK4 continues to produce the majority of cash crops within the commune. Field-corn production in 1966–67 amounted to only about 600 bushels (*tang*); peanuts remain the predominant cash crop. For peanuts the soil is prepared with hoes; for corn the seeds are dibbled in like swidden-field rice, after the ground cover has been slash-cleared and burned. Wood and some crops are still transported by motorized canoes, but river transport has decreased so much since the improvement of the road that the larger power boats have all now left Nan and returned to Uttradit Province.

While there is some dispersal of residences into orange-grove and garden sites, most families continue to maintain a house in the hamlet, where they feel safer. There may well be less need to fear loss of oranges now that most families have at last a few trees. At harvest time, people do stay in the groves or fields to guard the harvest against animal intruders and thieves. Hamlet solidarity has not yet been radically affected by this dispersal of homesteads. Greater use of wood for housing is apparent in PK4 and WM1, with some cement and brick being used in PK4. The more "permanent" construction may not have much effect on kinship and residence patterns. There is no indication that married children value the new houses of parents above their own bamboo house. In WM1 especially, a minimum of thought and skilled labor have gone into house design and construction, rendering the wood houses less attractive and livable than the traditional bamboo style. In the other hamlets there has been little change in housing materials. Nowhere has there been significant change in hamlet size, except that PT1 has become recognized as a "permanent" hamlet with several more families locating there.

Improvement of Schools

The most consistent and direct concern for Commune Baw by government agencies has been manifested by the malaria control unit of the Ministry of Public Health and by the Ministry of Education. Thorough spraying, done twice a year, has been generally appreciated. The Ministry of Education has increased the number of teachers assigned to the four Commune Baw schools from five to seven and has given financial help to three of these schools between 1962 and 1967 for school maintenance and construction. Each school building is now of permanent construction, adequate for the first four grades of primary school. In HY2 the bridge-construction company donated cement for the floor and the teakwood doors; elsewhere the villagers provided all the additional labor and supplies.

Nevertheless, the influence of education on the commune has probably decreased since 1958. Now only two teachers live in the commune, the rest using motorcycles to commute daily from town on the new road. It has been difficult to recruit and keep the added staff. With fewer teachers living in the commune, the chance of their having much influence on adult hamlet life has been reduced. In PK4 parents are less willing to have their children study than previously, and nowhere do the parents provide pencils, notebooks, and textbooks. Results of a comparative test of students in the rural schools of Mu'ang District showed that out of seventy-nine schools tested, Commune Baw schools had the following standings: WM1, 35th; HY2, 52nd; PK4, 59th; and PW3, 70th. Dropouts are still a major problem; WM1 loses about 50 per cent before fourth-grade graduation, and other hamlets probably lose more. The WM1 and HY2 schools, with only about half the potential to draw on, have almost as many students as PK4.

Joint programs for teachers and students have been increased, with the PK4 school joining in interschool activities with schools in Commune Tanchum of Pua District to the north, and the other Commune Baw schools sharing in interschool sports and other activities with schools of Commune PhaSing of Muang District to the south. Even were all Commune Baw schools to supply graduates, it is questionable if there would be enough fourth-grade graduates to make feasible an upper-primary-grade school for the commune. It was predicted that the improved roadway would help unite the commune by making it easier for the hamlets to keep in touch with each other, with the proposed commune upper-primary-grade school to be both a symbol and an instrument of the new unity. The improved road seems to have had the opposite effect.

A serious threat to the schools relates to the new roadway. It has been announced that the road right-of-way is to be sixty meters wide; this may be proper for the class of highway intended eventually, but it will upset the housing patterns in six of the ten hamlets in this commune. Two of the schoolyards, where new school buildings have just been completed, would be reduced to a few feet in width. Orchards and some improved fields would likewise be affected. The government will probably pay some small financial indemnity for the land taken. However, neither the Highway Department nor the Ministry of the Interior has shown any concern over the disruption of life caused by the routing and the width of the road.

Other Relationships with Government

The expectation that an improved road would bring more government officials to Commune Baw has not been borne out. True, more government officials travel on the road, but it is now possible to speed through the commune without even pausing to buy snacks in the hamlets, and to date officials have seemed to give even less attention to Commune Baw hamlets. This increased speed of travel has put several refreshment shops out of business; since trucks and buses no longer stop in HY2, sales have dropped to practically nothing. The Chinese food-shop owner there plans to move as soon as he receives payment for his land from the Highway Department.

None of the changes predicted because of government pressure or encouragement has yet come to pass. Specifically, no effort has been made to prohibit swiddening in Commune Baw; neither pressure nor convenient procedure has been forthcoming to encourage personal land claims; the national extension of required schooling from four to seven years has not been made applicable to Commune Baw (or to much else of rural Thailand); and the commune council has been given neither significant duties nor funds. Although the competence and concern of the district magistrate are important, his area is so large and his duties so many that the primary agent in government relationships with any commune is the commune headman. Thus the personality and ability of the commune headman are of considerable importance. During the past decade the former commune headman has died and the headman of HY2 has been chosen to replace him. The new commune headman greatly enjoys hunting and hiking through the forested areas of the commune, to the extent that he is frequently unavailable. He lets the hamlet headmen carry out their responsibilities without much supervision. No meeting of headmen has been held in the commune for two years, although they do see each other monthly at the district meeting of all headmen. Since the new commune headman lives at HY2, at the southern entryway into the commune, officials are less obliged to enter the rest of the commune. This has been particularly noticeable in PW3, the home of the former commune headman; very few government officers have visited there since the change of headmen.

The former headman was a lifelong resident of the commune and mixed easily with all, often staying overnight in each hamlet; the new headman is town-born and not at ease on lengthy visits. Neither has he concerned himself with accurate statistics (the PK4 head teacher complains that the villagers do not remember when their children were born, and he has a hard time convincing them that the year has come when the children should begin school). While the new headman does not have swidden fields as his predecessor did, nor order the villagers to continue giving free labor to tend such fields, neither has he tried to enforce the laws limiting swiddening. In brief, the new commune headman exercises neither the prohibitive nor the stimulative functions of government; during his tenure, laissez-faire government attitudes will probably prevail.

There are new hamlet headmen in PK4 and PW3. The former PK4 headman was murdered one afternoon on the roadway just outside his hamlet in 1966. Commune gossip is that his own villagers may have hired two outsiders to shoot him because they had wearied of his alleged involvement in blackmailing and shady deals and the charging of illegal fees. Some characterize the new PK4 headman as a dullard chosen to reduce the probability of interference in the affairs of his hamlet residents.

The commune council meets only one day a year when it votes on how to spend the returned land taxes, quadrupled in ten years but still only amounting to twelve dollars a year. This group of representatives from each hamlet has never been challenged to think of itself as a commune government responsible for planning and carrying out locally determined and supported development projects or for discussing common problems. Nan Province is now participating in the Accelerated Rural Development Program of the Thai government and thus receiving personnel, financial, and materiel aid from the United States, but the ARD program to date has had no effect on Commune Baw. Perhaps there is a bit of truth in the joke current around Thailand, that the best way to stimulate government aid for an area is to import a few Communists. Commune Baw has yet to try this.

Two new kinds of aid have been given to Commune Baw in the last few years: a hand pump has been installed on the hamlet well in HY2 by the village health and sanitation unit, and a midwife has been stationed in the same village. The pump has broken twice, and since it is considered government property and an unnecessary frill, no one wants to spend money to repair it. The midwife was stationed in this hamlet when she was appointed in 1964 because she was responsible for serving the commune to the south as well. Most village women have been unwilling to pay for prenatal care. Theoretically the midwife's services are free, but she is allowed to charge for medicines; in the eyes of the villagers, this means that the service is not free. Now with a small child of her own, the midwife does not visit other hamlets unless requested. Most of her assistance in HY2 relates to relief for minor ailments.

There has been a significant increase in the number of those willing to go to the government hospital in Nan Town for treatment, as the visits of the commune public health officer have become quite rare. It is also reported that there is much less recourse to spirit propitiation as a method of healing.

The government has increased the number of radio broadcasts designed to influence villagers. In Commune Baw, the villagers switch off both news and commentary. Although practically everyone now has access to a radio, music is the preferred choice of all, so the radio has not proved significant in molding public opinion. With the closing of the coffee shops due to the improved road, fewer newspapers will be available in the commune. Increased visits to town and speedier regular communication via the road, however, should make most hamlets better informed than previously. The government has located a two-way radio at the home of the commune headman, but with his absences and the convenient regular buses, little use is made of it.

Changes Relating to Religious Orientation

Buddhist lay and clerical organizations, while stronger and more active in town, have yet to have any effect on Commune Baw. Within the commune, Buddhist influence has waned: the HY2 temple has been for three years without any resident priest and thus without novices; there is only one priest in each of the other three temples, and only eight novices in all. All the priests and novices in the priesthood in Commune Baw ten years ago have returned to common life, with the exception of the present PK4 abbot who was then the HY2 abbot. The temple buildings at HY2 and PK4 have been improved, but the HY2 temple is still unfinished. No work has been done on it for three years, except for the new ceiling donated by the bridge-construction company. Temple buildings at PW3 and S3 need extensive repairs. No new ceremonies have been introduced, and the only special annual Buddhist observances held in the commune are at the beginning and end of the Buddhist Lent and at the time of the Songgran Festival. Sermons in northern Thai printed in Chiengmai are now available on stiff paper folded like the old palm-leaf manuscripts, and each of the three temples with a resident priest has several for use by the novices for study and memory work.

In PW3 and S3 there has been an increased observance of animist practices to try to end the recent trend of poor harvests. HY2, PN2, and RPW2 have had very infrequent visits of a priest, and their observance of Buddhist ceremonies has declined almost to the level of WM1. Buddhist ethics are taught in each of the primary schools.

The most significant change relating to Christianity in Commune Baw is that two-fifths of HPH1, including the headman, have been converted. Six of the ten hamlets now include Christians. Listed in order of number of members, these are HPS1, WM1, HPH1, PT1, RPW2, and HY2. Church membership in 1967 by families was 100 per cent in HPS1, less than 50 per cent in WM1, HPH1, and PT1, and about 10 per cent in RPW2 and HY2. In several of the past ten years there have been resident youth workers stationed in HPS1 or visiting there regularly, and the children and youth groups have become fairly strong. With the help of visiting Christian youth from other parts of the province, a work camp was held in early 1967 which succeeded in digging a community well in front of the church.

A project sponsored by the Rural Life Division of the national church and the provincial church Rural Life Committee has had an interesting outcome. In early 1962, the twenty-eight families who were then members of the HPS1 church were offered loans to aid them in switching to permanent field agriculture, with the minimum goal being one acre of paddy land and two acres of orchard. Of these, twenty-three families accepted small loans of rice given out as each stage of work was completed (finding potential field sites, getting local rights to this land, clearing the trees and other plant life, preparing the paddies, planting, and so on). The majority attempted only orchard sites, and sixteen succeeded in beginning small orchards. Twelve families attempted to create paddy fields, of which seven gave up after one year. Three families have become relatively prosperous with approximately three acres each of paddy plus varying amounts of orchard, and two others have an acre or more of paddy. A small stream has been dammed to provide year-round irrigation, making possible at least two crops. The total investment in this loan program was about $1,000, consisting of rice loans to a maximum of only about $40.00 per family, plus buffalo and tool loans that totaled about $300. Individual families here with the will to do so could make the switch to permanent-field agriculture with an average loan of about $100.

The majority of HPS1 families were satisfied with their swidden agricultural system, and in the absence of government pressure, they were not motivated enough to make the change. Most of the sixteen who started small orchards continue to claim them, neither significantly enlarging them nor giving adequate care. A few have received a few hundred *bhat* of income from selling their oranges, others from selling their sites. Three families in PK4 have been stimulated to establish paddy fields on the sites given up by the HPS1 villagers, and other PK4 villagers have told the HPS1 residents that if they do not start making use of other paddy-field sites that have been claimed, next year these sites will be taken over.

It is thus probable that there will be a few more families with paddy fields in the coming decade. However, the limited number of level areas and an even more limited supply of dammable water restrict the expansion of paddy farming to a small percentage of Commune Baw families even if they have the motivation. So far there has been no attempt to introduce terracing, contour plowing, or the use of any mechanical farming equipment into this commune. Those few with paddy fields have acquired new understanding of the relationship of plant cover to year-round water in the streams and so have attempted to influence the locations of swiddening and lumbering.

Analysis and Conclusions

Clearly, change has come to Commune Baw in the past decade; evaluating its significance, judging its permanence, and categorizing its nature are our challenges.

It appears that most change has arisen as unrelated side effects of a mixture of imposed conditions, necessitated responses, and opportunities offered, rather than according to any consciously motivated plan of either the villagers or the government. Even the principal government effort in this commune (improvement of the road) was not done specifically to aid Commune Baw but as part of a larger program considered a military necessity. The villagers' lives do change, even though they seldom plan and work toward that particular change. Government initative, whether it be purposely directed at the commune or purely incidental, triggers much of the change.

Many government laws and policies that relate directly to conditions that exist in the commune have been formulated in Bangkok during the past decade; that they have not been applied is due partly to budgetary limitations and the lower priority given to purely civilian needs, but a more basic reason is the nature of the civil service in Thailand. Implementation of any law depends on the energy and conscious interest of a long chain of civil servants. Inertia or unconcern at any stage of the administrative hierarchy can and does reduce these laws to mere ink on paper. Perhaps this is fortunate on the whole, for strict application of policies and laws that have been based on theoretical considerations far from the locality of application could cause even more trouble than the declaration of a sixty-meter right-of-way for the road through Commune Baw. (At the rate that cement drainage pipe sections, which with other construction material and equipment litter the roadway for several kilometers, are put in place, the marking and clearing of the right-of-way may take several years.)

The government also falters in the coordination of efforts, and it gives insufficient attention to the human factors that affect relations between officials and villagers. For example, much more emphasis is needed on the motivations, stated expectations, and after-hours influence of its staff. Specifically, in Commune Baw, at least the head teacher of the hamlet schools should be required to become a resident of the community; medical personnel should be paid on the basis of services rendered; headmen should be chosen on the basis of respect and ability; supervision of staff should be centered in the area served rather than at the district headquarters; and local councils should be given responsibility and assistance. Some agency of government, with at least some local representatives, should regularly review each political unit as a whole to understand the effects both of what is done and what is left undone by government agencies. Restructuring of administrative boundaries should take place when changes in communication patterns make it advisable. Without such considerations, Commune Baw residents and many other rural people will continue to think of government as "it" or "they" rather than "us," and to feel it capricious if not actually hostile.

Each hamlet of Commune Baw retains its basic character as of 1958 except as noted. Technological changes have mostly been superficial. When planting an orchard or a cash crop, villagers continue to use swidden principles and techniques of cultivation. If and when income from cash crops is more than sufficient to cover expenses for food, travel, and medicines, more fundamental changes in technology in both the production and consumption sectors may take place.

Most social changes to date reflect the personality differences of individuals and changes in their place of residence rather than change in the social structures themselves. The basic hamlet cohesiveness persists, and no wider loyalty has yet developed, except somewhat in Legal Hamlet 1 which is partially integrated due to common church membership. Clearing of the road right-of-way, if carried through, could cause major social disruption.

Ideological changes appear to be taking place in religious orientation in most of the hamlets, but it is still too early to detect the permanence of the trends. Nowhere in the commune are Buddhism and Christianity in direct confrontation. Acceptance of secular urban values has definitely increased in Legal Hamlet 2 and with the improved communications is apt to become a fact throughout the commune. Swidden culture is being challenged at several points, and in some hamlets modification is underway in the interpretation of the major swidden values. For instance, personal ownership of orchard land is now generally recognized, although formal ownership papers are not often sought; rice is still a primary value, but cash income is now likewise desired; spirit-propitiation ceremonies related to crops are still performed but are not so frequently used for medical care; some permanent housing is being constructed; a few villagers have shown readiness to try permanent-field agriculture. Still, in most aspects, the swidden value system continues to furnish the norms of daily life, at least in legal hamlets 1, 3, and 4. Unless government brings specific pressure against it, swidden culture may persist for some time in Commune Baw.

References Cited

Conklin, Harold C.
    1957 Hanuoo Agriculture. Rome: Food and Agriculture Organization, United Nations.
Judd, Laurence C.
    1961 *Chao rai*: Dry Rice Farmers in Northern Thailand. Unpublished doctoral dissertation, Cornell University.
    1964 *Tham rai*: Dry Rice Agriculture in Northern Thailand. Ithaca, N.Y.: Southeast Asia Program Data Paper No. 52, Cornell University.
Sharp, Lauriston, Hazel Hauck, Kamol Janlekha, and Robert B. Textor
    1953 Siamese Rice Village. Bangkok: Cornell Research Center.
Willmott, Donald E.
    1960 The Chinese of Semarang: A Changing Minority Community in Indonesia. Ithaca, N.Y.: Cornell University Press.

9. Culao—A Vietnamese Fishing Cooperative and Its Problems

HOWARD K. KAUFMAN

In 1963, Saigon officials involved with cooperatives believed that a well-administered cooperative had a high probability of succeeding, and were disturbed to discover that the fishing cooperative in Culao District (Khanh Hoa Province) was not performing according to expectations. The Commissioner General of Cooperatives requested the assistance of a foreign specialist in assessing the causes. I was assigned the task.

Following a preliminary review of all available documents and a brief visit to Culao, I concluded that good administration, of itself, was an oversimplification and by no means the answer, even were the term "administration" defined so broadly as to include competent assistants capable of carrying out socioeconomic research, capable of organizing and conducting group meetings, and knowledgeable concerning the processes of fish marketing and community purchasing.

The research undertaken for this paper was based on the hypothesis that the quality of management is only one contributor to the success of a cooperative and that such factors as adequate funding, proper orientation of potential members, and the recognition of the roles of middlemen and fishmongers are also required. Also, each variable would have to be considered in terms of its contribution to the success or failure of the cooperative.

There were four objectives in my assignment:

1. To introduce a small group of Vietnamese government employees to the methodology of socioeconomic research.

2. To discover and to document objectively the reasons for the lack of success in the Culao District Fishery Cooperative.

3. To gather sufficient additional local socioeconomic data to enable the cooperative research staff program planners to gain an adequate picture of the economic activities and problems of both the cooperative staff and the fishermen. From these data it was hoped that the involved Vietnamese officials would acquire a broader perspective from which to plan a pilot project and to evaluate the role of their respective departments might play in the future of the proposed pilot project in Culao in particular, and in the fishing cooperatives of Vietnam in general.[1]

4. To provide a preliminary study to serve as a basis for more detailed studies on specific aspects of the Culao fishing configuration by the staff of the Cooperative Research and Training Center of the Ministry of Agriculture and Fisheries.

Scope of the Research

Because of limitations of both staff and time, the scope of the research was limited to probing the various attitudes held by the Culao fishermen and staff members of the cooperative vis-à-vis the cooperative itself and to exploring the socioeconomic aspects of the village and the economic aspects of the fishing configuration. For purposes of contrast, and to serve to affirm some of the tentative conclusions, an additional brief study was made at Ham Tan, where the cooperative was reputed to be unique in its success.[2]

---

[1] After reading my report, the Commissioner General of Cooperatives, who had long experience in cooperative work, indicated that conditions and problems in Culao appeared to be typical of those encountered in other fishing villages of Vietnam.

[2] The bulk of the research was undertaken by Mr. Nguyen Van Thuan and the writer. Five other cooperative officials received three months of training in the methodology of socioeconomic research and were placed at the latter's disposal when not occupied with administrative duties.

The Village Economic Setting

Culao[3] is located on National Route 1 to Hue, three kilometers from Nha Trang, the provincial capital. The village is divided administratively into three hamlets comprised of 1,206 houses, with a total population of 7,440. Culao, the most important and largest of the three hamlets, contains about 120 small shops and stalls, the better homes, a maternity clinic, the main market, the quay, the cooperative office, the administrative office, the village meeting hall, and a Buddhist temple.

Because of its proximity to the provincial capital, the inhabitants of Culao represent a rather heterogeneous occupational group: government employees, pedicab drivers, schoolteachers, mat weavers, carpenters, mechanics, and others primarily dependent upon work issuing from Nha Trang.

About 10 per cent of the fishing population are transients, residing in Culao only during the fishing season and returning to their own island villages during the off-season (mid-October to mid-January). Many fishermen living in other towns fish in the general area and sell their fish at Culao. A high percentage of fishermen have immigrated in recent years because of military insecurity and plan to return to their original villages as soon as the war ends. All of these groups play an integral role in the local economy.

The bulk of the village economy centers around fishing and tangential activities. Five hundred and thirty families are directly involved in the fishing industries, and 296 families are concerned indirectly through processing (*nuoc-mam*[4]), purchasing, marketing, or trucking of fish; lending money to the fishermen; boatbuilding; selling fishing equipment; crushing ice for packing. The

---

Owing to limitations of space most of the socioeconomic information has been omitted.

[3] Though Vinh Phuoc is the official name of the town, Culao, its more popular name, will be used throughout this paper.

[4] *Nuoc mam,* made from the juices of fermented fish, is the food sauce par excellence for Vietnam.

number of men actually going to sea varies from 300 to 1,350, depending upon the weather, their health, and the time of year.

Roughly 20 per cent of the fishermen have secondary occupations during the off-season. There are many who at the termination of their primary fishing season join an off-season fishing group, or merely fish in the channel in their small *Cau* boats, earning 80 piastres per day.[5] Many others serve as porters in Nha Trang, earning 30 piastres per day; some work as carpenters or masons; and some drive pedicabs, earning from 50 to 60 piastres per day.

The consensus of the nonfishing population is that Culao fishermen are spendthrifts. The hazardous life, combined with an erratic supply of income, tends to produce a "live today" philosophy. It is not unusual for a fisherman to spend a month's earnings in a single evening of eating, drinking, gambling, and the purchasing of black-market first-row tickets for the folk theater. Some purchase clothing for the family; a pair of western pants and shirt for himself, in emulation of the city dweller; or a pair of shoes, another symbol of affluence. On another day, gold earrings, a gold necklace or bracelet may be purchased by the wife, knowing full well that within two or three months these probably will have to be resold at a 10 to 15 per cent loss in order to obtain rice and fish. Following such an experience the fisherman may purchase other prestige items such as a watch, a pen, or a small transistor radio, fully aware that these, too, may soon have to be returned to the merchants at a loss of 30 to 50 per cent. However, a few boatowners do manage to save money in order to build a brick home, send their children to school in Nha Trang, buy a larger boat, better nets, or a motor.

The Fishing Configuration

Three occupational groups that play integral roles in the fishing configuration are the *Nau*, the moneylenders, and the *Roi*.

---

[5] One hundred piastres (1964) equals $1.00 U.S.

The *Nau*

Nau is a term employed uniquely by the fishermen of central Vietnam and refers to those moneylenders who are also involved directly or indirectly with the marketing activities of their clients. The *Nau*, in contrast to the ordinary moneylender, makes a portion of his loan interest-free (*Nau* money) in exchange for the prerogative of buying and selling a percentage of his debtor's catch. The *Nau* is respected not only because of his role, but also because of his status, a result of his wealth. In most cases, the *Nau* is not a "calloused individual," as he is sometimes referred to by the urbanite, but quite amiable and often personable.[6] If a debt cannot be paid on time, he may lend an additional sum to tide the borrower over until such time as the fish are more abundant. He may, on occasion, invite the boatowner and his crew to a sumptuous repast. If a debtor is sick, he may pay him a visit and bring medicine. If these actions are instigated by ulterior motives, most fishermen are unaware of them. Without the *Nau*, to whom could they sell their fish and be assured of receiving their money? The *Nau*'s acquaintances among the *Roi* facilitate his ability to collect the money after the *Roi* have resold the fish. Without the *Nau*, who would provide substantial loans? Ordinary moneylenders deal only with the more affluent fishermen and do not desire to become involved in fishmongering. The fishermen cannot turn to the cooperative, which lends a maximum of only 5,000 piastres, requires many papers to be filled out, and even then delays from three to four months before the money is made available. The cooperative never makes loans for sickness. Even those few sophisticated fishermen who realize that they are being exploited are dependent upon the *Nau* and appreciate his existence. The *Nau* is always nearby with money available, and willing (except in the case of the small *Cau* fishermen) to accept the potential catch as collateral.

[6] His role and relationship vis-à-vis the fishermen is reminiscent of the Chinese middleman in Thai rural society.

The Moneylenders

In addition to the *Nau,* there is a group of wealthy villagers, government officials, and merchants who wish to supplement their incomes by lending money to the more affluent boatowners to supplement the inadequate amounts available from the *Nau* or from the cooperative. Amounts lent range from 30,000 to as much as 300,000 piastres. The rate of interest varies from 3 to 20 per cent monthly according to the solvency of the borrower, his reputation as a fisherman, and the intimacy of the relationship between borrower and moneylender.

The *Roi*

The fishmongers, known as *Roi,* number between 150 and 200 depending upon the abundance of fish during a particular season. Nearly all are women, of whom the majority are wives of the local villagers. Their ages vary from twenty-five to sixty. The amount of fish any one of them buys each day for cash or credit (usually the latter) varies in value from as little as 200 to as much as 30,000 piastres. Some *Roi* have regular sources of supply in that agreements are made (with certain *Nau* or boatowners) in which the *Roi* promise to purchase a specified percentage of the catch at all times.

The *Roi* who buy on a regular basis are those with long experience and are known as professionals. Representing the larger markets of Nha Trang, Ninh Hoa, Van Ninh, Banmethuot, Dalat, and occasionally Saigon, they may earn from 50 to as much as 3,000 piastres per day. Many *Roi* work sporadically, e.g., when the fish are plentiful or when they have saved a few hundred piastres and wish to speculate. They buy from other *Roi* and sell either to retailers in Nha Trang or directly to the consumers, netting between 15 and 100 piastres per day (with the mode around 50 piastres).

The great majority of *Roi* deal in certain species of fish, haggling with and bidding against the other competitors for the cargo. The haggling during the bidding often terminates in rather violent arguments, in spiteful damaging of the fish in dispute, and occasionally in an exchange of blows. The fishermen frequently express a genuine fear of these shrews and are grateful to the *Nau* for acting as their intermediaries.

The Fishing Groups

At Culao, the number of fishermen, boats, motors, and nets employed varies with each month. The number of men employed by any one boatowner, the wages paid, bonuses provided, and size of loans all vary from boatowner to boatowner, and sometimes from month to month. There is wide variation in the amount of fish caught in any one day by two different boats employing the same technique, or by the same boat in two consecutive days.

Furthermore, though the duration of a particular fishing season may be five, eight, or ten months, rough seas and illness result in an individual average of only twenty days of fishing each month of the season. Thus fishermen are unemployed, or underemployed, on an average of 160 to 180 days of each year. However, during many of these nonfishing days, some are partially occupied in the various tangential activities mentioned earlier.

This paper deals with the economic rather than the technical aspects of the fishing groups. It commences with the fishing operations requiring the greatest outlay of capital and proceeds down the scale. The terms used refer to various fishing configurations which include the kinds of boats, equipment, and techniques employed. The fishing groups that play a basic role in the economy are: (1) the *Dang;* (2) the *Gia Tau;* (3) the *Manh;* (4) the *Luoi;* (5) the *Cau;* (6) minor *Cau* groups.

The Dang

The *Luoi Dang,* commonly referred to as *Dang,* is the most complex of the fishing operations and is practiced only in the central coastal region of Vietnam. It requires the greatest capital outlay and the most capable management. It carries the most prestige, and stands to result in the greatest loss or gain in any one season. Though there are but four *Dang* groups residing in Culao, there are another eight groups operating within the provincial area, all of whom utilize the port facilities at Culao.

Two large boats are required for the actual fishing operation. These boats, each with a crew of twenty men, are stationed at sea throughout the entire eighteen- to twenty-week season. Some groups own their own boats, and others rent them for the season at a cost of 10,000 piastres each. Along with the large boats are two small auxiliary boats for laying out, gathering in, and making repairs on the heavy 300-foot nets. In addition, each *Dang* group has two large motorized boats which are used to jockey the fishing boats into position and to haul the twice-daily catch from the stationary boats to the quay market. These motorized boats, in most cases, are rented from the *Gia* fishing-boat owners (see below) for 60,000 to 80,000 piastres a season.

The more common *Dang*[7] group corporation has an administrative board (all of whom have been fishermen) comprised of a president, a vice-president, a treasurer, a supply man, and two secretaries. Each of the administrative staff receives a stipend of 600 piastres per month to cover transportation and miscellaneous expenses.

Each of the members (the fishermen as well as the administrative staff) buys or pledges to buy shares (depending upon the system employed by the group) from the treasurer at a fixed sum, usually 15,000 piastres, which provides a portion of the working capital. The more affluent members of the group pledge or buy more shares, always in denominations of 15,000 piastres. The group may thus begin a season with a working capital of between 600,000 and 800,000 piastres. When the system of pledges is

---

[7] In the less common *Dang* operations, the proprietor hires his crew and takes all profits for himself. Members of his administrative staff receive 2,000 piastres each per month and a bonus at the end of a successful season. The fishermen receive 1,500 to 1,800 piastres per month.

employed, the group will borrow this sum of money against the pledged collateral. In either case, from the profit realized at the end of the season, members receive a dividend in proportion to the number of shares purchased or pledged.

In addition to its capital assets, the group usually requires an additional 200,000 to 400,000 piastres to see it through the season. This covers such expenditures as food for the fishermen, boat rentals, boat and net maintenance, and the exorbitant auction price of the fishing-pool rights. The additional sum is also sought in case the first month's catch is small and expenses have to be met.

If an additional loan must be made, each member of the corporation pledges an additional sum which he guarantees to make good should the season's proceeds be insufficient for repayment of the loan. These pledges are signed and given to the money-lender. The loan may draw interest of 3 to 4 per cent per month. If a portion of the loan is made with the *Nau*, 10 to 20 per cent of this loan may be interest-free (*Nau* money) on the condition that the *Nau* have exclusive rights to purchase the fish, from which he will earn his 2-per-cent commission.[8]

The *Dang* groups frequently prefer to borrow from several moneylenders. This better enables them to negotiate extensions and places them in a more favorable position for borrowing money the following year. The *Dang* groups fear that dependency on only one moneylender will enable him to exercise too much control, obligating them to accept his decisions concerning their monetary affairs. Although the treasurers have had no formal courses in bookkeeping, they have a systematic and rather sophisticated approach to accounting, even employing double-entry bookkeeping, which becomes quite involved as the season draws to a close.

Once the fish have been unloaded and sorted by species and size, the *Dang* president calls out his asking price based on the

[8] The 2-per-cent commission is only for the *Dang* group. The *Gia* groups pay 2½ per cent, and all others pay 5 to 10 per cent.

quantity, the price received the previous day, and his estimate of the next day's catch.[9] The *Roi* who first accepts the price is entitled to 25 per cent of the entire catch. The second 25 per cent is then available to any *Roi* (or group of *Roi*), or to *Nau* willing to meet the price offered by the first buyer. The purchase and resale of the remaining 50 per cent of the catch is always the prerogative of the *Nau* who has lent money to the group. If the *Nau* feels the price is too high or if he is too busy to devote time to resale, he announces his disinterest, and the *Roi* begin haggling. The *Nau* having the 50-per-cent prerogative receives his 2-per-cent commission regardless of whether or not he exercises his prerogative. This 2 per cent is collected after the total sales have been tabulated at the termination of each two-week period.

Where no *Nau* money is involved, the *Dang* group president or vice-president assumes responsibility for the sale of the fish. In these instances, he receives the 2-per-cent commission on the gross sales. All sales are on credit and funds are not collected until the fish have been resold to the retailers by the *Nau* or the *Roi.*

The great disadvantage of the *Dang* fishing configuration rests in the exorbitant price that the fishermen must pay for the fishing-pool rights as measured against the high financial risk. *Dang* fishing requires special areas where there are ocean deeps. These deeps have been commandeered by the provincial government and are auctioned off to the various *Dang* groups as a means of acquiring additional revenue for administrative expenses. (The fishermen are highly suspicious of the uses to which these revenues are put.) Auction prices paid by the *Dang* groups vary from 100,000 to 1,000,000 piastres per season, depending upon the reputed quality of each fishing area.[10] Any one year's catch varies

[9] Small fish are sold by the basket, larger fish by the piece. No scales are used; the weights are skillfully determined by sight.

[10] Each *Dang* group bids on the pool of its choice. The highest bidder must pay 25 per cent of his bid within one week, and an additional 25 per cent every three months until the bid is paid in full. The losing bidders are informed immediately and permitted to bid on another pool.

considerably from that of the previous year. In 1963, for example, the choicest pool provided only 60 per cent of the income needed to pay for the concession. Including the money owed to the *Nau*, this group lost over 600,000 piastres.

After observing the *Dang* operations, one is impressed by: (1) the high degree of initiative displayed in the operation as a whole; (2) the degree of imagination displayed in the various forms of administration; (3) the complexity of the bookkeeping; (4) the large number of individuals working together as an economic unit.

The *Gia Tau*

The second most important type of fishing when ranked according to capital outlay, gross income, and prestige is the *Gia Tau*, four of whose dozen groups reside in Culao. All twelve groups utilize the port facilities. It is primarily an off-season fishing technique practiced during the months of October through January when the ocean is too turbulent for the other boats to venture out. Since 85 per cent of the fishing boats of Culao are inoperative during the off-season, the competition at the quay market is minimal, and the *Gia* fishermen receive relatively high prices for their catches.

The boats and equipment used for *Gia Tau*[11] are usually the same as those used by the *Dang* groups. Two boats are utilized, each employing a crew of seven. The *Gia* enterprise is always totally financed and managed by a single proprietor. The fishermen receive a percentage of the profits. During the off-season, the proprietor has the advantage of being able to select his crew from among the better fishermen. Because the competition for these few jobs is very strong, the proprietor is not obliged to offer

[11] The *Gia Ghe*, which employs boats with sails instead of motors, is rapidly becoming extinct, owing to the difficulty in obtaining crews. The fishermen prefer to sign on with a motorized boat. The work is less fatiguing and the profits much greater since the motorized boats can reach the fishing areas and return to port more rapidly, thus allowing more time for fishing.

the gifts of money or bonuses required when hiring crews during the regular season. The ramie nets, which cost between 100,000 and 120,000 piastres, are continually in need of repair and a great deal of time and expense goes into their maintenance.[12] The two boats used for the *Gia* are equipped with twenty-five-horsepower motors, which cost 200,000 piastres each. In addition to the 10,000 piastres of *Nau* money, the *Gia* boatowner must usually borrow from the *Nau* an additional sum ranging from 30,000 to 50,000 piastres.

Gross income is handled in the following way. Let us say that the catch during a two-week period has grossed 110,000 piastres. The *Nau* receives his 5-per-cent commission (5,500 piastres) plus 2.5-per-cent interest on the loan (one-half month on 40,000 piastres)—1,000 piastres. The boatowner then deducts 4,200 piastres for food for the crew (20 piastres per day per person) and 3,300 piastres for gas and oil. Cost of materials for net maintenance is 1,500 piastres. Fifteen hundred piastres goes as partial repayment for 10,000-piastre outlay at the beginning of the season for the preparation of boats and nets. The remaining 93,000 piastres are then divided into ten equal parts. The boatowner takes six parts for himself. The remaining 37,200 piastres are divided evenly among the fourteen crew members. Thus the individual net earnings for the two weeks' work is 2,650 piastres, a tidy sum when compared to an average of 450 piastres for fishermen during any two-week period of the regular season.

This relatively lucrative type of fishing is not practiced by many because the physical risk is very great during this season of inclement weather, the season is short, and the capital outlay is relatively high.

The *Manh*

Manh fishing is divided into nine categories determined by the characteristics of the nets employed: the length, the breadth, and,

[12] According to the late R. J. Schoettler, Fisheries Advisor, United States Agency for International Development, Saigon, similar nets of nylon would cost double this amount, but would last twice as long, and because of their translucence would ensnare 60 to 80 per cent more fish.

most important, the diameter of the mesh. Two medium-sized (twenty-five- to thirty-foot) boats are used simultaneously, the principal and the auxiliary. Each boat employs at least nine crew members depending on the number of nets provided by the proprietor. Some boats operate with four nets, others employ as many as sixteen. Capital investment for the *Manh* shows wide variation, ranging from 60,000 to 160,000 piastres depending upon size, number of nets employed, and whether or not the boat is motorized.

Several months prior to the fishing season, the boatowner provides each fisherman with an interest-free loan of from one to two thousand piastres, depending upon his skills, which is later deducted from the fisherman's share of the catch. This loan serves three purposes: it partially supports the fisherman and his family during the nonearning season; it serves as an additional guarantee that the boat owner will employ him the following season; reciprocally, it usually assures the boatowner that the fisherman will be available to him when the fishing season begins. For one month prior to the fishing season, the boatowner and his crew repair the old nets and prepare for operation. For these services, each of the crew members receives only his food.

Once the *Manh* boats have returned and are moored at the quay, the *Roi* begin their cacophonic bidding, sometimes joined by the *Nau*. The boatowner decides on the price. All sales to the *Roi* are on a short-term (three-to-five-day) credit basis. If *Nau* money has been provided the boat owner, the *Nau* will collect his 5-per-cent commission on the gross sales.

Once a month the books are brought up to date. All deductions are tabulated, including 25 per cent for boat and tug rentals when applicable. The remainder is divided into two equal parts, the boatowner receiving one, and the crew members dividing the other. The average seasonal net income earned by *Manh* boatowners is estimated at roughly 60,000 to 70,000 piastres; that earned by the fishermen, 14,000 piastres a season. This last figure includes the estimated 1,500 piastres of fish the fishermen are allowed to take home throughout the season, and the meals provided by the boatowner.

A portion of the boatowner's share must be set aside for the necessary loans made at the end of the fishing season to the next season's crew. Since this sum is almost never available when needed, the boatowner perennially must turn to the *Nau* for help. The average amount of a seasonal loan made to *Manh* proprietors is approximately 25,000 piastres. The interest rate varies from 5 to 10 per cent per month.[13]

The *Luoi*

The *Luoi* employs one or two boats. In 1964 only 20 per cent were motorized and the majority of boatowners resorted to renting a tug to pull them to and from the fishing areas, for which the tug owners received 25 per cent of the catch.

A preseason gift or bonus of 1,000 to 2,000 piastres is provided by the boatowner to each crew member. Boatowners can obtain *Nau* money of from 5,000 to 10,000 piastres, with the accompanying rights of the *Nau* to market the fish with the usual 5-per-cent commission.

The average daily catch for the *Luoi* grosses 5,000 to 6,000 piastres. The division of the gross sales profit is similar to that for the *Manh*. The average net income for boatowners is 50,000 to 60,000 piastres per season. A crewman averages 12,000 a season, including his food and bonus.

The *Cau*

Cau is the fishermen's generic term for all fishing techniques employing hook and line. The number of Culao fishermen whose primary source of income is derived through *Cau* fishing is approximately 280, utilizing a total of 85 boats.

[13] For those *Manh* proprietors who have emigrated from the region of My Giang the interest on loans is 10 per cent per month, and the sales commission 8 per cent. It is thus not surprising to learn that marketing of fish on the open seas is most prevalent among the *Manh* fishermen who thereby avoid this 8-per-cent commission.

The average *Cau* boat costs roughly 8,000 piastres,[14] or it may be rented for 3,000 to 4,000 piastres per month. The necessary fishing paraphernalia (hooks, lines, and the like) cost from 3,000 to 4,000 piastres—a sum usually borrowed for this purpose. Because the relatively small catch is easier to tabulate and the fishermen are in more immediate need of funds, the books are tallied daily and the fishermen are paid at that time. If the boatowner serves as crew member, he receives a crew member's share of the catch in addition to his share as boatowner.

Minor *Cau* Groups

There are, in addition, variously shaped small *Cau* boats— *Tay, Chay,* and *Muc*—managed by only one or two persons, frequently a father and son or two brothers. The average daily haul for the small boats is 350 piastres gross. Because of the small size of the boats, many earning days are lost during inclement weather, and maintenance costs are relatively high owing to the amount of punishment the boats and cotton lines receive. Because they are considered poor risks, owners of these *Cau* boats are rarely offered *Nau* money.

Provincial-Level Fisheries Organization

Overseeing all district cooperatives and acting as the liaison with Saigon is the provincial cooperative, headquartered in Nha Trang. In addition, there are two other fishing organizations located in the city: the Fishermen's Trade Union (Syndicat des Pecheurs) and the Government Provincial Fisheries Service (Service de Peche).

The primary responsibility of the Government Provincial Fisheries Service is the welfare of the fishermen through the provision of equipment and information concerning improved fishing tech-

---

[14] The exceptions are the very few large *Cau Soi* and *Cau To* boats which cost as much as 50,000 piastres, employ twenty-horsepower motors, 15,000 to 20,000 piastres worth of equipment, and a crew of six to eight fishermen.

niques. They are also responsible, in theory, for the annual gathering of statistical data concerning the number of motors, boats, fishermen, and tonnage of fish caught throughout the province. Each month approximately twenty fishermen visit the office to request information concerning the means of procuring nylon nets and motors at government prices.[15]

The Fishermen's Trade Union, with a branch office in Nha Trang, is a private organization of boatowners, boasting 1,500 members. Again in theory, the trade union acts as intermediary between the fishermen and the government, and between the fishermen and the local merchants. Letters are written on behalf of the members concerning the ordering of needed fishing materials, and assistance is provided to members for special fishing operations such as boat building and financial arrangements.

The Culao Fishermen's Cooperative

The district cooperative located in Culao was established in April 1960. It was set up, under the auspices of the Directorate of Cooperatives in Saigon, primarily to provide financial assistance to the fishermen in the form of restricted-purpose, low-interest loans. Though membership (943 persons) in 1964 traversed all economic levels, the mode represented the upper income groups.

The Culao Cooperative administration comprised one manager and two assistants. The cooperative was directed by a board of directors composed of nine members (all boatowners) elected for a two-year term by the members. They were selected by the cooperative manager from the more affluent and more influential members of the village, and thus hardly represented the interest of the vast majority of fishermen. In principle, the board met once a month to hear reports by the manager concerning his activities and suggestions made by the board during the last meeting, followed by a recapitulation of problems. It was rare for all

[15] In 1963 these prices had doubled as a result of the United States Agency for International Development "buy American" policy.

members to attend, and rarer still for problems to be discussed and plans to be made in a constructive fashion.

Incentive to be a member of the board was lacking, for several valid reasons. Membership required a considerable expenditure of time for which there was no remuneration, and thus carried no status inasmuch as a government job with no salary "cannot be a very respectable one." The board members continually received negative criticism from the populace and were rarely given credit even for positive actions. The sole incentive for becoming a board member was the assurance of a loan. Also, the authoritarian manner of the board chairman inhibited vocal participation; thus the member role was a passive one. The board chairman was troubled by the disparity between his own level of education, which was low, and that of the cooperative manager, whose education and role as a "government official" enabled him to exert considerable influence over the board, and no one including the chairman dared refuse or refute him openly. The manager was respected but feared and held in suspicion as a spokesman for the government.

Every two weeks the manager visited the provincial cooperative office, not for assistance or advice, but to receive directives. The channel was always unilateral and there was never an opportunity for initiative from below. It is partially for this reason that many of the members claimed that the cooperative was simply owned by, and operated for, the government. The manager had never been a fisherman and knew very little about the problems involved in professional fishing. The fault lay with the authorities who had assigned him as manager, for although his nominal function was to serve the needs and wishes of the members of the cooperative, his background prevented him from doing so. In addition, the understaffed administration had neither the time nor the qualifications to carry out its multifarious duties.

Legislative Functions and Related Problems
of the Culao Cooperative

The prime objective of the cooperative was to develop an
esprit de corps via cooperative action. One method of attaining
the objective was through meetings and pamphlets. In general,
there had been a lack of proper orientation for the cooperative
members, which explained in part their indifference as well as
their lack of comprehension of the functions and potentials of
the organization. Since the rate of literacy was low, the great bulk
of literature distributed was either not read or not understood by
the target audience. Lacking personnel, the Culao Cooperative
was unable to institute a districtwide education program, at even
a minimal level. Finding a time when twenty or thirty fishermen
were free to meet for instruction was difficult. Among the reasons
for the small attendance at meetings was a pragmatic attitude
concerning the discrepancy between talk and action. The fishermen were not interested in discussing the nebulous future and
lacked the capacity to comprehend the advantages of a project
requiring immediate sacrifice while bearing fruit only some twelve
months later.[16]

Prerequisite abilities and training found lacking among the
cooperative staff members were: the ability to arouse the fisherman's interest sufficiently to bring him out to meetings, training
in special techniques, a certain degree of maturity and interest,
and a relatively dynamic personality.

A second objective of the cooperative was to lend money at the
low rate of 1 per cent per month to assist fishermen in purchasing
equipment essential to earning their livelihood. Unfortunately, it
was seldom the needy who received loans. In any case, the loans,
of 2,000 to 5,000 piastres, were rarely sufficient to serve their

[16] One fisherman expressed this attitude very aptly. When told that even
were he to join the cooperative this year he would probably not be granted
a loan until next year, he replied: "In that case, I will wait until next
year to join."

purpose, and the amount of money available was far below the amount requested. Only 30 per cent of the requests, and 20 per cent of the recipients' needs, could be met. Furthermore, the amount of red tape involved in procuring a loan produced a delay of three to six months and consequently was of little use in terms of its original purpose. In many cases, the tardy low-interest loans from the cooperative were used to pay off a part of a private high-interest loan, and the cooperative was the loser.

The screening of loan applications was a difficult undertaking since the cooperative had little data on its members and because of the large number of unpredictable factors, including the actual indebtedness of the applicant, the present condition of his collateral (boats and nets), the amount of illness to be anticipated, and the expected catch. The practice was to make loans to those fishermen who had been successful in the past and who were, of course, the more affluent.

A third objective of the cooperative was to provide, at reasonable prices, needed supplies such as nets, motors, cordage, lines, and hooks. Unfortunately, the budget did not permit stocking these items, and thus the fishermen were forced to purchase them from local merchants whose prices ranged from 20 to 100 per cent higher.

Problems Identified by the Cooperative Staff

The procrastination and the elusiveness of the debtors created an incessant headache for all. The cooperative had never been able to collect more than 40 per cent of its outstanding loans.[17] A commonly encountered excuse was, "Well, the loan was late in arriving, so why should I have to pay on time?" Actually, the fishermen had the money needed to repay the loan. However, they were worried that once the loan was repaid to the cooperative and they later needed money, there would be no opportunity to obtain another loan from the cooperative until their turn came

[17] As of April 1964 outstanding due debts amounted to more than 600,000 piastres.

around again. This would then place them in the undesirable position of having to borrow from the Nau at interest rates of 5–10 per cent monthly. Thus it was better to pay the 1 per cent monthly interest to the cooperative and hold on to the capital for any emergency which might arise. Other reasons for failure to repay debts were early misunderstandings concerning the loan procedures and interest rates; sudden departure to urban areas for employment; threats of retaliation by the National Liberation Front should the debt be repaid. For obvious reasons, the NLF in the area were not anxious to see the government cooperative succeed.

The salaries of the administrative staff were inadequate to meet living costs, resulting in a lack of initiative and a propensity for corruption at the provincial cooperative office.

Any expenditure of over 1,000 piastres required special permission from the Saigon office. Expenditures of over 500 piastres needed approval of the provincial office, resulting in a loss of face and respect for the cooperative manager vis-à-vis the board members, who realized that he was manager in name only. More important were the abundant paperwork and expenditure of time involved in each operation.

The provincial cooperative identified as their primary problems: lack of logistic support from Saigon, overwork resulting from understaffing,[18] inadequate salaries, and inadequate training for the responsibility of the position held.

Attitudes of the Fisherman Concerning the Cooperative

All owners of large boats felt that the cooperative served very little purpose. Loans were too small and supplies inadequate or nonexistent. Most owners of medium-sized and small boats expressed similar views less vehemently. Both groups considered the management to be weak. Boatowners who had never been able to secure a loan were critical of the entire loan procedure.

[18] Several of the cadre were spending between 30 and 50 hours in overtime every month with no compensation.

The aged members of the cooperative resented the management for not inviting them to attend board meetings, claiming that their "wise counsel" was being ignored to the detriment of all other members. The younger fishermen (aged eighteen to forty) were hired hands for the most part and expressed either mild negativism or indifference toward the cooperative. Many villagers had not joined the cooperative in the belief that only those who owned boats received loans.

There was widespread complete ignorance, on the part of members as well as nonmembers, of the purposes and functions of the cooperative. Those who claimed some understanding stated that its purposes were to lend money to the wealthy—"the poor could never receive loans since they have neither boats nor homes to offer as collateral"—and to provide motors "although they are never in stock."

In making a loan, the cooperative was accused of "cutting off one's head as well as one's tail." This referred to the 5-per-cent deduction made at the time the loan was transacted and the interest added at the time the loan was repaid. The purpose of the initial 5 per cent was to assist the cooperative in ultimately becoming financially self-sufficient. However, the psychological effect of this *modus operandi* was quite negative because the villagers had been improperly oriented to the function of the cooperative.

Many poorer members lamented the restrictive uses to which cooperative loans could be put. No consideration was given to crises such as hunger and sickness. Long-standing members felt that the procedure for granting loans was unjust in that new members were granted loans before all the older members had received them.

Those fishermen who expressed positive attitudes concerning the loan program were primarily owners of medium-sized boats who had received loans. Yet even they were critical of the diminutive loan size. Many boatowners suffered from the misconception that those who had received a boat-purchasing loan were not eligible for a motor. Others claimed that key money was needed to obtain a motor; that motors when available were sold to those who already possessed them, and occasionally to non-fishermen who rented them out at exorbitant fees. Those express-ing positive attitudes in this regard were the few who had re-ceived motors.

The majority of fishermen interviewed expressed disillusion-ment with the cooperative, stating that they had been led to believe that the cooperative would be a panacea, providing multi-tudinous benefits which thus far had not materialized. Many had been promised motors and nets, but the very few who had re-ceived them were seldom those most in need. Rumors were rampant concerning the need of key money to obtain both loans and motors. There were stories of embezzlement of funds by the "government-operated cooperatives" in other villages. Other rumors claimed that the Culao Cooperative was planning to monopolize all sales of fish and then lower, by 50 per cent, the price presently paid to the fisherman.[19]

The Ham Tan Fishermen's Cooperative

The Ham Tan Cooperative in Binh Tuy Province, in contrast with Culao, exemplified a relatively successful cooperative and, tending to affirm my earlier impressions, provided a further basis for many of the recommendations I eventually made to the Com-missioner General of Cooperatives.

The members of the board of directors, as well as the manager, were all experienced fishermen, and although they had had only three to six years of formal education, were quite competent. With each biennial election the less capable officers had been re-placed by those with more ability. At meetings the members, as well as the board members, aired their problems. All members felt that the cooperative was their own and not, as in Culao, a

[19] It was the writer's impression that the *Nau* were the source of these rumors, but the evidence is quite fragmentary.

government-run cooperative operating for the benefit of a small group of wealthy fishermen.

One of the more important functions of the cooperative had been to sell fish directly to Saigon, thus bypassing the middleman and greatly increasing profits. In the incipient stages of these innovative marketing procedures, the *Nau* (thirty in all) created a disturbance. Several tried exorbitant bribes to persuade the Province Chief to sabotage the cooperative. However, the Provincial Governor not only evicted most of the *Nau* from the province but went so far as to issue a circular which stated that any fisherman caught selling to the *Nau* would be heavily fined. Thus the successful eliminating of the middlemen was due mainly to the strong administrative support found at the highest local echelon.[20]

To handle the fish marketing the cooperative hired a group of ten persons comprising one director, four fish handlers, two accountants, one cashier, one supplyman (in charge of procurement of such equipment as gasoline, nets, ropes, and the like), and one messenger. The Province Chief stationed a policeman at the quay to keep order and to see that there was no interference by the *Nau*.

The fisherman brought his fish to the quay where they were sorted, weighed, placed in large baskets, iced, salted, and the baskets numbered. The fisherman received an itemized receipt. Preparations for payment to the fishermen began on the third day. The cooperative deducted its expenses, allowed for weight loss during the trip to Saigon, and deducted its 6½-per-cent commission.[21] The final amount due the fisherman was written

[20] Though the number of active *Nau* had been reduced to zero, the fight was not yet finished. Many of these *Nau* sent petitions to high government officials in Saigon claiming that the various administrative actions were unfair to free enterprise, were not in the spirit of democracy, and were actually detrimental to the welfare of the fishermen. Fortunately for the cooperative, the petitions were ignored.

[21] The provincial government received 1 per cent from the commission. One-half per cent served as a tax for the national government, and 5 per

on the receipt which could be presented to the cashier for payment.

A common practice of fishermen in need of ready cash was to sell their receipts to the *Roi* after the original weighing-in, usually at the Saigon price posted on the bulletin board—that is, a price of three days earlier. The cooperative still received its commission from these transactions. When the *Roi* purchased the receipts from the fishermen, they themselves collected from the cooperative on the day of payment.

The attitude of the cooperative's board of directors concerning the *Roi* had undergone some change during the years 1962 and 1963. Though at first resentful and suspicious of the actions of the *Roi,* the cooperative began to look upon them as a blessing in disguise. They actually helped both the fishermen and the cooperative in several ways: they helped to sort the fish; they bought all of the small, marginal-profit fish which the cooperative did not care to handle;[22] they provided the fishermen with ready cash, which the cooperative could not do, while still providing the cooperative its commission.

Ham Tan versus Culao

In Ham Tan, 88 per cent of the fishermen were cooperative members versus 47 per cent in Culao; 33 per cent owned or worked with medium-sized or large boats versus 18 per cent in Culao; 47 per cent of all boats were motorized in Ham Tan, only 16 per cent in Culao; 75 per cent of all boats employed nylon nets versus 28 per cent in Culao.

There were very many reasons for the economic disparity between the two areas. The conspicuous ones were: (1) The rela-

---

cent was returned to the fisherman at the end of the year after all administrative expenses had been deducted. Over the past two years, this dividend averaged out to a 1-piastre return to the fisherman for every 40 piastres received from the sale of his fish to the cooperative.

[22] The small fish are bought by the *Roi* for 2 to 4 piastres per kilogram and are sold to the *nuoc mam* manufacturers in Phan Thiet. The profit was very small in comparison with the amount of work involved.

tive proximity of the Ham Tan port to Saigon permitted a constant and ready market for their produce. (2) The relatively low density of the Ham Tan population resulted in much less competition. (3) The cooperative paid the fishermen 80 per cent more for their fish than had the *Nau,* thus enabling many boatowners to buy motors from the Saigon merchants despite the relatively high cost. (4) The dividends paid back at the end of the year served as incentives for continued membership and high morale. (5) A Ham Tan Cooperative subcontractor assumed the role of fishmonger, thereby permitting the fishermen to devote more time to their nets and boats. (6) The cooperative offered needed materials such as nylon filament, oil, and gas at reasonable prices.

Less apparent reasons for the disparity were: (7) The Ham Tan Cooperative was managed by dedicated, knowledgeable personnel, all of whom were or had been fishermen. (8) All fishing interests were represented on the board of directors. (9) The great majority of cooperative members were political refugees from North Vietnam who had learned to cooperate with one another in order to survive in a new and insecure area. They were entrepreneurs who brought with them a tradition of hard work combined with thrift. (10) The cooperative provided a one-month training course in maintenance and repair prior to selling motors to the fishermen. (11) There had been continued strong support by the Provincial Governor from the early stages of the cooperative's development.

Assumptions Underlying the Recommendations that Follow

The recommendations that follow were based on the conviction, substantiated by evidence, that the Culao Cooperative, if properly organized and managed, could become a successful one. They were generated with the understanding that: (1) they were pragmatic in that they fell within the expediting potentials of the various concerned agencies; (2) they were realistic in that they were based on the expressed needs of both the cooperative officials and the villagers of Culao; (3) they were also realistic in terms of the military situation in 1964 and the existing budget of the National Agricultural Credit Organization; and (4) not all recommendations were expected to be executed the first year. Priority was left to the judgment of the NACO staff.

It was hoped that the government would introduce a pilot project in Culao; if the project proved successful, it could be emulated in other fishing areas of Vietnam. The project would eventually encompass the entire district administratively, but the advocated changes in loan procedures, in supplying motors, and in elimination of debts would be limited the first year to members residing in Culao.

Some Observations and Recommendations

1. "Cooperation," in general, as is true of most rural peoples in Southeast Asia, does not rank high in the Culao fisherman's value scale. Fishing presents a highly *competitive* configuration. Boats compete for fishing areas, and for fish within these areas. Fishermen compete for hiring-on. The *Roi* and *Nau* compete for the right to purchase the fish and compete with the boatowners concerning the price.

Cooperation is a culture value that must be learned. This learning is not a short-term process. However, if it is to be taught to the fisherman, it must be demonstrated to be utilitarian in a short period of time if he is to be expected to maintain his adherence to, and interest in, a cooperative. The little cooperative spirit that exists among the fishermen on any one boat exists only because their livelihood, and perhaps their lives, depend upon it. It is a pragmatic operation. The cooperation found among the *Dang* was introduced through coercive means by the Vietminh as recently as 1950. If the fishermen can be shown a properly functioning cooperative which can perceptibly raise his standard of living or even tangibly alleviate his misery, then membership would double and a high degree of success would be assured. This has been demonstrated in Ham Tan, but has not as yet been properly tried in Culao.

2. Another important cultural factor to be considered is that the wealthy fisherman is the more aggressive one. He is wealthy because he is aggressive. The poorer fisherman is poor partially because he has been a relatively passive agent in a competitive milieu. Unfortunately, wealth forms a social barrier which makes cooperation between fishermen of varying economic levels a difficult though not impossible undertaking.

3. Good leadership is the key to cooperation. Respect is an attribute of good leadership, and wealth an attribute of respect. This combination of factors does pose a problem. Fortunately, there are many persons with potential leadership ability who lack wealth but who could rally supporters, given proper incentives.

4. An outstanding weakness in the cooperative movement in Culao is the lack of understanding on the part of the fishermen of the overall function and aims of the cooperative. The need for an education program is paramount. During the off-season, all efforts of the district staff should be concentrated on a village-wide re-education program, requiring a revitalization of the long-neglected adult literacy classes, a series of general meetings, lectures, posters, and pamphlets. Managers and members of the Ham Tan Cooperative should be invited to discourse on their successful cooperative. Concomitantly, a team of five or six influential members of the Culao community should visit families in their homes, explaining the aims, functions, and benefits of a cooperative.

5. The cooperative manager should be carefully selected. He should be neither a government official nor a retired government official. He should be an individual of integrity, as well as a natural leader. His formal educational background is *not* as important as the experience he has acquired as a fisherman.[23] Dur-

[23] Too many officials equated education with ability and intelligence.

ing his first month in office, he might be assisted by the cooperative manager at Ham Tan. An alternative, which was discussed
and approved by the Ham Tan Cooperative staff, would be to
transfer some of the Ham Tan staff to Culao for a one-year
period to manage the cooperative.

6. With a potential increase in cooperative membership of
more than 80 per cent, the size of the administrative staff should
be augmented to include a supplyman with the sole function of
determining the needs of the members and eventually investigating the end-use of the purchased supplies. The burden of the
debt collector could be alleviated if the cooperative were to begin
collecting debts through the marketing of fish. The actual marketing could be handled on a contract basis as in Ham Tan.

7. In each cooperative management and staff training course,
more emphasis should be placed on group dynamics and inter-
personal relations. To learn and preach a new idea is a relatively easy task; the difficulty arises in trying to sell the idea to
tradition-bound fishermen. All that he has learned is of little
value if the one-time student, now a field-staff official, creates a
barrier between himself and his audience. Each course, therefore,
should attempt to erode the Mandarin mentality of the officials.

8. If for no other reason than the rising cost of living in the
Nha Trang area, it is recommended that the salaries of all staff
members be increased. Adequate wages are necessary to attract
qualified personnel. Boatowners can earn more from fishing and
are reluctant to work for the cooperative without adequate compensation. In addition to this small salary increase, all staff members should receive a bonus based on $\frac{1}{2}$ per cent of the cooperative commission on net profits from all sales. This would
encourage efficiency while serving as an incentive for making the
venture successful.

9. The new board of directors should receive adequate compensation for their time. This could be derived from the $\frac{1}{2}$ per
cent of the net income mentioned above. Since cooperative laws
prohibit payment of a salary to board members, payment would

have to be in the form of a bonus given at the end of the year. There are no idealists among the fishermen. If they must work for the cooperative with inadequate compensation they will devote a minimum of their time to their duties.

10. The board of directors should be expanded to include one boatowner to represent each of the fishing techniques practiced in the district, and several retired fishermen whose prestige and influence in the village must not be ignored. The *Lach* chief[24] should be included, since his presence on the board would lend traditional dignity. To keep the board members informed of the various member activities is already one of his village functions. Also, insofar as he has always had to maintain direct contact with large numbers of fishermen, he would be in a position to obtain personal statistical data without offending the fishermen.

11. Since a part of the lethargy, frustration, and indifference among the staff of both the provincial and district cooperatives results from the paucity of independent action permitted by the next higher echelons, we recommended that the positions of provincial and district cooperative managers be strengthened. Only men of integrity and ability should fill these positions. The granting of loans and all other local expenditures up to 5,000 piastres should be at their discretion. As a checks and balances procedure,

[24] The *Lach* chief served a function unique to the fishing communities of central Vietnam. He was one of the most respected elders of the village; his position was usually held for a lifetime and transferred upon his death to his eldest son. He had the reputation of being a good fisherman and a man of high morals. In recent years, however, the responsibilities of the *Lach* chief have diminished as the village administrative services have expanded their activities. Despite the reduction in his prestige and status, his functions are still many: to give permission for all nonresident boats to fish in the area and to land at the quay; to see that all local fishing boats are registered; to levy taxes on all boats; to levy taxes to cover partial expenses for the maintenance of the "Mr. Whale" (the totem guardian spirit of fishermen throughout Vietnam) shrine and for the yearly ritual for "Mr. Whale"; to advise the government District Chief, when requested, on the integrity of individual fishermen; to settle disputes among the fishermen related to fishing activities; to organize rescue crews in case of disasters at sea.

the board of directors could pass on all loans and the chairman of the board could pass on all local expenditures. Although most educated Vietnamese government officials equate educational achievement with both ability and intelligence, there are among the fishermen in Culao—very few of whom have more than three years of formal education—some very intelligent and competent individuals who would be capable of handling greater responsibility to the satisfaction of all concerned.

12. The concept of a loan from one's government is relatively new in Vietnam. From time immemorial the fishermen of central Vietnam have depended on the local *Nau* and moneylenders, and the loan procedures have always been quite simple. Application for cooperative loans should be simplified: categories of loans could be divided into loans to wage earners and share-of-profit earners; loans to owners of small, medium-sized, and large boats; and emergency loans.

Wage earners are usually in need of funds during the off-season. The cooperative could set a maximum of 3,000 piastres for loans in this category. The fisherman's employer would be required to sign the loan papers and held indirectly responsible for repayment. These loans would require merely the signature of the boatowner and the borrower. Alternately, inasmuch as the boatowner usually has to borrow in order to lend money to his crew, the cooperative could make the loan directly to the boatowner who would, in turn, make the distribution to his crew. In this case, the ceiling would be based on the number of fishermen employed.

At the end of their fishing season, 40 per cent of the small *Cau* boatowners still owe an average of 1,000 piastres (based on a 3,000-piastre loan). The cosigner of these loans would be another *Cau* boatowner in the same "group of five" (see p. 268).

With few exceptions, the *Manh* and *Luoi* boatowners are able to repay their debts to the *Nau* or moneylenders by the end of the season. Their individual needs at the beginning of the following season are roughly 20,000 piastres. The maximum loan should be 25,000 piastres. The loan application would be signed by two other boatowners in the "group of five."

The *Dang* boatowners offer a somewhat greater risk to the cooperative because of the large auction fees paid to the provincial government. If these fees could be reduced and paid on a basis determined by a nominal percentage of the catch, the risk to the cooperative would be greatly reduced. Although the loan needed by these groups is relatively large, their catch is proportionately large, and the 6½-per-cent commission charged by the cooperative for marketing their fish would partially compensate for the risk.[25] Final authorization for loans of this size (300,000 to 500,000 piastres) would issue from the provincial cooperative chief.

The Culao Cooperative should have at its disposal an emergency fund of 300,000 piastres. In case of sudden or prolonged illness, a death, total destruction of a net, or a boat lost at sea, a fisherman could borrow from this special fund. The amount of the loan would be determined by the circumstances of each case, with the method of repayment the same as that for other loans.

13. Investigation of each loan application should be reduced to a simple determination that the applicant is a resident, owns a boat or hires out, and needs the loan. Since the boatowner also signs the application for nonowners—or, in the case of a boatowner, another in the "group of five" signs—the investigation would require no more than a day, and the loan would be granted without delay.

14. Each loan would require the borrower to sell his fish to the cooperative until the debt is repaid. In the case of nonowners, the cooperative would have the right to withhold a portion of his earnings until the debt is repaid.

15. For the pilot project, it is recommended that the coopera-

[25] For the pilot project, it was recommended that only the four *Dang* groups residing in the village were to be given assistance. The *Gia* groups were relatively well off and were to be excluded from the pilot project during its first year.

tive gradually assume the debts of its members. At the beginning of the fishing season more than 90 per cent of the fishermen are in debt; at the end of a normal fishing season more than 30 per cent are still in debt. The plan would be to enable the latter (mostly small *Cau* fishermen) to be extricated from debt by the end of the season, and to lend enough money to all fishermen toward the middle of the off-season to see them through the two-month period until they are again earning. This would also involve loans to all boatowners, enabling them to prepare their boats and nets for the new season. It would be useless merely to eradicate the fisherman's debt if the need for funds midway through the off-season or at the beginning of the fishing season were to be met again by the *Nau*. The total sum needed is estimated to be 6.5 million piastres, a sum well within the capacity of the National Agricultural Credit Organization.

With the better prices received through the sale of fish to the cooperative and the reduced interest rates on their loans (from 5–10% monthly with the moneylenders to 1% monthly with the cooperative), plus the rebate on the net profits, the fishermen receiving loans could very well become solvent by the end of two years. However, if the cooperative is to replace the *Nau* in the business of lending money and marketing fish, it must be prepared to assume a more social and personal role than it has hitherto been playing.

Some means would have to be found to prevent the fishermen from borrowing money from the *Nau*. As was the case in Ham Tan, the Nha Trang Province Chief would have to issue an order prohibiting the fishermen and the *Nau* from all mutual monetary relationships, with stiff fines levied on offenders. This is an essential measure, for when a fisherman's debt is assumed by the cooperative, he might well feel that a great burden had been lifted and make unnecessary purchases or indulge in relatively extravagant forms of recreation, turning again to the *Nau* for loans.

16. The most urgent need of the boat-owning fishermen is

motors. Since the use of a motor usually raises the catch by at least 80 per cent,[26] it is strongly recommended that the cooperative make available at least 100 motors to boatowners during the first year of the pilot project. These would cover approximately half the needs of Culao. The motors should be distributed by lottery to avoid any claims of favoritism. It is also recommended that the USAID policy of "buy American" be revoked for Vietnam. A Japanese motor sells in Vietnam at one-half the cost of a similar model from the United States.

For the great majority of fishermen who cannot pay cash, the cooperative would provide a loan requiring the borrowers to sell their fish to the cooperative. The cooperative would then deduct 20 per cent daily from the net sales until the loan is repaid. It has been estimated that approximately one season (two for the *Cau* fishermen) would be sufficient time for repayment to be made. As each motor loan is repaid the cooperative would provide another motor for another fisherman, resulting in a revolving motor fund. Fishermen who want motors would serve to pressure those who had obtained them into paying back their loans promptly.

17. Since there is a good deal of motor abuse through mechanical ignorance on the part of the boat operators, no motors should be distributed before each recipient has passed a practical examination on motor repair and maintenance. End-use checks to verify continued ownership of these motors should be made periodically by the cooperative. The cooperative must also stock parts.

18. An important adjunct of a loan program should be a savings plan: too often the fisherman tends to squander his pay or his bonus in a few days. With the commission on fish sales, the cooperative would, in effect, be saving for the fishermen in the form of dividends. However, an effort must be made to *encourage*[27] increased savings by both boatowners and wage earners,

[26] A motorized boat permits many more fishing hours.
[27] The author has found from personal experience in Korea that a *compulsory* savings program can be highly unsatisfactory.

perhaps only 5 per cent the first year, 10 per cent the second and subsequent years. This could be done by purchasing additional shares in the cooperative, which would also be earning interest for the fisherman.

19. The basis for all revisions in the cooperative's *modus operandi* is the underlying assumption that the cooperative must enter into the fish marketing—the *sine qua non* for success of the pilot project. Only by selling the fish will the cooperative be in a strategic position to recover money lent. It is recommended that a contract be let to handle the marketing. The *Dang* presidents are all qualified fishmongers, and two have expressed willingness to assume positions with the cooperative as brokers if the salary were adequate. One or two experienced *Roi* should also be interviewed to determine their willingness to organize the marketing of fish *for the cooperative*.

Unlike the Ham Tan Cooperative, which always had a ready market in Saigon, Culao would have to depend on several outlets: the local market and the markets at Nha Trang, Banmethuot, and Dalat.

The cooperative should pay the fishermen 50 per cent of the estimated value of the fish immediately, and the remainder following the receipts from sales. This would partially prevent clandestine selling by the fishermen on the open seas or to the *Roi*. In addition, the Province chief would have to issue an order prohibiting such transactions, with the accompanying heavy penalties.

Another way to diminish clandestine selling would be to organize the boatowners into groups of five, all of whom practice the same technique and fish relatively near to one another. Each member of the group of five would be held responsible for the actions of the others and would be expected to report any infringements to the cooperative, through his representative on the board of directors. This is an old Vietminh in-group surveillance system which was successfully adopted in Ham Tan. Any offenders automatically lose their cooperative membership at the termination of the fishing season. As mentioned earlier, this system of group responsibility should be extended to cover loan repayment, through pressures exerted by the other members of the group who would be collectively responsible.

20. To maintain a good price level for the fishermen's surplus catch during the peak months, March through May, the installation of a refrigerated room adequate to handle all surplus fish over a forty-eight-hour period is recommended. The maximum tonnage of surplus fish sold at a loss on any one day has been five tons. It is estimated that with the proposed motor program and increased use of nylon nets, the surplus would rise to between ten and thirteen tons. The room would also serve as a storage place for ice needed to ship fish during these months. However, a cost-effectiveness study should be undertaken before launching this operation.

21. There is functional overlapping and redundant staffing among the three provincial fishing agencies in Nha Trang, viz.: the trade union, the Fisheries Service, and the cooperative. Fishermen pay membership fees in two of these organizations, and all three vie for the distribution of the few government-purchased motors and nets as they became available. All three agencies are understaffed and lack operating funds. It is recommended that the three agencies be amalgamated under the aegis of the cooperative. This would serve three important purposes: it would increase the prestige and importance of the cooperative, it would centralize the various related fishing activities, it would help solve the perennial staffing problem in each agency.

22. There is also a need to reduce the number of fishing cooperatives in an effort to pool limited resources of funds and personnel, thereby enhancing the probability of success for those cooperatives that remain.

23. The little "research" carried out is assigned to untrained staff members on an *ad hoc, post facto* basis. Preproject research can assist the technician and provincial staff member in determining the character of the social milieu in which he is planning to work. Too often the authorities initiate projects without fully

understanding the socioeconomic environment and only later request help in determining what went wrong. The newly trained research cadre should be assigned on a permanent basis, and only when not actively engaged in research and its tangential aspects should they be expected to perform other administrative functions. This will offer continuity and consistency to the field work, not to mention the time saved in establishing rapport with the respondents.

24. The objective of this exercise is to design a successful pilot project which will eventually inspire emulation throughout the fishing areas of Vietnam. Inasmuch as these recommendations are by no means infallible, and unpredictable events may occur, it is recommended that a team from the Cooperative Research and Training Center in Saigon be sent to the pilot project periodically for the purpose of evaluating progress made and assessing the nature of problems encountered. This would provide the authorities in Saigon with timely information permitting them to remedy the situation post haste.

25. For every project discussed and agreed upon with the fishermen, the cooperative should be prepared to take immediate action. The fisherman's threshold of patience is low. Once he loses faith in the project, he loses interest, and this may well impede acceptance of subsequent project proposals.

Conclusions

The success of the Culao pilot project depended upon a set of interrelated factors. These ranged from the changing of those commonly held values and preconceived notions maintained by the vast majority of fishermen, to prejudices held by the district and provincial cooperative chiefs, on to the authorities in Saigon.

It was clear that an established fishing cooperative could be only as successful as the Vietnamese government and its representative, the Provincial Governor, wished it to be; only as successful as the manager of the cooperative was capable of making it through his ability and dedication; only as successful as the degree of enlightenment and allegiance of its current and potential members.

In terms of financial support, it seemed advisable to inquire into the short-term and long-term objectives of USAID for Vietnam. Should the "buy American" policy have been waived for Vietnam? How sincere was the desire of the Vietnamese government to help the fishermen? For example, should Japanese reparation money have been spent importing miscellaneous luxury items (as was the case) or could it better have been spent on motors, nylon nets, and loans to fishermen? There was also the critical issue of whether or not the welfare of the money-lenders, many of whom were high-level government officials, would be favored over that of the borrowers. Was it realistic to expect to recover money loaned at 12-per-cent interest per annum when the fishermen bore outstanding debts carrying interest rates of 60 per cent? Should the prices for fish paid by the voting consumer in the urban areas have been given greater consideration than prices paid to the fishermen? Was there any utility in supplying nylon nets and motors if the price offered for the additional fish caught was inadequate to allow payments toward the added capital expenditure?

An all-inclusive approach to the many questions and problems raised in this report was badly needed. Therefore, it was decided to recommend that all efforts be concentrated upon one pilot project, rather than to disperse limited resources ambitiously over too wide an area.

The success fo the Culao Cooperative depended upon mutual accord on both aims and methods. Success depended upon whether or not the authorities were sufficiently far-sighted to envision the necessity of helping the majority rather than a minority of their countrymen. It depended upon a mutually accepted set of values, a common philosophy, and a common goal. Whenever, in the march toward the attainment of this goal, opposition or conflict of interests were encountered, these obstacles would have to be removed and the problems resolved as rapidly as possible.

Bureaucratic delays created weaknesses throughout the structure and usually implied hypocrisy rather than inefficiency.

It was recommended, therefore, that in the best interests of the local development and local security program, a meeting be held of all interested Vietnamese government and USAID officials and representatives of private philanthropic organizations operating in Vietnam. For, unless all those concerned could reach an agreement on objectives and the most expedient means of obtaining them, there was little hope that the pilot project would become a success, or, once successful, would remain so. The National Liberation Front was not dallying and already was suspected of having members operating within Culao.

Postscript

Several meetings were held in Saigon and attended by representatives from CARE, Asia Foundation, the National Credit Bank, and the various departments in the Ministry of Agriculture, as well as the agriculture division of USAID. The pilot project was approved unanimously. However, disagreement arose concerning details of priorities and the project never came to fruition.

By 1966, the war had escalated to the point where the Culao Cooperative had virtually become defunct and the Cooperative Research and Training Center in Saigon was appropriated by USAID for office space.

10. In the Wake of Mechanization: Sago and Society in Sarawak

H. S. MORRIS

In the past half century no anthropologists working among people who have begun to feel the pressures of the industrial world on traditional culture have been wholly able to avoid discomfort at what they have observed. Not all have troubled to examine the exact conditions which have produced the situation, and of those who have done so few have recorded it with the perception and elegance that Lauriston Sharp brought to his analysis of the early stages of the disintegration of Yir Yiront culture in northern Australia. "The steel axe," he wrote, "is not only replacing the stone axe physically, but is hacking at the supports of the entire cultural system" (Sharp 1952). The Melanau of Sarawak were never as simple in their technology and handling of a very different environment as the Yir Yiront, but in the last hundred years the same kind of pressure has hacked away their cultural system until today they are in danger of becoming landless peasants in a social environment that offers them little chance of gaining an adequate livelihood. Few, if any, understand how in the course of three generations their culture has passed from subsistence agriculture into a cash economy in which most of their traditional values appear to have no relevance.

The Melanau today are a culturally diverse people living on the northwest coast of Borneo on the Rejang River and the coastal areas that stretch from its mouth to the northeast as far as Miri. Most speak closely related languages, not all of which are mutually intelligible. Traditionally they practiced shifting cultivation and had similar types of social organization. In the census of 1960 they numbered 44,661, of whom 31,770 were Muslim, and about 10,000 pagan. The coastal area, in which most of them live, is a low-lying and dense swampy jungle on poor soil that extends ten to twenty miles inland. Across this swampy ground slow-flowing rivers meander to the North China Sea. The sago palm flourishes in the poor soil, but, except on the slightly raised river banks, rice and other crops do not grow well.

In 1947 the Melanau of the Oya River numbered 6,852 and inhabited some dozen villages built on the banks of the river. Upstream, beyond the swampy area, live the Iban, who cultivate hill rice by shifting cultivation. According to legend these hills were once inhabited by the Melanau, but they had already moved down into the swamps before the arrival of the Iban from west of the Rejang in the middle of the last century. It is reasonably clear, too, that from very early times some of the Melanau had lived downstream, and had evolved a subsistence economy based on the cultivation of sago and dry rice grown on the river banks. Today only upstream villages grow the sago palm as a cash crop; those nearer the coast fish and grow rubber. Most of the pagans live in the upriver villages, and it is from them that the material in this paper is principally taken.

Traditional Social Organization

A Melanau village today forms a line of small rectangular wood and thatch houses on piles along both banks of the river. It usually stands on the site of a former longhouse settlement. Villages vary in size from 200 to 1,000 inhabitants and are separated from one another by three or four miles on the river, which is still the only practical route for travel. The swamp jungle on each side of it is dense and often dangerous, and for this reason the people of the different rivers have always tended to be culturally and politically distinct.

The earlier villages consisted of one or at most two longhouses.

These were massively built fortresses, often thirty feet above-ground, and situated at the confluence of a strategically important tributary stream and the main river. Each house was politically independent within its own territory, and was frequently on terms of active hostility with its Melanau neighbors and the Iban invaders upstream. The investment of labor and capital in the longhouses was so great that they were rarely moved or completely rebuilt. When raiding was suppressed under Charles Brooke's rule in the latter part of the last century, and the houses became overcrowded, the people simply abandoned them and built separate dwellings on the edge of the river.

Although physically one structure, a longhouse was made up of separately built apartments, each owned and inhabited by one married couple and perhaps one married child. Longhouses, constructed in the form of a row of terrace houses with a common covered verandah like a gallery in front and behind, might house 200 or more people. Much of the village life and many ceremonial activities took place on the front verandah, which was fifteen to twenty feet wide and up to three or four hundred feet long. When the houses were abandoned no central meeting place replaced the verandah, and much of the culture, especially the performance of communal ceremonies, fell into disuse because the newer houses were small.

In longhouse days the political control of a village was in the hands of a small group of aristocratic elders (a-nyat), whose families usually owned the central apartments, and who were the descendants of the village founders. On each side of this core were apartments owned by freemen (a-bumi), and at each end of the house were the apartments of freed slaves (a-dipan). Most slaves were owned by aristocrats (a-mantri). An elaborate set of customary rules (adat) regulated the behavior of the ranks to one another and most other aspects of social life. The adat, one of the community's most valued possessions, was in the custody of the aristocratic elders. No single elder was superior to the others, though he might have special knowledge that fitted him for particular tasks. A man with unusual abilities in war would be put in charge of raids, and another with knowledge of rituals might assume leadership on appropriate occasions. But leadership of this kind was not usually formalized as a permanent office, and there were no single political chiefs who ruled villages as of personal right.

Each household was economically independent. The members grew its rice and other crops and were primarily responsible for their own physical and supernatural safety and prosperity. There was, generally speaking, little specialized division of labor and a household could normally supply its own needs. Matters which affected other people in the longhouse either fell into the sphere of the *adat,* and were therefore regulated by the elders, or, if they were concerned with the supernatural, were in the hands of ritual experts, who might or might not be aristocrats.

Traditional Melanau society in the Oya River made use of three overlapping criteria in organizing social life. The first was that of local grouping; the second was that of kinship; and the third was that of hereditary rank. A Melanau thought of himself in each of these social dimensions. He was closely identified with a particular locality, especially with one longhouse whose inhabitants were thought to be, and often were, peculiar and unique in matters of dialect and custom. As an individual, a man or woman was the focal point of a kindred with whom he shared a wide range of social and economic interests regulated by principles of bilateral descent. Lastly, he had by virtue of birth a rank status. In any context the behavior of one man towards another was largely determined by the fact that the two men were neighbors or strangers, kinsmen or not, of equal or different rank. Within the social order his behavior was regulated by the *adat;* within the symbolic order similar principles governed his ritual behavior (Morris 1953).

The Sago Industry

According to folk history the Melanau have always eaten sago and cultivated it in the swamp areas for a very long time, though, as in the past, they regard rice, not sago, as their staple food. Their early ancestors, they say, felled a palm in the jungle, stripped the bark, and after making holes in the trunk pounded the pith to shreds by using wooden poles. The pith was then taken back to the village and washed in fine woven baskets so that the sago flour, suspended in the water, was caught in a canoe or trough. The process used in the last century was much the same in essentials. The felled palm was floated to the long-house and cut into logs. These were stripped of bark and placed in a long trough fixed to the house rafters. Men sat on a bench beside the trough and chipped the pith to shreds (*repo*), using an adze (*palou*) tipped with a "blade" of hard wood. The pith, which was coarse in texture, was then flailed on the longhouse verandah before being taken down to a trampling platform (*jagan*) at the edge of the river. The pith was placed on a finely woven mat on the slats of the platform above a wooden trough. Water was added to the pile of pith and the worker trampled the wet mixture so that the sago flour, suspended in the water, passed into the trough below. When the flour had settled, the clear water was drained away, and the wet flour (*lemantak*) was taken out and spread on mats to dry in the sun. More usually the wet flour was further washed in a tub of water and dried. The refined flour (*tepong*) was now ready for use, either for baking into a kind of biscuit or for export. Flour appears to have been exported from the Melanau coastal district at least since the eighteenth century, and probably earlier. Stories are told of aristocratically organized expeditions setting sail for Brunei, Pontianak, and even Johore for the purchase of brassware and ceramics.

The unsettled conditions of life in Sarawak before the Brookes imposed peace meant that the production of sago was largely an aristocratic enterprise. As far as living memory goes sago gardens appear to have been individually owned and there seem never to have been rules forbidding a middle-class man or even a freed slave from making himself a new garden in the jungle, but to work alone outside the village was dangerous. Only aristocrats were able to mobilize the protection needed by the workers.

When James Brooke became Rajah of Sarawak in 1841, the export of wet sago flour from the Mukah and the Oya rivers to Kuching for refinement and export to Singapore and the world market soon became an important industry. Indeed, a large part of the Sarawak government's revenue came from it. It was this fact as much as the hostility of local rulers and the help they gave to what the Rajah called pirates that led in 1861 to the annexation of the coastal district by the Kuching government.

Before the annexation merchants from Kuching were regularly hindered in buying wet flour and the factories in Sarawak were not able to refine sufficient quantities to operate profitably. After annexation Malay-speaking middlemen settled in the area. They bought *lemantak* and stored it in local warehouses (sometimes for weeks) until sailing vessels arrived from Kuching to take it away. The long storage of the *lemantak* evidently caused it to deteriorate sufficiently to affect the salability of the flour produced from it. Some dealers today believe that unless *lemantak* is immediately refined poor quality flour is produced. Chinese middlemen soon joined the Malay settlers; and in the years before 1900 the Melanau, in response to the expanding trade with Kuching, the government's increasing need of revenue, and their own growing reliance upon consumer goods brought in by the middlemen, were obliged to transform the whole of their social life and economy.

By 1900 they had practically abandoned longhouse life, and instead of the relative independence and safety of a subsistence economy, they now relied almost exclusively on the sale of one cash crop which was subject to fluctuations of price on the international market. They had also come to depend on middlemen to sell their crop and bring them the necessities of life. In certain respects the process was deleterious to the life of the Melanau and had been allowed to go forward unchecked by the administration, whose principal concern with the area was the maintenance of the steady revenue on which its existence depended.

The social and economic consequences of this process have continued unchecked down to the present day. In exchange for expanding the production of sago and providing Kuching with revenue, the Melanau were protected from most of the raids of the Iban marauders and the depredations of pirates. But the administration was thin on the ground, and as long as the supplies of sago were regularly and peacefully shipped from Mukah and Oya, it was assumed that all was well. Administrative officers interfered as little as they could in the economic affairs of the villages. The main exceptions were to make rules for the use of straining cloths between the trampling platform and the trough to improve the quality of the wet sago. The second exception was an attempt to regulate the activities of the Chinese traders who came into the district in large numbers. The attempt was not so much to regulate their economic affairs as to restrain the hostility which their commercial outlook provoked among the Melanau. After several incidents, all Chinese traders were compelled to live in lines of shops at specified bazaars and not in the longhouses or the newer types of village that were developing. In spite of the regulations, Chinese factories were eventually permitted to refine the wet sago outside most villages. The Melanau themselves found the inconvenience of paddling several miles up or down river to sell their wet flour greater than their dislike of the foreigners. During the whole period the slow deterioration of Melanau life went unobserved or at any rate unnoted.

Cultivation and Land

Sago flour is produced from a palm (*metroxylon sagus*) which grows, as observed earlier, well on the swampy and rather poor peaty soil characteristic of the coastal district. It is a perennial which, once planted and properly tended, does not need renewal. Nevertheless, certain types of soil, conditions of drainage, and methods of cultivation appear to favor its growth and yield of flour. Apart from the practical rules of horticulture employed by the Melanau themselves, there is no systematic body of knowledge about these matters.

Sago gardens are still individually owned, as in former days, but are now surveyed and registered by the administration. Only a Melanau may own sago land, and the Chinese middlemen, who have completely displaced the earlier Malay arrivals, can acquire gardens only with great difficulty. In the villages which cultivate the palm, land is evenly distributed among men and women (Morris 1953).

Production of Wet Flour

Until very recently the production of sago flour was organized as a cottage industry. In a household both husband and wife might own sago gardens, but it was the man who tended them, felled the mature palms, and prepared them for the woman to extract the wet flour. Having felled the palm, he cut it into conveniently sized logs and brought them to the village, where he stripped the bark and split the logs for reducing the pith in them to a coarse sawdust (*repo*). Early in this century the use of the adze and the flail was given up, and a nail-studded plank, used like a saw, was adopted instead. After 1945 this plank was replaced by a nail-studded wheel driven by an engine at refining mills just outside the villages, but the rasped pith was still brought back to the household for the women to process. The introduction of power-driven rasping greatly speeded production and allowed the industry to expand after the war in response to the world demand for cheap industrial starch. It also introduced for the first time the real danger of overfelling the sago crop. This did not in fact occur because of the accumulation of palms unfelled during the war, and because the market for Sarawak flour collapsed before the crop was exhausted.

When the pith of the palm had been reduced to sawdust the women processed it by mixing it with water and trampling it on a mat to express the starch from the woody part of the pith in the same way as it had always been done for the past century. When all the starch was expressed from the pith, the woody remainder was thrown into the river. The effectiveness of the process depended on the fineness of the weave of the mat, the use of a straining cloth, and the quality of the water used. In the Mukah and the Oya rivers the water is peat-stained and this is said to affect adversely the quality of the dry flour (*tepong*) produced.

Refining of Sago Flour

When the trough was full of *lemantak* a middleman, always Chinese and usually the owner or employee of a refining factory, came and bought it at a price based on the market quotations radioed from Singapore. The cash from the sale was divided in equal parts among the owner of the palms and the man and the woman who had produced the flour. All, even if they were husband and wife, took independent charge of their own shares.

In order to assure himself a regular supply of wet sago the Chinese dealer generally ran a small retail business in conjunction with his sago refinery. By retailing consumer goods on credit he bound a number of producing households to his factory by their need to pay for goods which they had received. As a rule he was careful never to clear the account completely at any sale of wet flour, so that if the family did not begin to work again after a reasonable rest he could bring pressure to bear on them by withholding further credit. In spite of a belief to the contrary held by the Melanau and the administration, the system produced little hardship. The Chinese dealers, because foreigners were not allowed to own sago land, could not convert a debt into land, and there was therefore no temptation for them to allow extravagant credit. The giving of it was simply a device needed to keep the workers on the job in order that a dealer, by withholding credit if necessary, could be sure of a steady supply of *lemantak*. The export market required regular and predictable quantities of the final flour (*tepong*), which he himself refined.

By 1950 the preparation of flour from wet sago was a Chinese monopoly. A small factory with vats for washing and straining the *lemantak* and a mat-covered open space for drying and bagging the *tepong* in the sun was all the equipment needed. A few Melanau laborers, often children, were hired. Their number and kind, Melanau or Chinese, depended on the size of the enterprise; but wages were low and relatively few employees were needed, so that openings for villagers as wage laborers were limited. In addition, the owner of a refinery required sufficient capital to stock and run his retail business. The conditions under which the factory operated were primitive, inefficient, and dirty. The profits came from keeping costs low and not troubling to produce flour of good quality.

The capital needed to open and run such an enterprise was not great, though it was beyond the resources and experience of most Melanau. It was usually beyond the resources of most local Chinese entrepreneurs as well, and they relied on bigger merchants in neighboring settlements and towns for capital loans and regular credit in the form of consumer goods. The merchants in the towns might not be the ultimate exporters of the sago flour and were themselves often tied to the exporters, a very limited number of firms, in similar relationships of credit. This "ladder of indebtedness" was an integral part of the structure of Chinese society and closely related to its internal political functioning, and suggestions for modifying any part of it, such as the sago industry, were likely to be resisted by every possible means (Tien 1953).

The price of Sarawak sago flour fell steeply in the middle of the 1950's, and the industry experienced a severe slump. The annual tonnage of flour exported declined from 38,247 in 1950 to 9,871 in 1955. During the same period the refiners began to introduce locally made machinery which allowed them to process the rasped sago pith into wet flour in their own factories. This innovation removed a principal source of Melanau income and had the effect of concentrating the whole process of manufacturing sago flour in a limited number of refineries which required very little labor for their operation. The *lemantak* produced by machinery was in no way superior to that manufactured by the older method and was frequently even dirtier; but the work was quicker, a little cheaper, and much less troublesome to the refiners. If the profits of the refiner's retail business are also taken into account, it is even doubtful that the new process brought him real monetary gain. By the middle of 1967 almost the entire cottage industry which had supported the Melanau population was gone; most of them were underemployed and harmful social effects were beginning to appear. In particular refiners now refused to buy *lemantak* from the trampling platforms, and most of the women were therefore without the employment which until then had filled their days. More serious was the fact that they were now without the regular income which had given them independence from and equality with the men.

For nearly a century, under pressures of which the Melanau were unaware and which were tacitly approved by the government, the people of the coastal district had come to rely on a single cash crop. Technical changes and a slow reorganization of the handling of the product had gradually reduced their share in the industry, and when this last innovation suddenly cut off one of their principal sources of income, they were bound to suffer. It was no longer possible to return to a subsistence economy. The full effects of the change have not yet shown themselves because the refiners do not yet own many sago gardens and the Melanau still do. But most Melanau have insufficient land to support themselves without work, and a minority own no sago gardens at all. Although a refiner will no longer buy wet sago from the trampling platforms, he still depends upon the owners of gardens to sell him palms and still requires men to fell and transport them to the factory. A certain number are therefore able to earn some cash for essentials such as clothing, tools, rice, dry and salt fish, schooling for their children, and so on, but it is an irregular and very uncertain income. Sago, it is worth reiterating, has never been eaten as a staple food except in times of hardship and is nutritionally deficient. Furthermore, the labor market is limited, and families without active men are beginning to suffer. It can only be a question of time, unless the process is checked, before sago gardens are sold in quantity to refiners or a few rich Melanau who are in the earliest stages of becoming large-scale landlords. The result would be an industry based on plantations in the hands of a few people, mostly factory owners. The Melanau population would then be reduced to a landless peasantry with very few ways of earning a living.

Other Types of Work Open to the Melanau

The Lumber Industry

The effects of the new economic and social situation in the sago industry have been partly disguised by new openings for men as lumber workers in the swamp forests of the coastal areas; but this work is no real substitute for the sago industry, for it is organized in such a way that the money which comes from it into the villages is relatively very small. In addition, the cash which does come in is mainly in the hands of young men and not the older heads of families.

An area of forest is granted, usually to a Chinese entrepreneur, for the extraction of certain types of timber under the supervision of the Forestry Department. The entrepreneur in turn demarcates the area into blocks, and grants one or more of these to a gang leader whose responsibility it is to recruit men for felling the timber. At all stages the entrepreneur deals only with the gang leader, who undertakes work according to his estimate of the size of the gang he can recruit, the amount of fellable timber in the block, and the length of time he can hold together his group of workmen. The entrepreneur makes him an advance in cash and he returns to his village to recruit men. He naturally prefers the young and strong without ties to make them want to return home quickly, but he may not be able to build up a whole gang of such men. He makes cash advances for the maintenance of dependents during the men's absence, and these are deducted from the final share in the gang's profits.

The success of the group's work depends on the organizational ability of the leader and on his judgment in selecting men. If he recruits too many, the profits will not be worthwhile; if he has too few he will fail in his contract. The block of forest allocated to him may be short of fellable timber. He is responsible for all dealings with the company on behalf of his gang; he keeps a record of the timber they have felled and receives and divides the money finally paid for the work. He may also buy food and other consumer goods collectively for his men at the company's shop, though the more usual custom is for each man to be issued a book by the store and to buy his own necessities on credit. These books are written in Chinese and therefore cannot be checked by their holders, who if they are literate read only the Roman script. If a gang leader is dishonest or his judgment faulty at any stage, if his education is insufficient to keep clear records, or if he is not able to stand up to the clerks of the timber company, then the whole gang suffers and is in practice without redress. The rewards of the work are variable, but never very great. A man usually takes an advance of $30 to $50, and after six to eight weeks away from the village may return with anything from $70 to $200. He can return with much less. If his dependents have not been able to manage on the money he left, they may have endured considerable hardship, because retailers, without the security of the former regular sales of wet sago, are no longer willing to extend household credit.

The organization of this industry is, of course, finally conditioned by the government's overriding need to have the timber extracted and exported as cheaply as possible. As much as 5 to 10 per cent of the revenue now depends upon it. In order to achieve this end it is necessary to tempt entrepreneurs with favorable terms, for in the context of local finance the capital invested is very large, and the risks are considerable. It was feared, probably without real foundation, that unless the rewards were correspondingly high the timber might remain unfelled or the government might have to enter the business itself. Even so the share of the total profits received by the workers is disproportionately low, and they have little protection in the form of a basic wage, effective inspection of working conditions, company shops, or prices.

Rice Growing

Various alternatives to replace sago in the economy of the Melanau have been suggested and partly implemented by the government. Any diversification is clearly good. In the lower reaches of the Oya and the Mukah rivers rice-growing schemes have been inaugurated and could profitably be extended; but to transform the district into an extensive rice-growing area, even if the soil permitted it, would require very large capital investment and most careful consideration of the economic and social consequences.

Coconut Growing

It has also been suggested that coconuts, planted on a large scale and combined with small factories for processing, should replace sago as the main crop of the district. It is worth noting that the coconut industry, like the sago industry, has always been subject to booms and slumps; but as a supplement to and diversification of the present economy, the scheme undoubtedly has merit. If, on the other hand, it is intended to displace sago and make Melanau once again dependent on a single cash crop, then it has less to recommend it.

Work as Migrant Laborers

The market for migrant labor in the lumber industry has already produced a few of the undesirable social consequences familiar in African countries where entire rural districts have been reduced to a condition close to disaster by the prolonged absence of large numbers of young men. Nothing on this scale is yet observable in the Melanau coastal areas, and it is clear that the government of Sarawak is aware of the dangers. A scheme for establishing a palm-oil industry in Sabah, for example, requires labor, and the government of Sarawak has been at pains to persuade whole families of Melanau, not just individual laborers, to emigrate on most favorable terms. The response has been negligible. This is perhaps not surprising in the light of Melanau history. For more than a century they endured the control first of Malays from Brunei, and then of the British; for several decades they were attacked by the Iban and learned to live with them as neighbors; and finally they saw their living and their fortunes come to depend on the good will of Chinese arrivals. Notwithstanding all this they remain Melanau, speaking their own language, and still living in the villages that their ancestors founded many generations ago. They can see no reason why they should leave their rivers and their homes to other people. They will have to become much poorer than they yet are before they can be persuaded to migrate in numbers.

Fishing

Fishing has always been one of the means of livelihood open to the Melanau, but their methods are primitive and not very productive, and are open only to those villages near the seacoast. In its present form fishing cannot significantly fill the need for either food or cash. Although the South China Sea is one of the richest fishing grounds in the world and the potential market for fish in Southeast Asia immense, no full attempt to develop this resource has been made in Sarawak; there is not even a department of fisheries in the administration.

All these schemes and any others that can be devised are highly desirable as means of diversifying the economy, and they could do much to mitigate the growing poverty of the sago-growing areas. But the real problems of the sago industry itself would remain. It is still, in spite of present conditions, a national capital asset of great value, and it would be unwise—economically, politically, and socially—simply to write it off. The introduction of alternative means of livelihood should obviously be accompanied by a vigorous redevelopment of the sago industry, but before discussing some of the suggestions for doing this that have been advanced at different times it is convenient to summarize here the social and economic results of what has occurred in the past.

The Social Consequences of the Present Situation

The undesirable consequences of recent slumps in the price of sago and of the latest technical and economic changes, most of which have already been mentioned, fall under seven heads.

1. With the concentration in a few privately owned factories of all stages in refining sago flour, the principal source of income for the Melanau has been removed.

2. A large number of formerly independent self-employed peasants has therefore had to look for work as wage laborers hired irregularly by refineries or as migrant laborers in the lumber industry.

3. The problems of migrant labor and chronic underemployment, familiar in more extreme forms in Central and South Africa, are as yet only incipient, but there is evidence already of neglected and broken families and potential political unrest.

4. The complete removal of the women's main occupation and their traditional independence, combined with an almost total lack of alternative employment, has forced them and their children to rely wholly on the husbands' seriously impaired earning powers. This situation, to which neither the men nor the women are accustomed, leads to distress and friction and still further disruption of Melanau society.

5. Sago refineries employ only a small number of women, and these have no domestic responsibilities that demand their presence at or near their homes. They also employ an even smaller number of men. Child labor is adequate and often cheaper.

6. The refusal of the owners of the refining factories and retail businesses to buy wet sago from the trampling platforms has

meant that almost all domestic credit facilities have been with-drawn from Melanau households. A family without sago gardens in which there are mature trees or one whose men are unable to find work now suffers hardships never previously known.

7. Owners of refineries safeguard their supplies by purchasing palms before they are mature, and a Melanau with few trees to sell may find it difficult to obtain a fair price from a factory owner, who is in a position to beat him down. Moreover, the only method now open to a Melanau of raising a large sum of money for some necessary purpose is to sell his whole crop, often several years ahead. Formerly he could have obtained the money on credit against the regular sale of wet sago. He can, of course, and frequently does sell a garden to obtain the needed cash; but if the present trend continues, the area is likely to become one of refineries and associated plantations. A few Melanau might be employed in cultivating the plantations and felling the palms, but even this is not certain. The owners of refineries are Chinese, and unemployment in their own communities in the coastal and adja-cent districts is high. Judged only in economic terms these de-velopments might be considered as improvements which would ultimately add to the efficiency of the industry, but a profit-and-loss account which neglects social factors does not always con-tribute to efficiency. It is more likely to lead to disaster. Racial tensions in Sarawak are already sufficiently inflamed to make any additional irritations undesirable.

The Economic Consequences of the Present Situation

Recent changes in the economic organization of the industry have occurred (1) at the level of primary production, and (2) at the level of international marketing.

Primary Production

As we have seen, the most significant recent change here is in the development of machines for processing raw sago (*lemantak*) from the rasped pith of the palm (*repo*). These machines are crude and inefficient, and the quality of flour produced by them is, if anything, poorer than that which came from the trampling platforms. Little care is taken in their use, and impurities of all kinds, including the novel one of machine oil, frequently find a way into the flour. A machine, it is said, can process the palms more quickly than a woman, but since work is limited in the end by the supply of palms available at any one time, this fact may be less important than it first appears.

Sarawak flour has always had a bad reputation for being dirty, and in the past the blame has usually been put on the quality of water used in refining or the conditions of trampling, but the introduction of machine-processed wet sago has not produced flour of any better quality. There is no reason why it should, because, given reasonable care in the early stages, quality depends on subsequent refining, and because it has always been possible to sell Sarawak flour, though at a lower price than that of better quality produced elsewhere. Local refineries have consequently not thought it worth their while to make flour of the same quality as that produced in Singapore or to bother about the industry's reputation. What they were able to sell gave their sector of the industry sufficient profit, and they were little concerned with the welfare of the Melanau peasants. Sago has been, and still is, regarded by nearly everybody except the Melanau more as an extractive industry than as a permanent asset that requires careful management and conservation.

The concentration of refining sago flour in factories has probably reduced costs slightly: it certainly makes the management of the factories easier, and it could, in the right circumstances, ensure a better final product. The ultimate reasons for the poor quality of Sarawak sago flour are to be found, not in technology, but in the structure of the refining and marketing sections of the industry. In the washing, drying, bagging, and rebagging of the flour, impurities are not removed and may even be inserted; the reasons for this lie in the need for keeping an unnecessarily large number of middlemen solvent. Every stage between production and export increases the risk of contamination and reduces the economic efficiency of the industry.

Marketing

In 1950 there were about a dozen sizable firms which under license exported sago flour from Sarawak. Most of it went to Singapore for re-export to Britain and Europe. The distance of these markets and the heavy cost of freight made the flour competitive as a source of cheap starch for the food and textile industries only if its quality was reasonably good or if it was noticeably cheaper than other sources of starch. Such a concentration on a distant and narrow market also meant that any slight political or economic changes in the purchasing country could have the most serious consequences in Sarawak. In 1950 a large proportion of Sarawak flour was bought by one food-producing firm in Britain which was subsequently taken over by an American enterprise closely allied to maize-growing interests. Although sago flour has chemical and physical properties which will always make it preferable to other types of starch in the production of some kinds of food, this firm nevertheless turned to maize flour, and the Sarawak sago industry was almost ruined. The private firms which the government had permitted to handle the marketing of a commodity that produced between 2 and 10 percent of the revenue had apparently been content to watch the slow contraction of their traditional markets, and had made no serious earlier attempts to open new and diverse outlets in food and textile industries nearer home.

At present only three firms are significantly concerned in exporting sago. When the market for Sarawak flour collapsed, one of these firms with immense difficulty found new purchasers in Japan who manufactured a type of foodstuff in great demand in Southeast Asia and who have subsequently opened factories in Singapore and Malaya. These Japanese manufacturers had earlier made an investigation into the possibility of opening a refining factory in Sarawak in order to be sure of obtaining a reliable and uniform flour. They met with hostility from the local refiners and exporters, and little encouragement from the government. The firm therefore bought expensive and up-to-date equipment from America and established a refinery in Japan. They would have liked to import dried *lemantak,* as prepared by the Melanau, but eventually agreed to buy the poorest and cheapest quality of refined flour that the industry in Sarawak was willing to export. The compromise was just profitable enough to keep the refining and exporting sections of the industry alive, but it reduced the Melanau peasants to near poverty. The combination of new machinery and a new trade agreement was sufficient to preserve the Chinese in the district, but not the Melanau.

By 1963 the annual export of sago flour from Sarawak had once more reached its approximate maximum of 30,000 tons annually. At the beginning of 1964 and for some time afterward the price of sago rose considerably and showed no immediate signs of dropping. The rise was caused by the interruption of supplies from Indonesia, which had annually exported about the same quantity of sago to Singapore as is produced in Sarawak. It is worth noting that unlike the Sarawak sago this Indonesian sago had always been exported in the crude form. There is no doubt that the Singapore refineries would be very willing to import *lemantak* from Sarawak too; but although this might have the effect of eliminating some of the steps in the ladder of indebtedness previously referred to, there is no certainty that this would happen, and local opinion in Sarawak doubted the wisdom of allowing one of its industries to be treated solely as a source of raw material for an industrially developed area in another state.

Conclusions

The interests of a student of social and cultural change do not necessarily lead him to look beyond the social and cultural correlates in a case history of this kind. His interest is largely exhausted when he has understood the system and the way in which it is altering. But in the role of applied anthropologist his interests are close to those of politicians and administrative officials, who are concerned to control and guide the direction of change in the light of their own particular sets of values. Although the interests of the anthropologist and the official may partly coincide at this point, nevertheless the anthropologist, who is often outside the immediate local system that he is studying and the official system in which it is set, may find that his values do not correspond with those of the politicians and the officials who seek his advice.

Until the end of World War II the Sarawak government was little concerned to control the sago industry or to take active measures to promote the welfare of the Melanau people. In the years that followed the war officials were anxious to found schools and set up institutions of local government. In doing this they wished, if possible, to build on existing institutions and to find local money for the new bodies to handle. In this task the officials consulted a number of outsiders as well as officials in the government of Sarawak. Several of those consulted pointed out that a careful regulation of the sago industry was essential to the stability of the area; but it was not until the industry was ruined and armed hostility across the borders with Indonesia caused political anxiety about the loyalties of some of both of the Chinese and Muslim inhabitants of the area that serious thought was given to the condition of the whole district and its resources, including the sago industry.

In Kuching, the state capital, there were a number of views on the most useful and practical way of handling what was now seen as the problem of the sago-producing area. Probably the most widespread opinion was that there was in fact no problem except the difficulty of adjustment by peasants to the modern world, and that the matter would solve itself, though while it was doing so a careful watch might be needed on the political loyalty of the people. Another view was that the difficulties of the sago industry could best be solved by writing it off. In economic terms the industry was inefficient, and social efficiency, considered by yet other people as an important item in the account, was not measurable and therefore, in the view of those who held this opinion, could not be seriously taken into account. Most governments, of course, are aware that views as limited as both these cannot always been entertained, and many officials in Sarawak were aware that to write off the sago industry might be politically unwise for several reasons.

Many of those who believed that the problems of the sago industry would solve themselves held this opinion because they were convinced that, if the industry were to survive at all, it could only do so as a privately owned factory and plantation industry. Such a development was not only economically desirable, it was also inevitable, though it could be delayed by official interference. Those of this view, who thought that there might be social and political dangers in the process, suggested that some of the measures of diversification of the local economy described earlier would be sufficient to ease the transition of the Melanau people into the modern world.

There was a third body of opinion which held that the process of unguided change might be politically too dangerous and that the sago industry was too valuable a national asset to discard or neglect. Out of many discussions with proponents of these different views came various suggestions, some of which were implemented by the government. At least two anthropological reports formed part of the discussion, though it is impossible to say how far they influenced official decisions. The suggestions that were made at different times were roughly of two kinds: recommendations at the national and at the local levels.

Recommendations at the National Level

Marketing

The international marketing of Sarawak sago flour had fallen into the hands of two or three private firms, and although they handled their responsibilities with some sense of public duty, a state of affairs of this kind was felt by some to be inherently undesirable. In the political context of contemporary Southeast Asia it laid the government open to the charge of permitting monopoly capitalism and all the connotations that go with the term. In the economic sphere it made it harder for the government to be sure that national resources were being well used, and to perform its proper functions in safeguarding the welfare of the smaller workers in the industry. However public-spirited a trading organization may be, its ultimate aim must be the making of cash profits and not public welfare. In its marketing arrangements it therefore necessarily looks for the easiest market to operate. Once having secured it, a private enterprise tends to turn its attention to its other interests, and only when a crisis arises does it review its long-term policy in a wider context, perhaps with regret that it did not disperse its contracts more widely when dispersal was still possible. A margin of profit which is sufficient for a few firms to continue in business may not in fact be beneficial to the industry as a whole, but because of their control they are able to impose their own terms on dependent businesses. In the view of some of those involved in the discussions it is seldom wise for a government to permit effective control of important resources to pass out of its hands in this way.

One recommendation put forward for the consideration of the government was that it should establish a national sago board on the lines of similar organizations in other countries whose governments had faced problems in the production and disposal of a primary product of national importance. As the sago industry alone was not likely to be able to support such a board, and as the rubber and pepper industries also had closely related problems it was suggested that a national joint-marketing board might be set up.

Such a national marketing board, it was argued, would be able to keep the state of an industry under continual review in the light of political and social, as well as purely economic, developments. If adequately based it would also be able to maintain and manage a floating fund to regulate the internal price of the product in periods of boom and slump alike. Indeed, such a fund would be necessary if the board were to regulate the industry for the benefit of the country as a whole. By a system of licenses the board would be able to keep under constant review the ultimate destinations of the crops it handled. Within Sarawak it would also provide a means of modifying the system of middlemen whose numbers had grown too large for the industry to carry without sacrificing the interests of the Melanau growers of sago. In place of the many middlemen a few centralized refining and collecting depots would probably save enough to go some way towards paying the expenses of the board. A national marketing board, it was argued, would have more incentive than most private firms to keep national marketing policy under constant review. In could insist on contracts for the sale of sago being placed widely and could make serious and sustained efforts to open new markets in the rapidly developing industries of Asia, rather than in the distant marginal markets of established industry in Europe and North America.

Quality of Sago Flour

In spite of the many official and private efforts that had been made over the previous seventy-five years to control the quality of Sarawak sago flour, it was still the poorest on the international market. There were no technical reasons why it should not be as clean and reliable a product as that made in Singapore or elsewhere. The industry in Sarawak had simply not been compelled to do better. In the past sufficient flour could always be sold to keep the main structure of the industry alive, even in periods of slump, and thus there was no real incentive to improve either the organization or the product. In the past the government had relied on inspection by customs officers to check that a uniform flour was being exported, but experience had shown that it was impossible to control quality in that way. The problem needed to be attacked at the point of production.

On various occasions it had been suggested that the simplest and most reliable way of ensuring a flour of good quality would be to set up one central modern refining factory to handle the country's entire crop. The most practical method of doing this would have been to put the project into the hands of a sago board. The suggestion of one large factory was first made in 1922 by the Resident of Oya (Sarawak *Gazette,* vol. LII, no. 820). The sago-producing district of Sarawak is small in area, and, as the Resident observed more than fifty years ago, the existing modes of transport, with slight additions, would be sufficiently cheap and adequate. If the factory were built close to a center such as the town of Sibu on the Rejang River, where shipping facilities for export have existed for some time, the reduction in the cost of production would be very great indeed. In 1922 it would not have been expensive to build such a factory; today it would be, and it would take a number of years to reimburse the expense of the investment.

Those who advocated this scheme also pointed out that both before and after the formation of the Federation of Malaysia development funds had existed for the improvement of the economic and social standards of the inhabitants of Sarawak, but that virtually nothing had been allocated to the Melanau coastal District. The building of an efficient refinery was seen as an essential step in reorganizing and preserving the sago industry, for it would allow an active central control in the production of a flour of uniform quality. It would also allow the government to secure a proper share of the benefits of the industry to the Melanau producers.

Others believed that the building of two or three less ambitious factories on the Oya, the Mukah, and the Bintulu rivers might achieve the same ends, although less efficiently in economic terms. The water in none of these rivers is said to be good for refining flour, but it can easily and very cheaply be purified. The required conditions of cleanliness and honesty of management of such factories would not have been difficult to attain, and the refineries would not have needed elaborate equipment or organization. Factories in Singapore produce good quality flour with simple apparatus. Well-designed buildings and open, brick-covered drying grounds or special kilns to replace the present mat-covered muddy clearings would have ensured the required minimum of cleanliness. It would have been necessary, however, to have diverted a large part of the wet sago or sago palms to these refineries, though a sufficient and calculated quantity could have been left for the more reliable firms already in business to handle. These government factories, besides handling the bulk of the refining, would also have acted on behalf of the sago board as the only official depots for collecting and dispatching the flour to a central depot. In addition to these functions, it would have been essential for the factories, in close consultation with the sago board, to set the daily prices of sago and to see that they were known and observed locally.

Some of those who favored the building of smaller local factories felt that because the initial expenses would be less, there would therefore be less temptation to seek financial assistance from private industry in their construction and operation. They feared that a private interest in the factories might lay the way open to some possible loss of control in the wider regulation of the industry.

Recommendations at the Local Level

The institution of a national sago board and factories belonging to it in order to control the quality and marketing of Sarawak sago was only part of what many felt would be needed to reorganize the industry and set it on a satisfactory footing. Such bodies could hardly operate successfully unless certain local matters were also taken in hand. These matters fell under four heads.

Research into the Growing of the Sago Palm

Little is known about the cultivation of the sago palm. Rules of thumb used by the Melanau indicate that some types of soil and conditions of drainage not only shorten its maturation period, but also affect its yield. As the palm requires twelve to sixteen years to grow, an adequate body of knowledge cannot be quickly built up. Government departments have on occasion suggested setting up a permanent sago scheme for basic horticultural research directed by the Department of Agriculture, with Sago Officers stationed on the Oya, the Mukah and the Bintulu rivers to advise on and inspect the management of sago gardens and assist in the control of the industry generally. Such a scheme, it was argued by those making the suggestion, might also help convince the Melanau that their interests were not being wholly overlooked by the government.

Yield of Sago Palms

Before the refineries could operate satisfactorily, and before any realistic control of internal prices was possible, exact knowledge of the yield of flour from palms of different sizes and kinds would be needed. An initial and not very expensive piece of research in which a few hundred palms were processed in carefully controlled conditions would give provisional tables of the yield to be expected from a palm of a known type, girth, and height. Subsequent observations and records kept by the factories would finally produce a set of tables which would allow the setting of a quick and fair price. By the use of such tables the recurrent danger of overfelling would be removed by forbidding the sale of palms below a stated yield capacity. Moreover the keeping of such records and the use of such tables would also permit a reasonably accurate estimate of the value of standing crops and allow the allocation of realistic quotas of palms, or *lemantak* from the trampling platforms, to the remaining private refineries.

Sale of Land

With the advent of Malaysia and the concept of common and equal citizenship, discriminatory protection of Melanau landowners is likely to become increasingly objectionable. Already the Chinese owners of refineries in the coastal district have in one way or another acquired control of considerable areas of sago garden and the standing crops on them. They are not slow to point out that it would be easier to run their businesses if they had still more control, and that to own large plantations would be a good way of assuring a predictable supply of palms. But the social dangers of an industry based solely on plantations were sufficient to make many both in and out of the government reluctant to sanction such a development. The temptation for a Melanau in need of capital to sell his land had already become almost irresistible. Administrative officials said, with some truth, that when the owner of a refinery sold a garden, he would sell it only to another refinery owner, even though a Melanau peasant was willing, able, and anxious to buy. If all sales of land were publicly and widely announced beforehand in the villages and at the administrative centers, and if sales of land were handled by public auction at regular intervals, some of the disadvantages to the Melanau might be avoided. In any event all sales would need to be carefully scrutinized in the light of the sago scheme.

Policy Concerning the Cottage Industry

The almost complete elimination of domestic production of wet sago was the immediate cause of the present distress among the Melanau peasants. The effects were cumulative and had not yet fully developed. The situation had therefore not attracted the attention it merited. It could become dangerous, both politically and socially. With these dangers in mind those who recommended the institution of a sago scheme also recommended that all refineries should be required to buy a quota of wet sago from the villages. A proviso of this kind would not have proved unduly costly, and the expense would have been in the interests of social if not of economic efficiency. Such a quota could always be reviewed as circumstances required. In no other way, it was argued, could a barely adequate standard of life be assured to the Melanau people in the immediate future.

Postscript

By 1967 none of these suggestions for the regulation of the sago industry, which had at different times been suggested by government officials, anthropologists, and officers of independent development organizations, had been implemented. Some measures for the diversification of the economy had been set in train, but no serious attempt had yet been made to support the main props of traditional Melanau culture, which had been hacked away as the villages entered a full cash economy. Instead of living in politically independent villages they now lived in a modern federated state. In it they commanded neither the education nor the power to compel their rulers to undertake measures to preserve their livelihood, and many were convinced that those same rulers would not be altogether displeased if the process of hacking away at the supports of their independent language and culture were to continue. Most had indeed already recognized and accepted this fact by becoming Muslims, and most were aware that it was probably only a matter of time before they ceased altogether to be Melanau and became Malay in every sense of the word.

References Cited

Morris, H. S.
1953 A Report on a Melanau Sago Growing Community. London: Her Majesty's Stationery Office.
Sharp, Lauriston
1952 Steel Axes for Stone Age Australians. *In* Human Problems in Technological Change. Edward H. Spicer, ed. New York: Russell Sage Foundation. Pp. 69–90.
T'ien, Ju-k'ang
1953 The Chinese of Sarawak: A Study of Social Structure. London: London School of Economics and Political Science.

11. An Epicycle of Cathay; or, The Southward Expansion of the Sinologists

MAURICE FREEDMAN

This conception of civilizations as recognizable objects in the landscapes of time and space coincides nicely with the conventional view of culture which the anthropologists have so thoroughly and, in my opinion, too successfully promulgated during the past thirty years, and which is by now so widely accepted that most of us use the term, it would be my claim, without thinking sufficiently about what its referents might be. . . . Equipped only with the conventional cookie-cutter concept of culture, we find ourselves in grave analytical difficulties when we turn to Southeast Asia, lying between the great creative but self-producing civilizations of India and China. . . . Though we know all too little about it, Vietnam in itself may perhaps be seen as a cultural continuum in time in the Brown, Reischauer, and Fairbank sense, a suborder within Southeast Asia; or, with more emphasis on space, simply as a branch of the great Chinese civilization extending southward as an intrusion into an adjacent region [Sharp 1962:4, 5].

The scholar whom we salute in this book here speaks with nice caution, for, expert on "culture," he knows what many other such experts, anthropological and other, do not know: cultural boundaries are not unambiguously given in culture; they are chiefly the artifacts of our classifications. And of course our classifications change. But surely there can be no difficulty about seeing that Vietnam does not belong in Southeast Asia, where it is by convention placed, and that it ought to be put among the

East Asian countries, the area of "Chinese" civilization?[1] Well, we might (especially under Professor Sharp's eye) want to hesitate before offering an answer, but while we are arguing or pondering the point we could consider how our redrawing of the cultural map might affect our vision of the political relations between China and Southeast Asia. If Vietnam is in that region, then any exercise of Chinese power within that country is an invasion, and a further proof that China drives south. If it is in East Asia, it may well mark the furthest southern limit of Chinese influence. Anthropological arguments and considerations aside, some people may sleep more peacefully for Vietnam's being classified in the region of Chinese civilization.

But the sinologues will disturb them. Just a little while before Professor Sharp delivered the presidential address to the Association for Asian Studies from which I have quoted, a symposium had been held in Hong Kong in the published proceedings of which we find a section entitled "The Southward Expansion of the Han Chinese in Historical Times." In that section there appears an abstract of a paper read by Professor F. W. Mote, the eminent sinologist, on "Cities in North and South China," where he says:

[China's] geographical South in the last thousand years has been absorbing Annam and Kwangsi, pushing into Southeast Asia, and crossing seas to the Philippines, Malaya and the Indonesian Archipelago. Despite Australia's immigration laws, Singapore's determination to become "Malaysian," and tensions on the Sino-Burmese and Sino-Indian borders, it is possible to imagine, or almost impossible not to imagine, the continued sinicization of Asia lying further to the South. For although most Chinese have not yet conceived of these regions as parts of China, in terms of the long and unabating Chinese advance, they clearly appear to be outposts like many others further north that China absorbed gradually throughout the centuries [Mote 1967:153].

[1] For recent work showing the Chineseness of Vietnam see Woodside (1971) and Langlet (1970).

But there is a fuller and more recent version of the sinological thesis to tackle. I mean Professor C. P. FitzGerald's splendid new book, *The Southern Expansion of the Chinese People* (1972).[2]

I think it may be useful to begin with to try to site Professor FitzGerald's thesis within the general tradition to which I believe it belongs. Of course, the view is by no means novel that Chinese culture and power drift (or drive) south, and the reappearance of a unified China (Taiwan aside) since 1949 has for many observers brought the southward movement closer to being resumed. With the thesis of the southward trend many people couple the thesis that in the Overseas Chinese, China has a ready-made spearhead or fifth column. Those Overseas Chinese are held, in the thesis, to be a people set apart from where they live, and in consequence, a guarantee of an effective intervention by China in the region. One remembers the argument as it has appeared in the newspapers from time to time, and in the books that bear some family likeness to the newspapers.

And one remembers it in its scholarly forms. In these latter, the thesis is, of course, hedged around with qualifications and made more subtle. One remembers Herold J. Wiens. His version of the southward drive from China is clearcut. Having spoken of the "direct threat from the colossus of the north" as something being "graver than at any time in history, more serious than during the southward drive of the empire of Ghengis Khan," he goes on to plead for the cooperation of the Southeast Asian countries with the "Free World nations" (how quaintly it reads) "that lead the vanguard of the opposition to Communist enslavement" (Wiens 1967:351). Yet his view of the role of the Overseas Chinese in the great drive is mild: "Thailand, which aside from Vietnam, perhaps has the closest historical ties with China, at the same time fears the influx of the Han-Chinese the most. And well it

[2] I have reviewed this book (1972a) and assessed some of its arguments in my paper (1972b). Inevitably, there is some considerable overlap between that paper and the present essay. I should like to thank Professor Myron Cohen for helpful comments.

might, when it reviews the historical pressures of the Han-Chinese upon their [sic] cultural forefathers from the days of the Ch'u Kingdom down to the present " (Wiens 1967:345). That from a geographer.

A sociologist writing upon the Chinese in Thailand and explaining very well how in one sense they are assimilated and in another sense not, concludes his book with a section entitled "China's March South" where he speaks of the growth of the population of China and the likelihood that that country will "turn to Southeast Asia for living space, for markets, and for raw materials and food." "Historically," he proceeds,

the lands south of China have served as outlets for China's population. . . . Because of their fear of overseas Chinese economic and political influences, all Southeast Asian governments, Thailand included, have erected immigration barriers against the Chinese. None welcomes the revitalization of its Chinese communities by a new wave of immigration. But one must ask whether small nations like Thailand can resist the tremendous pressures exerted by China's expanding population, and if that, whether they can also resist the extraordinary cultural dynamic that China represents in Asia today. . . . Perhaps it is more realistic to think of China assimilating all the lands to the south, with a gradual, but determined penetration, the first stage of which is now taking place [Coughlin 1960:204f.]

The chief features of nearly all versions of the theory is that China is a menace (Dulles and dominoes . . .) and that the Overseas Chinese in Southeast Asia, willingly or unwillingly, act as agents of (to borrow Wiens's language) the colossus of the north. But it is not necessary that the theory be anti–Overseas Chinese, although it is usually so: a moving and generous plea in the Philippines for a fairer treatment of the Chinese in that country falls within the range of variations of the theory. That cry in defense of the Philippine Chinese says that unless they are better treated and so encouraged to identify themselves more closely with the country where their home is, they may align themselves with the enemy without.

The dilemma of the rich Chinese has always been whether to integrate with Filipinos and not be really accepted by them or to stay as they are, aliens forever. We must solve the dilemma not for some but for all. We have caused them to coalesce by discrimination and, particularly, by legislative discrimination. That discrimination must be removed. . . . Our country now faces the possibility of an armed invasion. In 1946 the communists were at Mukden. . . . Today, they are at the outskirts of Saigon. At this rate, it is no exaggeration to say that in the next few years, we ourselves may have to face them. When the time comes, union shall be essential. We cannot afford to have the Chinese portion of our population disloyal and ready to give aid to the enemy [Felix 1966:11].

Against this background Professor FitzGerald's version may be a surprising variation. For him of course China is hardly a menace, and he does not fear an imminent burst of Chinese power into Southeast Asia. The two elements in his general argument (eloquently set out in his new book) that bring it fully within the compass of the present are: (1) the stress put upon the southward movement of Chinese culture; and (2) the contention that the presence of large numbers of Chinese in the Nanyang (Southeast Asia) will in the long run involve the government of China in that region, Chinese power being extended perhaps even with the greatest reluctance. If the other versions may be said to represent China as a fire-breathing dragon, Professor FitzGerald's seems to suggest a huge but mild-mannered dragon unwillingly stirred to action. We may call this latter a "left" version to match the more common "right" one.

Professor FitzGerald writes as a historian, but to the extent that as anthropologists we approve his work we may want to claim him as one of us. And we should be in part justified in doing so. As a matter of fact, his anthropological interests are chiefly represented by the book he wrote many years ago on the Min Chia of Yünnan (1941), the field work for which was done after he had been taught by Malinowski at the London School of Economics. And now in his new book we can see how im-

portant a role Yünnan plays in his thinking about the spread of
Chinese culture. That province and Vietnam are for him two key
variations on the theme of sinification. Yünnan is now in China,
Vietnam now out of it. The former is in a sense less Chinese than
the latter. While China now looks from north to south across the
frontier between the two, it once looked north from a "Vietnam"
(a fraction of the present country of that name) in China to a
"Yünnan" (Nanchao) outside it.

These captivating paradoxes spring, to speak very briefly, from
the following historical circumstances. The kingdom of Nanchao,
roughly on the site of the present-day Yünnan, and the Tali
kingdom that succeeded it in the tenth century, had come under
heavy Chinese influence and included Chinese (Han) people
within their frontiers. But partly sinicized, Nanchao/Tali lay
outside China until the Mongol conquest in the middle of the
thirteenth century, undertaken in a movement to outflank the
Sung empire, brought it within its great neighbor's frontiers,
where it was to stay. On being hauled into China it was an
ethnically mixed country, imperfectly sinicized; and so in some
measure it has remained to this day. Vietnam, in contrast, had
been thoroughly sinicized during a long period of Chinese rule
before it broke free in the tenth century; and never again to come
under the rule of China for any great length of time, it was not
until the present day to abate its Chinese culture.

Yünnan and Vietnam furnish us, on Professor FitzGerald's
reasoning, with models of two quite different processes of cultural
and political domination by China. In the first model, Yünnan,
we have a territory holding a population of mixed origins which
acquires some Chinese culture before it passes under Chinese rule.
It makes a nuisance of itself to China, and in the end is forced
to join it. (The Mongols captured it and left it to a China that
would not part with it.) The second model, Vietnam, involves a
country which, although it has a tribal population, is overwhelmingly of one ethnic group. It receives Chinese culture, but few
Chinese people. Having at last attained independence from

China, it refrains from harassing its erstwhile ruler, now its suzerain. Indeed, it turns into a sort of miniature copy of its great neighbor and begins its own march to the south, having to clear out of the way and expropriate, or absorb, great numbers of Chams and Khmers before it reaches the modern limits of the country.

The People's Republic of China has pushed Han civilization and control outward from "China Proper" toward the corners of the vast territory bequeathed to it, at one remove, by the Ch'ing dynasty, although of course some of the Ch'ing lands (much of Mongolia among them) have been lost. Far-flung as they are, the modern frontiers of China might well have been more extensive. They might have included a large area to the south and west if, for example, the naval power culminating in the Ming ventures of the early fifteenth century, and which made possible the magnificent expeditions as far west as the east coast of Africa, had not been dispersed.[3] And even if we suppose that the territory ruled over by China had not been extended by the maintenance of great sea power, then at least we may assume that that power would have changed the relations between China and the many countries lying near it. As things turned out, Ch'ing China looked upon many of its neighbors as tributary states, and they performed the rites required of them in that status; but its political influence upon those states which lay to the south was on the whole weak. And when the West set out to drag China screaming into the nineteenth century, she was left defenseless for lack of strength at sea.

It is a commonplace of the writing on Ch'ing China that that dynasty principally faced north, whence it had come.[4] And it was

[3] See chapters 5 and 6 of C. P. FitzGerald (1972) and, for other important recent work on the subject, Needham (1971) and Ma (1970). Wang (1970) furnishes the background of economic history.

[4] As an example of the ineffective discovery in Ch'ing times of the past Chinese influences in the Nanyang, see Leonard (1972). The paper deals with a Chinese work that appeared in 1847.

precisely when official Chinese eyes were turned away from the Nanyang that for the first time large groups of Chinese began to build up in that region. Of course, Chinese had settled in places in Southeast Asia before Ch'ing times, but never before that dynasty had they settled in large numbers, and never before the middle of the nineteenth century had they emigrated (mainly from the southeastern provinces of Fukien and Kwangtung) in a flood. The Western occupation of Southeast Asia, which at its fullest extent (attained early in the twentieth century) covered the whole of the region with the sole exception of Siam, created the conditions for a massive "diaspora" of the Chinese. Indeed, the rulers of China began to take official cognizance of its emigrants only in the very last years of the dynasty, and then partly under pressure from the Western powers.[5] We have reached the modern world into which the Communist regime of China was soon to enter.

Professor FitzGerald's new book opens: "Chinese influence, Chinese culture and Chinese power have always moved southward since the first stage of which we have historical knowledge" (1972:xiii). What he appears to mean is that when Chinese culture overflows the edges of China, Chinese power is likely in the end to be dragged in to regulate the consequences. "It is rather a pattern of seepage, of slow overspill from the great reservoir which was China" (1972:xxi). Of the two models proposed to us, Yünnan and Vietnam, the former exemplifies the process; and we can begin to see from this point how the model may be used to illuminate the Nanyang as we now know it. Once more (the sinologue says), as in the kingdom of Nanchao, there now exists "a large Chinese population established in an alien land." Once again "the rulers of this region are rather more hostile than friendly to the government of China." Once more the local Chinese "have developed the economy and brought a great

[5] The most comprehensive and convenient work on the general subject remains, alas, Purcell (1965). For a very useful survey of recent literature see Nevadomsky and Li (1970).

increase of trade and prosperity." And, as in Yünnan, "the majority of the immigrants have taken to urban life and occupations, leaving the ownership and occupation of the land to the natives" (1972:183f). This comparison of the Nanyang and Yünnan culminates in the assertion that "the immigrant community, at first poor, unsophisticated and often illiterate, has . . . been culturally enriched both by its own growing prosperity and by the advent of a significant number of Chinese of the educated classes" (1972:184).

I am not concerned in this essay to argue out fully the political implications of Professor FitzGerald's analysis and projections for the future; but I need briefly to say, as a preliminary to what follows, that I do not accept the argument that China may expand into Southeast Asia as a direct result of the presence there of Overseas Chinese. Expand it may, especially if it recovers the sea power it once gave up, but, in my opinion, the Overseas Chinese will have nothing or very little to do with it.[6] To see why that is so we need to abandon the base in China from which the sinologists have been working and examine the Nanyang Chinese from much closer up.

They have been examined by some very distinguished historians and social scientists—one's mind jumps at once to Professor Wang Gungwu and Professor G. William Skinner. As for the anthropologists, it is now becoming easy to overlook the fact that for the longish period between the end of World War II and (to fix upon a date which I shall not attempt to defend here) 1958, the Overseas Chinese were, or appeared to be, the only sort of Chinese among whom anthropologists might practice their traditional craft of field work. (Of course, although the study of Overseas Chinese was not confined to those in Southeast Asia, it was concentrated on them.) I said "appeared to be" in

[6] This argument is strengthened by Stephen FitzGerald (1972), an amazingly detailed account of the willed disengagement of China from the *Hua-ch'iao*. And see Freedman (1972b). Purcell (1965:567f) argued against the thesis that the Overseas Chinese were a fifth column for China.

the sentence before last because I have in mind the possibility that Hong Kong and Taiwan could have been exploited much earlier than they in fact were; academic blindness as well as political myopia must be held to account.[7] Whether the anthropologists were justified in looking upon the Nanyang as a substitute for a China from which the international situation had excluded them may be interestingly debated.[8] But I do not think it could be reasonably argued that they brought to their perception of the Overseas Chinese a model of Chinese society and culture into which the Nanyang data had to be forced. On the contrary, it is chiefly to the anthropologists, although not to them alone, that we owe our realization and understanding of the extent to which Chinese culture has been whittled away in Southeast Asia and how great numbers of people of Chinese descent have been totally absorbed into non-Chinese society. It would be interesting to speculate on the reasons why the anthropologists in the Nanyang showed themselves to be considerably more history-minded than those who had preceded them in the study of China and,

[7] Cf. Freedman (1970:8f).

[8] A good case can be made out for Nanyang studies precisely on the ground that they have contributed to our understanding of the homeland society. For examples see Willmott (1970:160–174) and Crissman (1967: 200–203). Doubtless too a more thorough understanding of society in China, with particular, but not sole, reference to the provinces of Kwangtung and Fukien, would make for a clearer view of the society and culture of the Overseas Chinese. A more direct approach to the interaction between the two branches of study was pioneered in Chen (1939)—see also Hsu (1945)—but it has never been taken very far. The most recent work along this line I know of is to be found in Chang et al. (1957) and Chuang et al. (1958). The latter article is especially interesting. S. FitzGerald (1972), chapter 4, "Domestic Overseas Chinese Policy: 1949–1966," offers tantalizing glimpses, as when, for example (p. 62), we learn of a phase when the dependents of Hua-ch'iao "were officially permitted to use their remittances on the upkeep of ancestral graves, geomancy, and other 'feudal superstitious practices.' " As a matter of fact, it might be pointed out that the decline in remittances from overseas to dependents at home must have followed fairly rapidly from the turnover of the generations, as we can see from the systematic analysis of the Chinese family and its economic arrangements. Cf. Cohen 1970, especially pp. 23f.

more strikingly, than those who were immediately after them to study the "residual China" of Hong Kong and Taiwan. Indeed, one begins to wonder, as the prospect of field work in mainland China itself seems to get closer, whether one ought to view it with some alarm, instead of with the more usual messianic enthusiasm; perhaps the harvest will prove to consist of quite unhistorical and very old-fashioned "community studies." But let that pass.[9] We must turn to the data on the *Hua-ch'iao*,[10] "the Chinese so-journers overseas," as the Chinese term prejudicially calls them.

In one sense there is an entity to be called the Nanyang Chinese; in another sense, no such entity exists. Let us begin with the latter assertion. If we list the countries/territories of Southeast Asia as they are at the present time—Burma, Thailand, Malaysia, Singapore, Indonesia, Portuguese Timor, Brunei, Cambodia, Laos, the two Vietnams, and the Philippines—we shall discover that they all number Chinese people in their populations, the proportions formed by these Chinese varying enormously. Consider Table 11.1,[11] in which the territories are arranged in order (lowest to highest) of the percentages formed of their populations by the Chinese. If we rearrange the territories by the size of their Chinese populations (greatest to least) we get: Malaysia, Indonesia, Thailand, Singapore, South Vietnam, the Philippines, Cambodia, Burma, North Vietnam, Laos, Brunei and Portuguese Timor. In only one country, Singapore, are the Chinese in the majority. In two others, Malaysia and Brunei, they form very substantial minorities. Elsewhere their minorities are small, some

[9] Of course, the prospect may be a mirage. Perhaps the time will never come. The barrier that came down in 1949 might be said to have restored a normal state of affairs that had been merely interrupted for the previous hundred years. China does not know the tradition of freely opening its social life to close inspection by the outside world (Dawson 1967:167f), and it may well be that the students of China who have been perfecting the techniques of study at a distance are better advised than the optimistic field workers who imagine that before long (I write in mid-1972) the barrier will be raised.

[10] See Nevadomsky and Li (1970).

[11] Based upon the table in S. FitzGerald (1972:196).

Table 11.1 Chinese Population in Southeast Asia, 1972 (estimated in thousands)

Country or territory	Chinese population	Chinese as % of total
Portuguese Timor	5	1
North Vietnam	200	1
Philippines	450	1.5
Burma	400	1.5
Laos	45	2
Indonesia	2,750	2.5
South Vietnam	850	5
Cambodia	430	7
Thailand	2,600	8.5
Brunei	25	26
Malaysia	3,300	35
Singapore	1,400	75

very small indeed. Political accident and political design (for the latter one thinks of Singapore) have produced an enormous range of percentages.

But that is merely the beginning of the variation. The name "Chinese" does not carry the same meaning throughout the table: one is in the grip of a spurious category if one supposes the contrary. Obviously, if one starts from a legal point of view then one notices at once that in each country "Chinese" includes people of Chinese nationality/citizenship (but not just of *one* China) and those of the relevant local nationality/citizenship[12]— not to mention those holding the passport of some third country. But there is far more to it than that. In any one country some of the people listed as Chinese are, in terms of their culture (and perhaps their descent), likely to be more Chinese than others so listed; and the gap between the extremes may be very great, a point we may illustrate by the distance between a Malay-speaking Baba Chinese in Malaysia or Singapore and his Mandarin-

[12] On this cf. Coppel (1972).

speaking compatriot. And if there were such a thing as—in cultural terms again—an average Chinese in each country, then he would not be the same from country to country. Countries differ in their non-Chinese respects, and their Chinese with them. Countries contain and condition their Chinese.[13] That is a fact that observers afar (especially from China perhaps) find it particularly difficult to assimilate. And they find it hard partly because there is also a Chinese Nanyang although we can see that there are in fact separate Chinese communities scattered through Southeast Asia. The Chinese Nanyang manifests itself in part in the interconnections among Chinese in the different countries of the region, in part in the organizations that purport to speak in the name of the Overseas Chinese of the region or in that of some special interest group among them, and in part in the attempts by various Chinese governments to treat the Chinese in Southeast Asia as a whole.

The international character of the Chinese in the Nanyang has clearly been an important feature of their lives and a crucial element in their commercial success. Links across frontiers of family and kinship, as well as of common origin in China, have made them quick to receive economic intelligence and to respond to the opportunities it might suggest. And perhaps Professor Fitz-Gerald is right to give importance (1972:165) to the fact that in their written language the Chinese in Nanyang have a special instrument for the "coded" transmission, in their newspapers, of information of commercial value. But these are matters that belong to the past more than the present. In precolonial and colonial times the barriers between countries were for the most part more permeable than they are now, when nationalism has taken

---

[13] Go (1971:564) speaks, surprisingly, of all the Overseas Chinese in Southeast Asia "sharing a common way of life distinct from the indigenous cultures of the host nations." But of course he shows himself sensitive to the differences from country to country. For an interesting attempt to isolate some organizational principles underlying the surface variety see Crissman (1967).

frontiers and turned them into formidable obstacles. One has observed during the past twenty years or so how the growing individuation of the countries of Southeast Asia has progressively isolated from one another their Chinese communities. Of course, the process does not go so far that all links are severed; and in favorable circumstances (as is at the moment the case with Chinese in Singapore and Indonesia in the important role they play in the trade between their countries) older ties may be re-activated. Certainly, enough of the old internationalism of the Nanyang Chinese survives to lend color to the accusation made against them that they lack a full commitment to the countries where they live. A former strength is a present weakness.

Now, it will have been seen from the summary offered earlier in the essay of Professor FitzGerald's application of the Yünnan model to the Nanyang that it supposes in the latter a culturally vigorous Chinese community—or, more correctly, a series of such communities. It would be grossly unfair to Professor FitzGerald to suggest that he has shown himself unaware of some of the important differences among the Nanyang Chinese groups and of the fact that assimilation, in varying degrees, has taken place, sometimes in its extreme form on a large scale. But it is fair, I think, to say that he has not brought his awareness of these differences into harmony with his general propositions. The sketch of Yünnan-in-the-Nanyang demonstrates that defect. Professor FitzGerald considers it possible that China will one day need to intervene in Southeast Asia precisely because there are Chinese there, not necessarily because they stand in need of suc-cor: He suggests the possibility that a flourishing alternative "China" in the Nanyang (Singapore—where else?) might pro-voke from China a hostile intervention (1972:209). And the general argument assumes that somehow the Chinese in South-east Asia will have grown more Chinese than they are, just as they are now more Chinese than they were. The assumption follows from Professor FitzGerald's version of the history of Chi-nese emigration.

In the beginning the emigrants were humble, poor, and often illiterate. (So far so good. That will certainly do for a generalization.) But as they grew richer, their Chinese cultural standards rose: "As the Overseas Chinese steadily become predominantly native born, and immigration ceases the level of transplanted Chinese culture has risen, not fallen, so that communities which were mainly illiterate only a century and less ago, are now steeped in the culture of their ancestral homeland, and unwilling to forego this heritage" (1972:119). The *Hua-ch'iao* were helped in the attainment of these new standards by small numbers of educated emigrants who came over to raise the general level. One can suggest how in this Professer FitzGerald has been forced into his version of Nanyang history by his attachment to his (seductive, one may freely admit) Yünnan model. "In Yunnan these latter [i.e., a significant number of Chinese of the educated classes] were more often political exiles sent to the remote province by the government of the day; in the Nanyang they are more likely to be exiles who have preferred to live abroad rather than remain in, or to return to China under Communist rule" (1972:184).

This view of the history of the Nanyang is difficult to reconcile with the evidence normally considered. In the first place, such elevation of Chinese cultural standards as occurred (by the spread of Mandarin and the nationalist culture that went with it) happened in the first half of the twentieth century, and precisely before China turned Communist. Since that great event, the parallel rise of nationalist regimes in the Southeast Asian countries has generally led to a decline in what I suppose Professor FitzGerald would regard as Chinese culture; certainly, at the present time in the Nanyang there must be less Chinese-language education and less use of the Chinese language for literary purposes than in 1949. (Professor FitzGerald is aware [p. 119] that English is a challenge to Chinese; but he clearly underestimates the extent of the challenge. Perhaps however, since English is widely used as a practical, not literary, language,

Professor FitzGerald would not want to allow it within the limits
of his somewhat austere definition of "culture.")

One wonders too about the political exiles said to have been
cultural leaveners, and one might suspect that there is in the analysis some confusion of social status and level of culture, whatever
that latter may mean precisely. There is no doubt that the intensification of Chinese culture among the Nanyang Chinese at
various times from about the beginning of this century (which
produced among other things the resinification of some highly
acculturated Chinese in Malaya)[14] has made for a strengthening
of bonds with China. But the bearers of the means of cultural
renewal were by no means generally of high social standing. For
many decades they were for the most part poor and socially depressed schoolteachers and, in more recent times, often poor and
socially depressed university teachers (from Taiwan). It is true
that there is now in the Nanyang a higher regard for education-
without-riches than there used to be, but it still seems to me to
be a distortion of Nanyang life to give the impression that educated newcomers from China have appeared to their overseas
fellows as a sort of wondrous cultural saviors. The sociology of
Chinese culture in the Nanyang is far more complex than Professor FitzGerald's formulae allow for.

We must recognize the break between the system of social
stratification in China and that developed in the Nanyang. *Shih,
nung, kung, shang:* scholar-administrator, farmer/peasant, arti-
san/worker, merchant—that idealized hierarchy represents for
traditional China the differential worth of occupational groups
in terms of the distribution of the values of civility and productivity. Civility marked off *shih* from the rest; productivity ranked
nung before *kung* and *kung* before *shang*. The hierarchy does
not represent the distribution of power within traditional Chinese
society, for it is obvious that *shang*, a category embracing everybody from petty trader to great merchant, could not be at the

[14] Cf. Freedman (1969:436f).

bottom of a scale of power. The hierarchy rejects in *shang* the value of what is taken to be unproductive, uncivil, and possibly luxury-inspiring activity.[15] By this formula moral and political leadership is to vest in *shih*. We may see at once that *Hua-ch'iao* society must by its arrangements contradict the ancient formula. It lacks *shih*. Leadership falls (or at any rate fell until quite recently) to *shang*.[16] A traditional hierarchy is then stood on its head when the few *shih* who find themselves in the Nanyang are treated as mere instruments (schoolteachers, clerks) of the *shang*. If we ignore the small farming population among the Overseas Chinese, we might go so far as to say that the Nanyang hierarchy came at times to be *shang, kung, shih*. And even when, in more recent decades, one has been able to detect a more traditionally arranged system of occupational statuses, such that educated men stand at the top and take on positions of leadership (professionals: lawyers, doctors, and the like), they have by no means been the sort of men that Professor FitzGerald seems to have in mind.[17]

The Chinese "wherever they have settled, have brought with them their own culture, at first in simple forms suited to a mainly illiterate migrant population, but as the level of their wealth and standard of living rose, they turned without hesitation to the more sophisticated art and literature of their ancestral land" (C. P. FitzGerald 1972: 138). Did they? Much depends upon what is meant by "they turned without hesitation to." The outward signs might be displayed without attachment on the part of their displayers to the artistic or literary values they might be thought to enshrine. I remember, from British Malaya, one of the richest men in the country (of distinguished Baba lineage), who knew no Chinese, assuring me that the splendid calligraphic scroll that

---

[15] But see Metzger (1970) for a reappraisal of the attitude of the Confucian state to commercial activity.

[16] On this matter see Skinner (1968) for a characteristically pointed paper.

[17] Cf. Wang (1968, especially pp. 209–213).

hung upon his wall had been done entirely by hand. And in the past one has watched the surprise on the face of newcomers when first in the presence of what they soon learned to categorize as nouveau riche style. It is not for the anthropologist to pass judgment: his point must be that Overseas Chinese culture, varied as it is from time to time and place to place, is not a mere approximation to the culture of the homeland. It grows from its special social circumstances, and none of these predisposes it toward the progressive adoption of the "higher" cultural values and styles of China.

Professor FitzGerald's argument will be seen to rest fundamentally upon the supposition that Chinese culture is endlessly viable. That is an assumption that must certainly come very naturally to a sinologue and sinophile. The Chinese in China (there is no secret about it) have a very high opinion of their cultural achievements and of their general superiority to the peoples around them. And sinologists often take on the prejudices of what they closely study. Indeed, to go by the advice offered by Professor Owen Lattimore in his Inaugural Lecture at Leeds in 1964, "the student of modern China, even when doing his research and teaching outside of China, should cultivate an intellectual method of seeing China from within, and looking from China outward at the world" (Lattimore 1964:2). Well, anthropologists will be among the first to recognize the methodological desirability of working outward from the categories of the people they study, insofar as that task can be achieved without abandoning categories which make sense of more than one society. They may be suspicious of a sinological aim to pose the student on one spot; in assimilating the Chinese point of view he may easily come to forget that there are others.

That China has been and will almost certainly continue to be one of the great civilizations is indisputable. Only a shortsighted peering at the century following 1840 could explain the failure to see that truth. But it does not follow that Chinese emigrants and their descendants must forever reflect the glory of their homeland or neglect to take advantage of the cultural and political opportunities open to them where they live. In the course of living outside China many have in fact already disappeared as Chinese, and many more will surely go the same way. We cannot predict exactly how Chinese the Nanyang Chinese will be in, say, twenty years from now; but, short of an effective presence of China itself in Southeast Asia, the chances are that there will be less Chinese culture than there is now. The continued creaming off of Chinese leaders in Thailand, when there can be no accession of new cultural strength from China;[18] the erosion of Chinese culture in Singapore under the stern antichauvinist policies of Mr. Lee Kuan Yew's government (so much so that the only possible candidate for the position of a China-outside-China seems likely to manage in the end with only a residual Chinese cultural apparatus); the destruction of Chinese cultural institutions in Indonesia—all these point to a desinification in the Nanyang. I should add, to avoid a common misunderstanding, that the acculturation to which these facts point is by no means to be taken as a sign of increasing social and political adjustment; the Chinese in Malaysia and Indonesia, for example, may well find that their relations with their respective compatriots get worse as they come more and more to resemble them in their cultural lives. But that is another matter.

Professor FitzGerald's view that the fate of Southeast Asia is that of Yünnan and not Vietnam can be turned on its head: we may say that if Chinese culture is to come to dominate in (parts of) the region, then it will be because of conquest by China. The correct model will have proved to be not Yünnan but Vietnam (*absit omen*). Violence will have led to Chinese culture, not Chinese culture to violence.

But as the argument progresses one grows uneasy with the word "culture," and one's mind returns to Lauriston Sharp's words quoted at the beginning of this essay. We know, as long

[18] Cf. Skinner (1968:203).

as we remain reflective anthropologists, that *a* culture is a classification that we impose upon the data. Vietnam is in or out of
China depending upon the arrangement we choose to make at
different times of the facts at our disposal. Certainly, whatever
else it may be, a culture is not a homogeneous substance with the
power to spread, like butter or treacle. But that is how Chinese
culture seems to be presented in the arguments for its inevitable
expansion—except that Professor FitzGerald allows for the possible dilution of the culture as it moves: "The March to the
South [by the Vietnamese], especially in its later phases when
some proportion of the conquered population was assimilated
into the victorious Vietnamese people, had the effect of diluting
and subtly altering the character of the Chinese culture which the
northern Vietnamese had so long adopted" (1972:31).

Consider other statements, already quoted in this essay: southern expansion "is rather a pattern of seepage, of slow overspill";
"Chinese influence, Chinese culture and Chinese power have always moved southward." We were invited by language of that
sort to accept a physical (sometimes hydrographical) theory of
Chinese culture. And if we have before us in our mind's eye a
wall map of Asia, north conventionally at the top, we may be
tempted to imagine Chinese culture oozing and dribbling down
under the pull of gravity. Our anthropological defenses lowered,
we may be lulled into the confident belief that we are the recipients of a great key to human history.

Of course the frontiers of Chinese power and culture have
advanced southward, the two frontiers not always coinciding
(Vietnam and Nanchao/Tali). Of course vast tracts of territory
and huge numbers of "barbarians" have been made Chinese[19]—
some of them in fact were probably ancestors of the Overseas
Chinese we are now discussing and among whom many have

[19] Cf. Miyakawa (1960), especially perhaps the delightful expression of
the Confucian point of view at p. 31. "An important way in which Confucianism civilized the southern natives was by improving their marriage
systems."

desinified themselves. But are we obliged to believe that the process of southward movement must continue? Obviously not. There is no inevitability about it. Population pressure could conceivably make China turn hungry eyes upon empty spaces in Thailand, where there is an opportunity to reproduce a Chinese agricultural way of life—there being few other candidates in the South. But in fact, within the frame of the political conditions that we can envisage for Asia in the near future, Chinese power is more likely to manifest itself in the revived form of a Chinese suzerainty that, in the abnormal conditions of the last hundred years, we have tended to forget.

China is not simply *Chung-kuo*, a state/country with clearly drawn boundaries, but also (in one sense of the term) *T'ien-hsia*, All-under-Heaven, a civilization (*the* civilization in its own estimation) embracing its neighbors without imposing its culture upon them. At the center of *T'ien-hsia* stood the bureaucratically controlled state presiding over the area of intense Han life and culture. Around this area were arranged others where control was exercised through a more personal form of rule,[20] the emperor acting now as overlord to local chiefs and rulers. At the periphery of this outer part of the civilization we find territories and rulers whose obligations were no more than to acknowledge the overlordship of the emperor and to send envoys who would make obeisance to him. The characteristic of the central area, China Proper, was that it was an agricultural country whose inhabitants were preferably engaged in administration and farming. Beyond the edges of the central realm lay barbarous peoples whose economic life was opposite (pastoralists, nomads), in which case they were unassimilable to Han culture, or similar but rudimentary, in which case their primitive forms of tilling the soil made them

---

[20] Of course, the more personal element in the exercise of imperial power was not entirely lacking within the political system of the central, bureaucratically regulated, realm. See Wakeman (1970:9). "A county official could, and sometimes did, receive instruction directly from the palace."

potential recruits to that culture. To the north and west the central realm could not traditionally expand; to the south it might. But the total range covered by the imperial overlordship could more easily be enlarged; and when relations were established with Western powers within the only system that traditional China could recognize, the list of tributary states could include some in the West, although because of their bases abroad, they might be thought of as being closer to China. The roll of regular tributary states given in the 1818 edition of the *Ta-Ch'ing hui-tien,* administrative statutes of the Ch'ing, reads: Korea, the Ryukyus, Annam, Laos, Siam, Sulu, Holland, Burma, Western Ocean (Portugal, the Papacy, England).[21] Out of context, that list looks comic, but it is far from being so. And one may imagine a new context in which the list, suitably modified, would resume its meaning . . . indeed, take on more meaning than the Ch'ing, in their preoccupation with the north, were able to give it. Chinese culture may have attained its furthest geographical limits; Chinese political influence may yet have a great distance to go.

If the Chinese survive in the Nanyang until the time when such a rearrangement of the political map appears likely—and China is seen to be on the point of becoming the great patron to a collection of Southeast Asian client-states—then obviously their position will be peculiar. One hesitates to say "privileged" because they might then be so different from the Chinese of China as to make them to the latter a dubious asset. But, more important, the imposition of such an order in Asia would in no way depend on there being recognizable Chinese in the Nanyang. The government of China seems intent, as the recent book by Dr. Stephen FitzGerald (1972) cogently argues, on desinifying the *Hua-ch'iao* by a combination of integration overseas and, if necessary, repatriation to China.[22] There could come a movement of Chinese power to the south, but Professor FitzGerald notwith-

[21] Fairbank (1968:11). On the general matter see this book *passim* and cf. Ginsburg (1968).
[22] Cf. Freedman (1972b).

standing, if it does come, it will not have been caused by a drift of Chinese culture. The sinologist may be tempted to make culture the pioneer dragging politics in its train. The anthropologist (is it a paradox?) puts politics in the van, culture trailing.

But it is not only "culture" that creates difficulties for us in our attempt, as anthropologists, to assess the value of the various models used to explain the position of the *Hua-ch'iao*. If Professor C. P. FitzGerald's Yünnan model links the fate of the Overseas Chinese too closely to China, another model, which also makes a fleeting appearance in his new book,[23] may put too much emphasis upon the permanent marginality of the *Hua-ch'iao* as an explanation of their position. I refer to the model called "the Jews of Asia." Professor FitzGerald sums up a good deal of the Jewish analogy when he writes: "Situations comparable to the Middle Eastern conflict of Arab and Jew would have been more than possible. . . . It is no accident that King Rama VI of Thailand and other sharp critics of the Chinese in the Nanyang had described them as 'the Jews of the Far East.'[24] It is also perhaps no accident that the rulers of the new Republic of Singapore, when seeking instructors for its new armed forces, found Israelis to their liking" (1972:197). (One might have supposed that Israeli military expertness of a special kind had something to do with it.) Of course, the Jewish analogy is everywhere found in the literature on the Overseas Chinese; it is a tribute paid by the East to the West; and one may be forgiven for being so bored with it that one has forgotten to submit it to scrutiny.[25]

When Professor W. F. Wertheim, the eminent Indonesianist, published a newspaper article on the ejection of Chinese from

---

[23] Cf. C. P. FitzGerald (1965:84).

[24] Cf. Purcell (1965:120f) and Skinner (1957:164f).

[25] But see some sensible remarks in Heidhues (1968:339f). I must confess that I myself appear to have been guilty of slapdash thinking on the subject: Freedman (1959:68). But I stand by the statement made there: "What things are common and not common to Jews outside Israel and overseas Chinese would make an interesting and instructive study—if there is a scholar who commands the literature on both." Who does?

the West Java countryside, it appeared under the title "Exodus der Joden van het Oosten" (1960).[26] In his collection of essays *East-West Parallels: Sociological Approaches to Modern Asia* (1964) we find one entitled "The Trading Minorities in Southeast Asia," which is mainly concerned with the people "of Chinese ancestry, who are . . . a 'homeless' minority within most of the Southeast Asian states, and who, largely as a consequence of their dominant position in trade, today present a series of social, economic, and political problems in most of the countries of that area" (1964:41). Although (he argues) not all Chinese are traders, yet in the crowded rural areas where many of them settled they filled an occupational gap corresponding to that which accommodated the Jews in medieval Europe; and "they have still to bear the odium attached to the trading profession by a rural society in which aristocratic and feudal values are still strong" (1964:44). More generally, the Chinese in the Nanyang have got themselves into an awkward marginal position, and the root of their difficulty is to be found in the "economic competition between adjoining social groups. . . . The present outbursts of violence or organized discrimination on a mass scale are not comparable with the occasional pogroms or riots in past centuries" (1964:76). For we are now in a transitional phase in which the new independent countries are trying to transform their societies. In this phase the Chinese find themselves faced by economic rivals from among the indigenous population. Thus it "is not cultural divergence which is at the root of the tensions. The movements become virulent precisely at the moment when the cultural differences are waning to such an extent that competition becomes possible. Lack of assimilation . . . provides an excuse to select a special group of 'foreigners' as the target. . . . It appears to me that a similar line of reasoning could be applied if we wish to explain the emergence of anti-semitism and some

[26] Professor Wertheim has also published a paper entitled "Ahasverus in de Tropen" (see Nevadomsky and Li 1970:8), but I have not seen it.

changing attitudes and inconsistencies throughout European history" (1964:79).

What Professor Wertheim says is obviously in part true. The competitive frictions between ethnic groups must increase when non-Chinese aspire to the economic roles and positions hitherto monopolized by the Chinese, and that increase has long been foreseen. But one might wish to quarrel with Professor Wertheim over his apparent determination to find an economic cause of both anti-Semitism and anti-Chinese action in Southeast Asia. After all, the real problem (although it may not appear so to the victims) is to discover not so much why they are the envied occupants of valued economic niches, as why they are still classified as aliens to justify their being made legitimate targets. (In the national language of Indonesia the problem is well stated by the division within the general category of "Indonesian citizen" between Indonesian citizens who are indigenous, *asli,* and those who are not.)

But though we may fault Professor Wertheim's analysis by saying that it does not go deep enough, we of course recognize in it a serious and scholarly effort to pursue an analogy as far as the evidence will take it.[27] The less thoughtful versions of the model rest upon a much broader conception of what is common to Jews and *Hua-ch'iao,* or at least they are apt to excite in the reader's mind a fuller range of such common features. Jews/ Chinese wander about the earth; they are people of an ancient culture; for the most part they work their way into intermediate positions in economy and society, constrained to do so by the restrictions placed upon them; they are disliked and persecuted; and, rootless cosmopolitans, they look to Zion/China. . . . We get back to Professor C. P. FitzGerald's speculations. In another context he possibly refers to the Jews without mentioning them: "The existence of discrimination in some degree in all the Nanyang except Singapore tends to make the Chinese, no longer

[27] Cf. Eitzen (1968).

'alien' nor 'transient,' into a peculiar people, a separate nation within the nation" (1972:191). Is one justified in hearing in this passage some resonance from Deuteronomy 14:2? "For thou art an holy people unto the Lord thy God, and the Lord hath chosen thee to be a peculiar people unto himself, above all nations that are upon the earth." Well, the analogy has of course broken down at that very point. The Chinese are not a chosen people. They have in fact no Almighty God to choose them. In reality they have not wandered the earth for centuries bereft of a home and keeping themselves to themselves in the name of a religious duty. The people who left China centuries ago have few descendants now who think of themselves as Chinese. The Chinese "diaspora," by comparison with the Jewish, is an illusion created by a mere hundred years or so of history. It has no deep roots and may indeed soon fade away. Certainly, we must expect to see "Chinese" survive as the name for a political bloc in Malaysia, and as the label of small ethnic minorities in many other Southeast Asian countries. But there may be no "diaspora" of the Chinese, organized and oriented to China.

Interesting and illuminating as they are, neither "Yünnan" nor "Jews" can in the last analysis help us to a complete understanding of the fate of the Chinese in Southeast Asia. As anthropologists, we know that in trying to study one complex phenomenon from all sides we are forced in the end to acknowledge its uniqueness. Perhaps we shall never succeed in fully understanding the Overseas Chinese, try as we may. But in making the effort we may be able to clear a number of intellectual errors out of the way (some of them may be bound up with our use of "culture"), and with the aid of such salutary cautions as that with which this essay opened we may learn to be critical of the most pleasing of the solutions offered to us.

References Cited

Chang Chen-ch'ien, Ch'en K'o-chien, Kan Min-chung, and Ch'en K'o-k'un
    1957 A Study of the Rural Economy of the Principal Home Districts of Fukien Overseas Chinese. Hsia-men Ta-hsüeh Hsüeh-pao, She-hui K'o-hsüeh Pan (Universitatis Amoiensis Acta Scientarum Socialium) 1:31–36. (In Chinese.)
Chen Ta
    1939 Emigrant Communities in South China: A Study of Overseas Migration and Its Influence on Standards of Living and Social Change. Bruno Lasker, ed. London and New York: Oxford University Press.
Chuang Wei-chi, Lin Chin-shih, and Kuei Kuang-hua
    1958 Report on a Survey Carried out in the Chin-chiang District of Fukien for the Purpose of Studying the History of the Overseas Chinese. Hsia-men Ta-hsüeh Hsüeh-pao, She-hui K'o-hsüeh Pan (Universitatis Amoiensis Acta Scientarum Socialium) 1:93–127. (In Chinese.)
Cohen, Myron L.
    1970 Developmental Process in the Chinese Domestic Group. *In* Family and Kinship in Chinese Society. Maurice Freedman, ed. Stanford: Stanford University Press. Pp. 21–36.
Coppel, Charles
    1972 The Position of the Chinese in the Philippines, Malaysia and Indonesia. *In* The Chinese in Indonesia, the Philippines and Malaysia. London: Minority Rights Group. Pp. 16–29.
Coughlin, Richard J.
    1960 Double Identity: The Chinese in Modern Thailand. Hong Kong: Hong Kong University Press.
Crissman, Lawrence W.
    1967 The Segmentary Structure of Urban Overseas Chinese Communities. Man n.s. 2 (2):185–204.
Dawson, Raymond
    1967 The Chinese Chameleon: An Analysis of European Conceptions of Chinese Civilization. London and New York: Oxford University Press.

Eitzen, D. Stanley
1968 Two Minorities: The Jews of Poland and the Chinese of
the Philippines. Jewish Journal of Sociology 10 (2):221–240.
Fairbank, John King
1968 A Preliminary Framework. *In* The Chinese World Order:
Traditional China's Foreign Relations. John King Fairbank, ed.
Cambridge: Harvard University Press. Pp. 1–19.
Felix, Alfonso, Jr.
1966 How We Stand. *In* The Chinese in the Philippines, 1570–
1770. Alfonso Felix, Jr., ed. Manila: Solidaridad Publishing
House. Vol. 1:1–14. Quotations are reprinted by permission of
the publisher.
FitzGerald, C. P.
1941 The Tower of Five Glories: A Study of the Min Chia of
Ta Li, Yünnan. London: Cresset.
1965 The Third China: The Chinese Communities in South-East
Asia. Melbourne. Cheshire.
1972 The Southern Expansion of the Chinese People: "Southern
Fields and Southern Ocean." London: Barrie and Jenkins.
FitzGerald, Stephen
1972 China and the Overseas Chinese: A Study of Peking's
Changing Policy, 1949–1970. Cambridge: Cambridge University
Press.
Freedman, Maurice
1959 Jews, Chinese and Some Others. British Journal of Sociology
10 (1):61–70.
1969 The Chinese in Southeast Asia: A Longer View. *In* Man,
State, and Society in Contemporary Southeast Asia. Robert O.
Tilman, ed. New York: Praeger. (Originally published as Occasional Paper No. 14, The China Society, London, 1965.)
1970 Why China? Proceedings of the Royal Anthropological
Institute of Great Britain and Ireland, London, 1969, Pp. 5–13.
1972a Review of C. P. FitzGerald 1972. China Quarterly
52:742–745.
1972b China Facing South: Reflections on Two New Books. The
Round Table 248: 425–440.
Ginsburg, Norton
1968 On the Chinese Perception of a World Order. *In* China's

Policies in Asia and America's Alternatives: China in Crisis. Tang Tsou, ed. Chicago: University of Chicago Press. Vol. 2, pp. 73–91.

Go Gien Tjwan
1971 The Changing Trade Position of the Chinese in South-East Asia. International Social Science Journal 23 (4) :564–575.

Heidhues, Mary F. Somers
1968 Die chinesische Minderheit im politischen Leben Indonesiens. Zeitschrift für Politik, Organ der Hochschule für politische Wissenschaften München 3 (23) :337–352.

Hsu, Francis L. K.
1945 Influence of South-Seas Emigration on Certain Chinese Provinces. Far Eastern Quarterly 5 (1) :47–59.

Langlet, Philippe
1970 La tradition vietnamienne: Un état national au sein de la civilisation chinoise. Bulletin de la Société des Etudes Indochinoises (Saigon) n.s. 45 (2 & 3): viii, 395, vi.

Lattimore, Owen
1964 From China Looking Outward. Leeds: Leeds University Press.

Leonard, Jane Kate
1972 Chinese Overlordship and Western Penetration in Maritime Asia: A Late Ch'ing Reappraisal of Chinese Maritime Relations. Modern Asian Studies 6 (2) :151–174.

Ma Huan (trans. and ed. J. V. G. Mills)
1970 Ying-yai Sheng-lan, "The Overall Survey of the Ocean's Shores" [1433]. Cambridge: Cambridge University Press.

Metzger, Thomas A.
1970 The State and Commerce in Imperial China. In Society and Development in Asia. Martin Rudner, ed. Asian and African Studies (Israel Oriental Society, Jerusalem) 6:23–46.

Miyakawa Hisayuki
1960 The Confucianization of South China. In The Confucian Persuasion. Arthur F. Wright, ed. Stanford, Calif.: Stanford University Press. Pp. 21–46.

Mote, F. W.
1967 Cities in North and South China. In Symposium on Historical and Archaeological and Linguistic Studies on Southern

China, South-East Asia and the Hong Kong Region. F. S. Drake, ed. (Wolfram Eberhard, Chairman of the Proceedings.) Hong Kong: Hong Kong University Press. Pp. 153–155.

Needham, Joseph
1971 Science and Civilisation in China, Vol. 4: Physics and Physical Technology, Part III: Civil Engineering and Nautics. Cambridge: Cambridge University Press.

Nevadomsky, Joseph-john, and Alice Li
1970 The Chinese in Southeast Asia: A Selected and Annotated Bibliography of Publications in Western Languages, 1960–1970. Berkeley, Calif.: Occasional Paper No. 6, Center for South and Southeast Asian Studies, University of California.

Purcell, Victor
1965 The Chinese in Southeast Asia. London and New York: Oxford University Press. 2d ed.

Sharp, Lauriston
1962 Cultural Continuities and Discontinuities in Southeast Asia. Journal of Asian Studies 22 (1):3–11.

Skinner, G. William
1957 Chinese Society in Thailand: An Analytical History. Ithaca, N.Y.: Cornell University Press.
1968 Overseas Chinese Leadership: Paradigm for a Paradox. In Leadership and Authority, A Symposium. Gehan Wijeyewardene, ed. Singapore: University of Malaya Press. Pp. 191–207.

Wakeman, Frederic, Jr.
1970 High Ch'ing: 1683–1839. In Modern East Asia: Essays in Interpretation. James B. Crowley, ed. New York: Harcourt, Brace and World. Pp. 1–28.

Wang Gungwu
1968 Traditional Leadership in a New Nation: The Chinese in Malaya and Singapore. In Leadership and Authority, A Symposium. Gehan Wijeyewardene, ed. Singapore: University of Malaya Press. Pp. 208–222.
1970 "Public" and "Private" Overseas Trade in Chinese History. In Sociétés et compagnies de commerce en orient et dans l'Océan Indien (Actes du huitième Colloque International d'Histoire Maritime, 1966). Paris: Bibliothèque Générale de l'Ecole Pratique des Hautes Etudes, VIᵉ Section. Pp. 214–226.

Wertheim, W. F.

1960 Exodus der Joden van het Oosten. De Groene Amsterdammer August 13. P. 5.

1964 The Trading Minorities in Southeast Asia. *In* W. F. Wertheim, East-West Parallels: Sociological Approaches to Modern Asia. The Hague: W. van Hoeve. Pp. 39–82. Quotations are used with the permission of the copyright holder, Mouton & Co.

Wiens, Herold J.

1967 Han Chinese Expansion in South China. Hamden, Conn: The Shoe String Press. (Originally published 1954 as China's March toward the Tropics.)

Willmott, W. E.

1970 The Political Structure of the Chinese Community in Cambodia. London: Athlone.

Woodside, Alexander Barton

1971 Vietnam and the Chinese Model: A Comparative Study of Nguyen and Ch'ing Civil Government in the First Half of the Nineteenth Century. Cambridge: Harvard University Press.

Contributors

Raymond Firth is Emeritus Professor of Anthropology, University of London.

Ward H. Goodenough is Professor of Anthropology, Department of Anthropology, University of Pennsylvania.

David M. Schneider is Professor of Anthropology, Department of Anthropology, University of Chicago.

Jane R. Hanks is Visiting Lecturer, Department of Anthropology, State University of New York at Albany.

Arthur P. Wolf is Associate Professor of Anthropology, Department of Anthropology, Stanford University.

Charles Madge was until 1970 Professor of Sociology, University of Birmingham, and now resides in France.

Fred Eggan is Harold H. Swift Distinguished Service Professor of Anthropology and Director of the Philippine Studies Program, University of Chicago.

Laurence C. Judd is Associate Professor of Sociology and Chairman of the Asian Studies Program at Illinois College.

Howard K. Kaufman is Chairman of the Department of Anthropology-Sociology, Ripon College, Ripon, Wisconsin.

H. Stephen Morris is Reader in Anthropology, Department of Anthropology, The London School of Economics and Political Science, University of London.

Maurice Freedman is Professor of Social Anthropology, Oxford University, and Fellow of All Souls College.

Robert J. Smith is Goldwin Smith Professor of Anthropology, Department of Anthropology, Cornell University.

Index

335

Social Organization and
the Applications of Anthropology

Designed by R. E. Rosenbaum.
Composed by York Composition Co., Inc.
in 11 point Intertype Baskerville, 2 points leaded,
with display lines in monotype Baskerville.
Printed letterpress from type by York Composition Co., Inc.
on Warren's No. 66 text, 50 pound basis,
with the Cornell University Press watermark.
Bound by Vail-Ballou Press
in Holliston book cloth
and stamped in All Purpose foil.